fine Cooking
Chocolate

fine Cooking
Chocolate

150 Delicious and Decadent Recipes

Editors of *Fine Cooking*

The Taunton Press

The Taunton Press
Inspiration for hands-on living®

The Taunton Press, Inc.
63 South Main Street
PO Box 5506, Newtown, CT 06470-5506
e-mail: tp@taunton.com

Editor: Carolyn Mandarano
Copy editor: Diane Sinitsky
Indexer: Heidi Blough
Jacket/Cover design: Kimberly Adis
Interior design: Kimberly Adis
Layout: Kimberly Shake
Photographer: Scott Phillips, © The Taunton Press, Inc., except for the following:
p. vi, 57, 113, 135, 183: Colin Clark; p. 13, 14, 25: Mark Ferri; p. 18: MaryEllen Bartley
and Matthew Kestenbaum; p. 20, 71: Alan Richardson; p. 26, 131, 146, 224: Amy
Albert, © The Taunton Press, Inc.; p. 31: Carol Duncan; p. 53, 163: Suzanne
Roman, © The Taunton Press, Inc.; p. 73, 74: Karl Petzke; p. 122: Thomas Allen; p.
123: Maren Caruso, © The Taunton Press, Inc.; p. 126: Ben Fink; p. 166: Mark
Thomas; p. 171: Judith Hill; p. 197: Sloan Howard; p. 207: Carl Dunkin; p. 217, 219,
220: Ellen Silverman
Cover photographer: Scott Phillips, © The Taunton Press, Inc.
Cover food stylist: Adrienne Anderson

Fine Cooking® is a trademark of The Taunton Press, Inc., registered in the U.S.
Patent and Trademark Office.

The following names/manufacturers appearing in *Fine Cooking Chocolate*
are trademarks: Almond Joy®, Baileys®; Ben & Jerry's®, Callebaut®, Chambord®,
Cointreau®, Droste®, Fleischmann's® RapidRise™, Frangelico®, Ghirardelli®,
Godiva®, Grand Marnier®, Guinness®, Guittard®, Häagen-Dazs®, Heath®,
Hershey's®, Honey Maid®, Ibarra®, Jif®, Kahlúa®, Knob Creek®, Lindt®, Nabisco
FAMOUS® Chocolate Wafers, Nestlé®, Nilla®, Nutella®, Red Star® Quick-Rise™,
SAF® Perfect Rise, Scharffen Berger®, Simply Organic®, Valrhona®

Library of Congress Cataloging-in-Publication Data in progress

ISBN: 978-1-60085-958-8

Printed in the United States of America
10 9 8 7 6 5 4 3 2 1

contents

chocolate-covered sandwich
cookies with dulce de leche
(recipe on p. 17)

cookies, brownies & bars

banana split brownies

MAKES 16 BROWNIES

FOR THE BROWNIES

- 8 oz. (1 cup) unsalted butter; more for the pan
- 3 oz. (⅔ cup) unbleached all-purpose flour; more for the pan
- 1¾ cups granulated sugar
- ½ tsp. table salt
- 3 large eggs
- ½ cup coarsely mashed overripe banana (about 1 medium)
- ½ tsp. pure vanilla extract
- 2½ oz. (¾ cup) unsweetened natural cocoa powder

FOR THE TOPPING

- ¾ cup plus 2 Tbs. heavy cream
- ½ cup coarsely chopped ripe banana (about 1 medium)
- 7 oz. semisweet or mildly bittersweet chocolate (55% to 62% cacao), finely chopped
- 2 cups mini marshmallows
- ¼ cup sliced almonds

With a topping of marshmallows, crunchy almonds, and banana-infused ganache, these brownies are like a classic banana split, minus the ice cream. Adding an overripe banana to the batter keeps them moist for up to 5 days.

MAKE THE BROWNIES

1. Position a rack in the center of the oven, and heat the oven to 350°F. Line a 9-inch-square metal baking pan with foil, leaving an overhang on two sides for easy removal of the brownies. Butter and flour the bottom and sides of the foil, tapping out the excess flour.

2. Melt the butter in a 3-quart saucepan over medium heat until it smells nutty and turns golden, 4 to 5 minutes. Remove the pan from the heat and let cool for 5 minutes. Whisk in the sugar and salt, followed by the eggs, banana, and vanilla extract. Whisk in the cocoa powder and flour, mixing slowly at first and then more vigorously until the batter is combined.

3. Spread the batter in the prepared baking pan, smoothing it so it fills the pan evenly. Bake until a toothpick or a skewer inserted in the center of the pan comes out with just a few moist clumps clinging to it, 40 to 45 minutes. Let the brownies cool in the pan before topping.

MAKE THE TOPPING

1. While the brownies cool, bring the cream to a boil in a small saucepan over medium-high heat. Remove from the heat. Stir the chopped banana into the cream; let the mixture steep for 1 hour.

2. Put the chopped chocolate in a medium heatproof bowl. Bring the cream to a boil over medium-high heat, stirring occasionally. Pour the cream mixture through a strainer held directly over the bowl of chopped chocolate. Discard the banana. Let the chocolate mixture stand for 1 minute, then stir until smooth. Pour the ganache evenly over the cooled brownies.

TO FINISH

Position a rack 6 inches from the broiler and heat the broiler on high. Cover the ganache with the marshmallows and almonds. Broil, rotating the pan every 20 seconds or so to keep the marshmallows from burning, until browned. Using a knife, free the marshmallow topping from the sides of the pan. Let the brownies cool in the pan until the ganache is set, at least 1½ hours. Using the foil overhang, remove the brownies from the pan and cut into 16 squares (use a wet knife to keep the marshmallows from sticking). —*Nicole Rees*

PER SERVING: 370 CALORIES | 4G PROTEIN | 44G CARB | 23G TOTAL FAT | 14G SAT FAT | 7G MONO FAT | 1G POLY FAT | 90MG CHOL | 100MG SODIUM | 3G FIBER

bittersweet mocha cookies

MAKES ABOUT TWENTY-EIGHT 2-INCH COOKIES

- ⅓ recipe (about 12 oz. or 1⅓ cups) freshly made Cocoa Cookie Dough (recipe below)
- 3 oz. bittersweet or semisweet chocolate, very finely chopped or pulverized in a food processor to the size of coarse crumbs
- ¼ tsp. finely ground coffee beans, plus 28 whole beans (regular, not espresso roast), or as needed

  About ¼ cup granulated or coarse decorating sugar

Extra chocolatey and laced with freshly ground coffee, these cookies are slightly crunchy on the outside and chewy within.

1. Put the dough in a large mixing bowl. Add the chocolate and ground coffee, and mix them in thoroughly with a rubber spatula or your hands. Shape the dough into a log 14 inches long and about 1¼ inches in diameter. Wrap in waxed paper or foil and refrigerate until firm, at least 1 hour or overnight.

2. Position a rack in the center of the oven, and heat the oven to 350°F. Line a cookie sheet with parchment.

3. Put the sugar in a small bowl. Cut the dough into ½-inch-thick slices. Coat both sides of the slices with the sugar. Arrange the cookies 1½ inches apart on the lined sheet, and press a coffee bean into the center of each cookie. Bake until the cookies puff and show very faint cracks on the surface, 9 to 10 minutes (the cookies will feel soft to the touch). Slide the parchment onto a rack and let the cookies cool completely. —*Alice Medrich*

PER SERVING: 80 CALORIES | 1G PROTEIN | 11G CARB | 4.5G TOTAL FAT | 2.5G SAT FAT | 1G MONO FAT | 0G POLY FAT | 10MG CHOL | 15MG SODIUM | 1G FIBER

cocoa cookie dough

MAKES 4 CUPS DOUGH (ABOUT 2 LB. 5 OZ.)

- 10 oz. (2¼ cups) bleached all-purpose flour
- 1⅔ cups granulated sugar
- 3⅜ oz. (1 cup plus 2 Tbs.) unsweetened natural cocoa powder
- ⅜ tsp. table salt
- ⅜ tsp. baking soda
- 10½ oz. (1 cup plus 5 Tbs.) unsalted butter, slightly softened
- 4½ Tbs. whole milk
- 1½ tsp. pure vanilla extract

In a food processor, combine the flour, sugar, cocoa, salt, and baking soda. Pulse several times to mix thoroughly. Cut the butter into about 12 chunks and add them to the bowl. Pulse several times. Combine the milk and vanilla extract in a small cup. With the processor running, add the milk mixture and continue to process until the dough clumps around the blade or the sides of the bowl. Transfer the dough to a large bowl or cutting board, and knead with your hands a few times to make sure the dough is evenly blended. Portion the dough into equal thirds. If you have a scale, weigh each third; each should weigh about 12 oz.

chocolate chunk cookies with dried cherries and pecans

MAKES TWENTY-FOUR TO THIRTY 2-INCH COOKIES

- ⅓ recipe (about 12 oz. or 1⅓ cups) freshly made Cocoa Cookie Dough (recipe on p. 5)

- 2½ oz. (⅔ cup) toasted and coarsely chopped pecans

- ½ cup bittersweet or semi-sweet chocolate chips or chunks

- 3 oz. (½ cup) dried tart cherries, very coarsely chopped

Tart cherries and toasted nuts add flavor and contrasting texture to this double chocolate-chip cookie.

1. Position a rack in the center of the oven, and heat the oven to 350°F. Line a cookie sheet with parchment.

2. Put the dough in a large mixing bowl. Mix in the pecans, chocolate, and dried cherries. Drop more or less level tablespoons of the dough 2 inches apart on the lined sheet. Bake, rotating the sheet about halfway through, until the surface looks dry and the cookies are soft but not too squishy when pressed lightly with your finger, about 12 minutes. Slide the parchment onto a rack and let the cookies cool completely. —*Alice Medrich*

PER SERVING: 90 CALORIES | 1G PROTEIN | 11G CARB | 6G TOTAL FAT | 2.5G SAT FAT | 1.5G MONO FAT | 0.5G POLY FAT | 5MG CHOL | 15MG SODIUM | 1G FIBER

crunchy cocoa wafers

MAKES 28 TO 30 COOKIES

⅓ recipe (about 12 oz. or 1⅓ cups) freshly made Cocoa Cookie Dough (recipe on p. 5)

This very basic cookie offers a good hit of chocolate, yet it's not too rich and filling.

1. Shape the dough into a log about 7 inches long and 1¾ inches in diameter. Wrap the log in waxed paper or foil. Refrigerate until firm, at least 1 hour or overnight.

2. Position a rack in the center of the oven, and heat the oven to 350°F. Line a cookie sheet with parchment.

3. Cut the log into slices a scant ¼ inch thick, and arrange them 1 inch apart on the lined sheet. Bake for 12 to 15 minutes, rotating the sheet about halfway through. As they bake, the cookies will puff a little and then deflate; they're done about 1 minute after they deflate. The tops of the cookies will look slightly pitted, and they'll feel dry but soft when touched (the cookie will hold an impression). Slide the parchment onto a rack and let the cookies cool completely, at which point they should be perfectly dry and crunchy. —*Alice Medrich*

PER SERVING: 50 CALORIES | 1G PROTEIN | 7G CARB | 3G TOTAL FAT | 2G SAT FAT | 1G MONO FAT | 0G POLY FAT | 5MG CHOL | 15MG SODIUM | 0G FIBER

brownie bowties

MAKES 2 DOZEN COOKIES

- ⅓ **recipe (about 14 oz.) chilled Cream Cheese Dough (recipe on the facing page)**

- 1 **recipe chilled Brownie Filling (recipe on the facing page)**

- 1 **Tbs. granulated sugar; more as needed**

If you won't be serving these cookies within a couple of days, freeze them in an airtight container and let defrost at room temperature.

1. Position racks in the upper and lower thirds of the oven, and heat the oven to 350°F. Line two cookie sheets with foil.

To make the bowtie shape, pick up two corners of a square, moisten with water, and overlap one side over the other. Press on the dough to seal it and also to flatten the filling slightly.

2. Remove the dough from the refrigerator, stand it up on its rounded edge, and cut it in half (as if halving a bagel) into two equal rounds. Return one round to the refrigerator and, if necessary, let the other dough round sit at room temperature until pliable enough to roll. Square off the dough by pressing the round edge on the counter four times. Roll on a lightly floured surface into a 9x11-inch rectangle a scant ⅛ inch thick. As you roll, check frequently to be sure it isn't sticking and reflour lightly as needed.

3. With a pastry wheel or a knife, trim the rectangle to even the edges. Cut the dough crosswise into quarters and lengthwise into thirds to make 12 squares. Set 1 rounded tsp. of the brownie filling in the center of each square. Set a dish of water on the counter. Pick up two opposite corners of a square, moisten one with a wet fingertip, overlap the corners by about ½ inch, and gently press them together over the filling to seal the dough and flatten the filling slightly. Transfer to a foil-lined baking sheet. Repeat with the remaining squares of dough, arranging the cookies 1½ inches apart. If the dough becomes too soft to handle at any point, refrigerate briefly to firm it. Roll and fill the second piece of dough.

4. Sprinkle the cookies liberally with sugar. Put both sheets in the oven and bake until golden brown on the bottom, 17 to 20 minutes, rotating the pans from top to bottom and front to back about halfway through baking. Let the cookies cool on the sheets for a few minutes before transferring them to racks to cool completely. *—Alice Medrich*

PER SERVING: 130 CALORIES | 2G PROTEIN | 11G CARB | 9G TOTAL FAT | 6G SAT FAT | 2.5G MONO FAT | 0G POLY FAT | 30MG CHOL | 40MG SODIUM | 1G FIBER

cream cheese dough

**MAKES ABOUT
2 LB. 10 OZ. DOUGH**

17 oz. (3¾ cups) bleached all-
   purpose flour

 3 Tbs. granulated sugar

⅜ tsp. table salt

12 oz. (1½ cups) cold unsalted
   butter

12 oz. cold cream cheese

Don't chill the dough for more than a couple of hours, as it becomes too hard to roll. If you must chill it longer, leave it at room temperature until it's pliable before proceeding.

1. Combine the flour, sugar, and salt in the bowl of a stand mixer. Using a paddle attachment, mix briefly to distribute the ingredients. Cut each stick of butter into eight pieces and add them to the bowl. Mix on low speed until most of the mixture resembles very coarse bread-crumbs with a few larger pieces of butter the size of hazelnuts, about 3 minutes. Cut the cream cheese into 1-inch cubes and add them to the bowl. Mix on medium-low speed until a shaggy-looking dough begins to clump around the paddle, 30 to 60 seconds. Dump the dough onto the work surface, scraping the bowl. Knead a few times to incorporate any loose pieces. There should be large streaks of cream cheese.

2. Shape the dough into a fat cylinder, 6 inches long and about 3½ inches in diameter. Wrap the dough in parchment or waxed paper, and refrigerate until cold and slightly firm but not rock-hard, about 2 hours. Portion the dough by measuring the cylinder and cutting it into equal thirds. If you have a scale, weigh each third; each should weigh about 14 oz.

brownie filling

MAKES 1 CUP

 2 oz. (¼ cup) unsalted butter,
   cut into 5 or 6 pieces

 2 oz. unsweetened chocolate,
   coarsely chopped

   Scant ½ cup granulated sugar

½ tsp. pure vanilla extract

⅛ tsp. table salt

 1 cold large egg

 1 Tbs. unbleached all-purpose
   flour

Melt the butter and chocolate in a metal bowl set in a skillet of barely simmering water or in the top of a double boiler. Stir frequently with a rubber spatula until the mixture is melted and smooth. Remove the bowl from the water or double boiler. Stir in the sugar, vanilla extract, and salt. Stir in the egg. Add the flour, and stir until the mixture is smooth, glossy, and cohesive, about 1 minute. Cover and refrigerate until the filling thickens and is fudgy, at least 1 hour.

caramel-pecan brownies

MAKES 3 DOZEN BROWNIES

FOR THE BROWNIES

- 6 oz. (12 Tbs.) unsalted butter, cut into ½-inch-thick pieces; more softened for the pan
- 4 oz. unsweetened chocolate, coarsely chopped
- 4 large eggs
- 1¾ cups granulated sugar
- 1½ tsp. pure vanilla extract
- ¼ tsp. table salt
- 3⅜ oz. (¾ cup) unbleached all-purpose flour
- ¾ oz. (¼ cup) natural cocoa powder
- 1½ cups pecans, coarsely chopped

FOR THE TOPPING

- 1 recipe Basic Caramel (recipe on p. 12)
- ½ cup heavy cream
- 3 Tbs. unsalted butter, cut into 3 pieces
- 1 tsp. pure vanilla extract
- ¼ tsp. table salt

FOR THE GARNISH

- 2 oz. bittersweet chocolate, coarsely chopped
- 1 Tbs. heavy cream
- ½ cup pecans, toasted and chopped

Caramel adds a touch of gooey to these fudgy brownies.

MAKE THE BROWNIES

1. Position a rack in the center of the oven, and heat the oven to 350°F. Butter the bottom and sides of a 9x13-inch baking pan.

2. Put the butter and chocolate in a heavy-duty 2-quart saucepan over low heat, and stir constantly until melted and smooth. Remove from the heat and set aside.

3. In a medium bowl, whisk the eggs until well blended. Gradually whisk in the sugar and then whisk vigorously until well blended. Whisk in the melted chocolate mixture, vanilla extract, and salt. Whisk in the flour and cocoa powder until blended. Stir in the pecans and then scrape the batter into the prepared pan, smoothing it into an even layer with a spatula.

4. Bake until a toothpick inserted in the center of the brownies comes out with a few moist crumbs clinging to it, 20 to 22 minutes. Transfer the pan to a wire rack and, if necessary, gently press down any puffed areas with a spatula to make the top level. Let cool for about 5 minutes.

MAKE THE TOPPING

While the brownies are baking, make the Basic Caramel. Remove the pan from the heat and carefully add the cream—the mixture will bubble up furiously. Once the bubbling has subsided, add the butter and gently whisk until completely melted. Whisk in the vanilla extract and salt. Pour the caramel topping over the brownies, using a spatula to spread it evenly over the entire top. Let the brownies cool on the rack for 45 minutes, then refrigerate until the caramel topping is set, at least 1 hour.

GARNISH THE BROWNIES

1. Combine the chocolate and heavy cream in a small saucepan over low heat, and stir constantly until melted and smooth. Pour the chocolate into a small piping bag fitted with a ⅛-inch plain tip. (Or put it in a small zip-top bag and seal the bag. Using scissors, snip off a corner of the bag to make a small hole.) Drizzle the chocolate over the brownies in a zigzag pattern. Sprinkle the chopped pecans over the top. Refrigerate until the chocolate is set, about 30 minutes.

2. Cut the brownies into 36 rectangles. Serve chilled or at room temperature. (Well-covered brownies will keep at room temperature for up to 2 days and in the refrigerator for up to 5 days.) —*Tish Boyle*

PER SERVING: 210 CALORIES | 2G PROTEIN | 21G CARB | 14G TOTAL FAT | 6G SAT FAT | 5G MONO FAT | 2G POLY FAT | 40MG CHOL | 45MG SODIUM | 2G FIBER

continued on p. 12

basic caramel

MAKES ⅔ CUP

- **1 cup granulated sugar**
- **¼ tsp. fresh lemon juice**

1. Fill a cup measure halfway with water and put a pastry brush in it; this will be used for washing down the sides of the pan to prevent crystallization.

2. In a heavy-duty 2-quart saucepan, stir together the sugar, lemon juice, and ¼ cup cold water. Brush down the sides of the pan with water to wash away any sugar crystals. Bring to a boil over medium-high heat and cook, occasionally brushing down the sides of the pan, until the mixture starts to color around the edges, 5 to 8 minutes. Gently swirl the pan once to even out the color and prevent the sugar from burning in isolated spots. Continue to cook until the sugar turns medium amber, about 30 seconds more. (Once the mixture begins to color, it will darken very quickly, so keep an eye on it.)

making caramel

Brush down the sides of the pan to wash away any sugar crystals.

After about 5 minutes of cooking, the sugar mixture will start to turn color.

checkerboard cookies

MAKES ABOUT 18 DOZEN COOKIES

FOR THE VANILLA DOUGH

- 6 oz. (12 Tbs.) unsalted butter, softened at room temperature
- 3½ oz. (1 cup) confectioners' sugar
- ½ tsp. salt
- 1½ oz. (⅓ cup plus 1 Tbs.) finely ground almonds
- 1 egg yolk, at room temperature
- 1 tsp. pure vanilla extract
- 9 oz. (2 cups) unbleached all-purpose flour

FOR THE CHOCOLATE DOUGH

- 6 oz. (12 Tbs.) unsalted butter, softened at room temperature
- 3½ oz. (1 cup) confectioners' sugar
- ½ tsp. table salt
- 1 oz. (¼ cup) natural (not Dutch processed) cocoa
- 1 oz. (¼ cup) finely ground almonds
- 1 egg yolk, at room temperature
- 9 oz. (2 cups) unbleached all-purpose flour

FOR THE EGG WASH

- 1 egg, whisked well

You'll end up with a little chocolate dough left over. This recipe yields a lot of cookies, but the dough keeps for months in the freezer as long as you wrap it well.

MAKE THE VANILLA DOUGH

With the paddle of an electric mixer (or regular beaters), cream the butter on medium speed until soft and creamy but not melted. Add the confectioners' sugar and salt; mix on medium-low speed until thoroughly combined, about 5 minutes, scraping down the sides of the bowl as needed. Reduce the speed to low, and add the ground almonds, egg yolk, and vanilla extract; mix until blended. Add the flour; as soon as the dough comes together, stop the mixer. Roll the dough between two sheets of parchment or waxed paper into an 8½x11-inch rectangle that's ⅓ inch thick; try to get the thickness even. Transfer the dough to a baking sheet; refrigerate for several hours until hardened.

MAKE THE CHOCOLATE DOUGH

Follow the instructions for the vanilla dough, adding the cocoa along with the ground almonds. Roll and chill as for the vanilla dough.

ASSEMBLE THE COOKIES

1. Remove the dough from the refrigerator, peel off the paper from both sides, and set the dough onto a fresh sheet of parchment. Using a sharp, thin knife, slice both doughs lengthwise into square strips about ⅓ inch thick. If the dough starts to soften, freeze it briefly to firm it up.

2. Set up your workspace so that you have a baking sheet to work on in front of you, both doughs to one side, and the egg wash with a pastry brush to the other side. Lay a strip of vanilla dough lengthwise on the baking sheet; then lay a strip of chocolate dough next to the vanilla; finally, lay another strip of vanilla next to the chocolate. Press the three strips gently together so that they stick to one another. Brush the tops with the egg wash.

3. Lay a strip of chocolate directly on top of the first strip of vanilla, lay a strip of vanilla next to that, and lay a strip of chocolate next to that. Again, gently but firmly press together and down to ensure that all the strips are stuck to one another. Brush this layer with more egg wash. Finish with another layer of vanilla-chocolate-vanilla. Gently press the log together on all sides. Make more logs with the remaining strips. Chill the logs for at least 1 hour.

4. Position a rack in the center of the oven, and heat the oven to 375°F.

continued on p. 14

Line a baking sheet with parchment. When the logs are hard enough to slice, remove them from refrigerator. Slice into cookies about ¼ inch thick. Set the squares ½ inch apart on the baking sheet, and bake until the vanilla parts are lightly browned, about 8 minutes, rotating the sheet halfway through. Cool on the baking sheet until cool enough to handle (about 10 minutes) and then transfer the cookies to a rack. *—Joanne Chang*

PER SERVING: 25 CALORIES | 0G PROTEIN | 3G CARB | 1.5G TOTAL FAT | 1G SAT FAT | 0.5G MONO FAT | 0G POLY FAT | 5MG CHOL | 10MG SODIUM | 0G FIBER

shaping checkerboard cookies

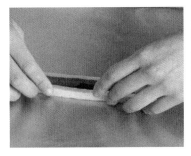

To build the first layer, sandwich one strip of chocolate dough between two strips of vanilla. Press the strips together.

Brush the pressed-together strips with egg wash to bind them and the next layer. Brush each succeeding layer with more egg wash.

Don't worry if the strips break; gently press the pieces together as you build a 3x3 checkerboard.

Press the log together firmly on all sides to join the strips and square it up.

With a sharp knife, cut the log into ¼-inch-thick slices and space them ½ inch apart on the parchment-lined sheet.

dried cherry and almond biscotti with white chocolate

MAKES ABOUT 3 DOZEN BISCOTTI

- 11¼ oz. (2 ½ cups) unbleached all-purpose flour; more as needed
- 1 cup granulated sugar
- 1¾ tsp. baking powder
- ¾ tsp. table salt
- 9 oz. (1¾ cups) dried cherries
- 3 oz. (¾ cup) slivered almonds, toasted
- 3 large eggs
- 3 Tbs. kirsch or brandy
- ½ tsp. pure almond extract
- 14 to 16 oz. white chocolate, chopped

Here, cherries jubilee—sweet cherries in a spiked syrup over vanilla ice cream—becomes biscotti with dried cherries, toasted almonds, and white chocolate.

1. Position a rack in the center of the oven, and heat the oven to 350°F. Line a large cookie sheet with parchment or a nonstick baking liner.

2. In a stand mixer fitted with a paddle attachment, combine the flour, sugar, baking powder, and salt on medium-low speed until well blended. On low speed, mix in the cherries and almonds. In a small bowl, whisk the eggs, kirsch, and almond extract. Slowly pour in the egg mixture. Mix until the dough comes together in large, moist clumps, about 1 minute.

3. Turn the dough out onto a lightly floured surface, and knead to incorporate any remaining dry ingredients. Divide into two equal piles. Shape each pile into a log 10 inches long and about 4 inches wide, lightly flouring your hands as needed (the dough will be sticky).

4. Position the logs on the cookie sheet about 4 inches apart. Bake until the tops are cracked and spring back slightly when pressed, 32 to 36 minutes. Transfer the sheet to a rack and leave until the logs are cool enough to handle, about 10 minutes. Reduce the oven temperature to 300°F.

5. Carefully peel the logs from the parchment and transfer to a cutting board. Using a serrated knife, cut each log on a sharp angle into ½-inch-thick slices. Return the slices to the cookie sheet, and arrange them cut side down. It's OK if they touch because they won't spread.

6. Bake until the biscotti are dried to your taste, 10 minutes (for slightly moist) to 20 minutes (for super-dry and crunchy), turning them over halfway through baking. Transfer the cookie sheet to a rack, and let the biscotti cool completely. They will still give slightly when pressed but will harden as they cool.

7. When the biscotti are cool, melt the white chocolate in a microwave or in a heatproof bowl set in a skillet of barely simmering water. Dip one end of each biscotti in the chocolate and place on a baking sheet lined with fresh parchment until set, about 30 minutes. Store in an airtight container for up to 2 weeks or freeze for up to 1 month.
—*Abigail Johnson Dodge*

PER SERVING: 160 CALORIES | 3G PROTEIN | 23G CARB | 6G TOTAL FAT | 2.5G SAT FAT | 1G MONO FAT | 0G POLY FAT | 20MG CHOL | 85MG SODIUM | 1G FIBER

thick and chewy chocolate chip cookies

MAKES ABOUT 9 DOZEN 2½-INCH COOKIES

10¾	oz. (1⅓ cups) unsalted butter, cold
1½	cups firmly packed light brown sugar
1	cup granulated sugar
2	large eggs, cold
1	Tbs. pure vanilla extract
17	oz. (3¾ cups) unbleached all-purpose flour
1¼	tsp. table salt
1	tsp. baking soda
12	oz. semisweet chocolate chips

Use butter and eggs right out of the refrigerator so the dough stays cool and the cookies maintain their thickness during baking; also use ungreased cookie sheets. To keep the cookies soft and chewy, store them in an airtight container along with a slice of bread.

1. Arrange oven racks in the upper and middle positions of the oven. Heat the oven to 375°F.

2. Using a mixer fitted with a paddle, beat together the butter, brown sugar, and granulated sugar, starting on low speed and gradually working your way up to high speed until the mixture is light and fluffy, about 3 minutes once you reach high speed. Scrape the bowl and beater. Add the eggs and vanilla extract, and beat on low until blended. Beat on high until light and fluffy, about 1 minute. Scrape the bowl and beater.

3. In a medium bowl, whisk together the flour, salt, and baking soda. Add this to the butter mixture and stir with a wooden spoon until just blended; the dough will be stiff. Stir in the chocolate chips.

4. Drop rounded measuring teaspoons of dough about 2 inches apart onto two ungreased baking sheets. Refrigerate any unused dough. Bake until the bottoms are golden brown, 8 to 10 minutes, rotating the sheets halfway through for even results. Remove the sheets from the oven, let sit for 3 to 5 minutes, and then transfer the cookies with a spatula to a wire rack to cool completely. Let the baking sheets cool completely before baking the remaining dough.
—Bonnie Gorder-Hinchey

PER SERVING: 70 CALORIES | 1G PROTEIN | 10G CARB | 3.5G TOTAL FAT | 2G SAT FAT | 1G MONO FAT | 0G POLY FAT | 10MG CHOL | 40MG SODIUM | 0G FIBER

chocolate-covered sandwich cookies with dulce de leche

MAKES ABOUT TWENTY-EIGHT 2-INCH SANDWICH COOKIES

- 9 oz. (2 cups) unbleached all-purpose flour; more for rolling
- 9 oz. (2 cups) whole-wheat flour
- 2 tsp. baking powder
- 1 tsp. table salt
- 8 oz. (1 cup) unsalted butter, softened
- ¾ cup granulated sugar
- 1½ tsp. finely grated orange zest
- 2 13.4-oz. cans Nestlé® dulce de leche
- 1 lb. bittersweet chocolate, chopped
- 1 pint heavy cream

These delicate shortbread cookies with a gooey dulce de leche filling and a coating of dark chocolate will become a holiday favorite. Store in a plastic container (separate each cookie with parchment) in the refrigerator for up to 2 weeks or in the freezer for up to 3 months.

MAKE THE COOKIES

1. In a medium bowl, whisk the flours, baking powder, and salt. In a stand mixer fitted with a paddle attachment, cream the butter and sugar on medium speed until light and fluffy, 2 to 3 minutes. Stir in the orange zest. Scrape down the bowl and paddle with a rubber spatula. With the mixer on low, gradually add the flour mixture to the butter mixture. After adding the last of the flour but before it's fully incorporated, add ¼ to ⅓ cup cold water and mix just until a smooth dough forms, 1 to 2 minutes. Divide the dough into two equal pieces, form into disks, and wrap in plastic. Chill overnight.

2. Position a rack in the center of the oven, and heat the oven to 350°F. Line two cookie sheets with parchment. Roll out the cold dough on a lightly floured surface until it's ⅛ to ³⁄₁₆ inch thick. With a 2-inch plain or fluted round cookie cutter, cut the dough in circles—you can gather and reroll the scraps once. Bake one sheet at a time until the edges are very lightly browned and the cookies puff up slightly, 8 to 10 minutes. Cool the cookies on a rack, and store in an airtight container for up to 3 days or freeze for up to 1 month, until you're ready to fill and coat them.

FILL THE COOKIES

Lay out the cookies, flat side down. Put a heaping ½ Tbs. of dulce de leche on half of the cookies. Cover each with a top cookie, flat side up.

COAT THE COOKIES

1. Put the chocolate in a deep, heatproof bowl. In a small saucepan over medium-high heat, bring the cream just to a boil. Pour over the chocolate; let sit for 10 minutes. Stir the mixture gently, incorporating the cream without overworking, until glossy and completely mixed.

2. Line two cookie sheets or rimmed baking sheets with parchment. Pick up a sandwich cookie with a small offset spatula. Immerse in the chocolate mixture, flipping the cookie to coat completely. Pick up with the spatula and tap a couple of times on the side of the bowl to get rid of excess chocolate. With another spatula in the opposite hand, gently smooth out the top of the cookie and then run the spatula along the bottom. Transfer to the parchment-lined sheet. Repeat with the remaining cookies. Allow the coating to set at room temperature for a few hours and then serve. —*Andy Corson*

PER SERVING: 370 CALORIES | 6G PROTEIN | 45G CARB | 19G TOTAL FAT | 12G SAT FAT | 5G MONO FAT | 0.5G POLY FAT | 50MG CHOL | 160MG SODIUM | 3G FIBER

chocolate cream cheese brownies

MAKES ABOUT 4 DOZEN BARS

FOR THE FILLING

- 4 oz. (1 cup) chopped bittersweet or semisweet chocolate or chocolate chips
- ¼ cup heavy cream
- ½ lb. cream cheese, at room temperature
- 1 egg
- 2 tsp. unbleached all-purpose flour

FOR THE BROWNIE BATTER

- 9 oz. (18 Tbs.) unsalted butter, at room temperature; more for the pan
- 1½ cups granulated sugar
- 5 eggs
- 1 tsp. pure vanilla extract
- ⅛ tsp. almond extract
- 7 oz. (1½ cups) unbleached all-purpose flour
- 2⅔ oz. (¾ cup) unsweetened cocoa powder
- ¼ tsp. baking powder

FOR THE ICING

- Approximately 8 oz. bittersweet or semisweet chocolate, finely chopped (about 2 cups)

With three different chocolate layers, these brownies are intense. The cocoa in them beckons for tall glasses of milk.

MAKE THE FILLING
Slowly melt half the chopped chocolate and cream together in a microwave or a double boiler. Set aside to cool. In an electric mixer fitted with a paddle attachment, beat the cream cheese and egg together until fluffy. Add the cooled chocolate mixture and mix well. Add the flour and the remaining chocolate and mix until incorporated. Chill the filling while you assemble the brownie batter.

MAKE THE BROWNIE BATTER
Position a rack in the center of the oven, and heat the oven to 350°F. Butter a 9x13-inch pan (a standard Pyrex® baking dish). Cream the butter and sugar in an electric mixer until fluffy. Add the eggs one at a time, making sure that each one is fully incorporated before adding another. Occasionally scrape down the sides of the bowl. Add the vanilla and almond extracts. Sift together the flour, cocoa, and baking powder and gently blend them into the batter.

ASSEMBLE THE BROWNIES
Using an offset metal spatula, spread half the brownie batter into the prepared pan. Spread the filling over the batter. Spoon the remaining brownie batter over the filling, and gently spread it into an even layer. Bake until a knife inserted into the center of the brownies comes out clean, about 35 minutes.

MAKE THE ICING
As soon as you remove the brownies from the oven, sprinkle about three-quarters of the chocolate on top. Let sit for about 5 minutes, until the chocolate has melted. Gently spread the soft chocolate into a thin, smooth layer. If it isn't enough chocolate, sprinkle a few more pieces on top and spread again, but be careful not to make the icing too thick. —*Patricia Ann Heyman*

PER SERVING: 150 CALORIES | 3G PROTEIN | 14G CARB | 10G TOTAL FAT | 6G SAT FAT | 3G MONO FAT | 0G POLY FAT | 45MG CHOL | 25MG SODIUM | 1G FIBER

dark chocolate crackles

MAKES ABOUT 5 DOZEN COOKIES

- 11¼ oz. (2½ cups) unbleached all-purpose flour
- 1 tsp. baking soda
- ¼ tsp. table salt
- 8 oz. (1 cup) unsalted butter, at room temperature
- 2 cups firmly packed light brown sugar
- 2 oz. (⅔ cup) natural, unsweetened cocoa, sifted if lumpy
- 2 tsp. finely grated orange zest
- 1 tsp. pure vanilla extract
- 3 large eggs
- 8 oz. bittersweet chocolate, melted and cooled until barely warm
- ¾ cup (4 oz.) chopped chocolate (white, bittersweet, or semisweet)
- ⅓ cup granulated sugar; more as needed

These cookies are fragile when hot, so be sure to let them cool on the cookie sheet for 5 minutes.

1. Position a rack in the center of the oven, and heat the oven to 350°F. Line three large cookie sheets with parchment or nonstick baking liners.

2. In a medium mixing bowl, whisk together the flour, baking soda, and salt. In the bowl of a stand mixer fitted with a paddle attachment (or in a large mixing bowl with a hand mixer), beat the butter, brown sugar, cocoa, orange zest, and vanilla extract on medium speed until well combined, about 4 minutes. Add the eggs one at a time, beating briefly between additions. Add the cooled chocolate and mix until blended, about 1 minute. Add the dry ingredients and mix on low speed until almost completely blended, about 1 minute. Add the chopped chocolate and mix until blended, about 15 seconds.

3. Form the dough into 1¼-inch balls using a small ice cream scoop or two tablespoons. (The balls of dough may be frozen for 1 month. Thaw them overnight in the refrigerator before proceeding with the recipe.)

4. Pour the granulated sugar into a shallow dish. Dip the top of each ball in the sugar, and set the balls sugar side up about 1½ inches apart on the prepared cookie sheets. Bake one sheet at a time until the cookies are puffed and cracked on top, 11 to 12 minutes. Let the cookies cool on the sheet for 5 minutes before transferring them to a rack to cool completely. *—Abigail Johnson Dodge*

PER SERVING: 110 CALORIES | 2G PROTEIN | 16G CARB | 5G TOTAL FAT | 3G SAT FAT | 1.5G MONO FAT | 0G POLY FAT | 20MG CHOL | 45MG SODIUM | 1G FIBER

chocolate cutouts

**MAKES ABOUT 4 DOZEN
2½-INCH COOKIES**

10 oz. (2 ¼ cups) unbleached
all-purpose flour

1½ oz. (½ cup) nonalkalized
cocoa

Pinch of salt

8 oz. (16 Tbs.) unsalted butter,
at room temperature

¾ cup granulated sugar

1½ tsp. pure vanilla extract

*Use nonalkalized (natural) cocoa, such as Hershey's® or Nestlé,
rather than Dutch processed for more chocolate flavor.*

Combine the flour, cocoa, and salt in a medium bowl. In a large bowl, beat the butter, sugar, and vanilla extract until well blended. Add the flour mixture; beat until well blended (if you're using an electric mixer, set it on low speed). Divide the dough and shape it into two flat disks; wrap one in plastic while you work with the other. Position a rack in the center of the oven, and heat the oven to 350°F. On a lightly floured surface, roll one disk ⅜ inch thick. Cut out shapes, and set them 1 inch apart on parchment-lined baking sheets. Repeat with the other disk. Combine the scraps, chill them if they feel warm, and reroll. Bake the cookies until the tops look dry and you see flaky layers when you break a cookie in half, about 15 minutes. Transfer to a rack to cool completely. Decorate the cooled cookies. —*Abigail Johnson Dodge*

PER SERVING: 70 CALORIES | 1G PROTEIN | 8G CARB | 4G TOTAL FAT | 2.5G SAT FAT |
1G MONO FAT | 0G POLY FAT | 10MG CHOL | 5MG SODIUM | 0G FIBER

Keys to Cookie-Baking Success

• **Weigh flour, cocoa, and confectioners' and brown sugars.** You'll get more accurate results. If you do measure by volume, fluff the dry ingredients before you spoon them (rather than pour them) into the measuring cup. Level off flour, cocoa, and confectioners' sugar; pack brown sugar firmly.

• **Blend ingredients when they're at room temperature.** Butter will be easier to cream, and all ingredients will be easier to incorporate.

• **Mix the dough just until well blended.** This is how you'll get tender cookies. The gluten in unbleached all-purpose flour gives body to the dough, which is a must for cookies to have "bite," but overmixing will make them hard and tough. An electric mixer is faster than mixing by hand, but either works.

• **Line baking sheets with kitchen parchment.** Parchment eliminates the need for greasing and makes cleanup easier. It's inexpensive, too. If you don't want to use parchment, grease your baking sheets lightly.

• **Rotate the baking sheets.** Most ovens have hot spots. To ensure evenly baked and evenly browned batches, rotate the sheets from side to side and from rack to rack during baking.

chocolate-dipped chocolate-apricot sandwich cookies

MAKES ABOUT 3 DOZEN SANDWICH COOKIES

FOR THE COOKIES

- 9 oz. (2 cups) unbleached all-purpose flour; more as needed
- ½ tsp. baking powder
- ½ tsp. table salt
- 8 oz. (1 cup) unsalted butter, softened
- 8 oz. (2 cups) confectioners' sugar
- 2¼ oz. (¾ cup) unsweetened, natural cocoa powder, sifted if lumpy
- 2 large egg yolks
- 1 tsp. pure vanilla extract

FOR THE FILLING AND GLAZE

- 1 cup apricot preserves
- 12 oz. bittersweet chocolate, finely chopped
- 2 tsp. canola or vegetable oil

The Sacher torte—chocolate sponge cake layered with apricot jam and covered in dark chocolate icing—becomes cakey cookies filled with preserves and dipped in bittersweet chocolate.

MAKE THE COOKIES

1. In a medium bowl, whisk the flour, baking powder, and salt. In a stand mixer fitted with a paddle attachment, beat the butter, sugar, and cocoa powder on low speed until blended, then raise the speed to medium and beat until light and fluffy, about 3 minutes. Scrape down the bowl and beater. Add the egg yolks and vanilla extract and mix on medium speed until well blended, about 1 minute. Add the flour mixture and mix on low speed until the dough comes together, about 1 minute.

2. Turn the dough out onto a work surface and divide into three equal piles on pieces of plastic wrap. Using the plastic as an aid, gently shape each one into a smooth, flat 5-inch disk and wrap in the plastic. Refrigerate until chilled, about 30 minutes. (The dough can be refrigerated for up to 3 days or frozen for up to 1 month.)

3. Position a rack in the center of the oven, and heat the oven to 375°F. Line two cookie sheets with parchment or nonstick baking liners.

4. Working with one disk at a time, roll the dough between two sheets of lightly floured parchment or on a floured work surface until ⅛ to 3⁄16 inch thick. Dust with additional flour as needed. Using a 2¼-inch cookie cutter, cut out shapes. Arrange about 1 inch apart on the lined cookie sheets. Stack the scraps and gently press them together. Reroll and cut. Repeat with remaining dough disks.

5. Bake, one sheet at a time, until the cookies look dry and slightly cracked and feel somewhat firm when pressed, 7 to 9 minutes. Let cool on the sheet for about 5 minutes, then transfer to a rack to cool completely. (The cookies can be stored in an airtight container at room temperature for up to 5 days or frozen for up to 1 month before filling and glazing.)

FILL THE COOKIES

Press the preserves through a fine-mesh sieve, discarding any large pieces of apricot. Arrange half of the cookies bottom side up on a work surface. Put 1 tsp. of the preserves in the center of each cookie. Cover each with one of the remaining cookies, bottom side down. Gently squeeze each cookie together to spread the preserves until it just reaches the edges.

GLAZE THE COOKIES

1. Line two or three baking sheets with parchment, aluminum foil, or waxed paper. Put the chocolate and oil in a small, deep, heatproof bowl. Heat in a microwave until almost melted, or set the bowl in a skillet of barely simmering water and stir until melted and smooth.

2. Dip each cookie halfway into the glaze until lightly covered. Lift the cookie out and gently scrape the bottom against the side of the bowl to remove excess glaze. Set on the prepared baking sheets. Let the cookies sit at room temperature or in the refrigerator until the glaze is firm. Serve immediately or store in an airtight container at room temperature for up to 2 days. —*Abigail Johnson Dodge*

PER SERVING: 180 CALORIES | 2G PROTEIN | 24G CARB | 9G TOTAL FAT | 5G SAT FAT | 2.5G MONO FAT | 0G POLY FAT | 25MG CHOL | 50MG SODIUM | 2G FIBER

chocolate-mint thumbprints

MAKES ABOUT 3 DOZEN COOKIES

This updated classic pairs the contemporary flavors of chocolate and mint.

FOR THE COOKIES

5¼ oz. (1 cup plus 2½ Tbs.) unbleached all-purpose flour

¾ oz. (¼ cup) Dutch-processed cocoa

6 oz. (¾ cup) unsalted butter, at room temperature

2 oz. (½ cup) confectioners' sugar, sifted

1½ tsp. pure vanilla extract

¼ tsp. table salt

FOR THE MINT FILLING

4 oz. (¾ cup) chopped semisweet chocolate (or chocolate chips)

1½ oz. (3 Tbs.) unsalted butter, cut into 6 pieces

Scant ¼ tsp. pure peppermint extract

MAKE THE COOKIES

1. Sift the flour and cocoa together into a medium bowl. With a hand mixer or a stand mixer fitted with a paddle attachment, cream the butter and sugar on medium speed until light and fluffy, about 2 minutes. Add the vanilla extract and salt; continue beating until blended and smooth, about 1 minute more. Add the flour-cocoa mixture and mix on low speed until a soft dough forms, about 1 minute. Chill the dough in the refrigerator until firm enough to roll into balls, 40 to 60 minutes.

2. Position a rack in the center of the oven, and heat the oven to 350°F. Line two cookie sheets with parchment or nonstick baking liners.

3. Using your palms, roll heaping teaspoonfuls of the dough into 1-inch balls. Arrange them 2 inches apart on the lined sheets. With a lightly floured thumb or index fingertip, press straight down into the middle of each ball almost to the cookie sheet to make a deep well. (Or use the end of a thick-handled wooden spoon.)

4. Bake one sheet at a time until the tops of the cookies look dry, 8 to 9 minutes. Gently redefine the indentations with the end of a wooden spoon. Let the cookies cool on the sheet for 5 minutes, then let them cool completely on racks.

MAKE THE FILLING

Put the chocolate and butter in a heatproof bowl set in a wide skillet of almost simmering water. Stir with a heatproof spatula until almost melted, 2 to 4 minutes. Remove the bowl from the heat, and stir until melted and smooth, about 30 seconds more. Stir in the peppermint extract. Let the filling cool, stirring occasionally, until slightly thickened and a bit warmer than room temperature, 30 to 40 minutes. Spoon the filling into a small pastry bag with a small, plain tip. (Or use a small plastic bag and cut a tiny bit off a bottom corner of the bag.) Pipe the filling into the center of each cookie. Cool completely before serving or storing. The cookies will keep in an airtight container at room temperature for 4 to 5 days. *—David Crofton*

PER SERVING: 80 CALORIES | 1G PROTEIN | 7G CARB | 6G TOTAL FAT | 3.5G SAT FAT | 1.5G MONO FAT | 0G POLY FAT | 15MG CHOL | 15MG SODIUM | 0G FIBER

chocolate-nut wafers

MAKES ABOUT 12 DOZEN
COOKIES

- **9 oz. (2 cups) unbleached all-purpose flour**
- **2 oz. (½ cup) natural (not Dutch-processed) cocoa**
- **½ tsp. ground cinnamon**
- **8 oz. (16 Tbs.) unsalted butter, at room temperature**
- **10 oz. (2⅔ cups) confectioners' sugar**
- **¾ tsp. table salt**
- **1 large egg, at room temperature**
- **8 oz. (scant 2 cups) chopped walnuts**
- **4 oz. (scant 1 cup) chopped pistachios**

> **For the best results, measure your flour by weight instead of volume (1 cup of all-purpose flour equals 4½ oz.). If you don't have a scale, use the proper technique when filling your measuring cups—stir the flour to aerate it, spoon it lightly into the cup, and sweep the cup level with a straightedge.**

A very sharp knife makes it easy to slice the nutty dough into neat squares.

1. Blend the flour, cocoa, and cinnamon in a medium bowl; set aside. With the paddle of an electric mixer (or regular beaters), cream the butter on medium speed until soft and creamy but not melted. Add the sugar and salt; mix on medium-low speed until thoroughly combined, about 5 minutes, scraping the bowl as needed. Reduce the speed to low and add the egg; mix until blended. Add the walnuts, pistachios, and flour mixture; as soon as the dough comes together, stop the mixer. Scrape the dough onto a large sheet of plastic wrap. Using the wrap to help shape and protect the dough, gently press it into a 6-inch square that's 1½ inches thick. Wrap in plastic and refrigerate until the dough is firm enough to slice, at least 4 hours.

2. Position a rack in the center of the oven, and heat the oven to 400°F. Line a baking sheet with parchment. Unwrap the dough, trim the edges, and slice the square into four 1½-inch-square logs. Slice each log into square cookies between ⅛ and ¼ inch thick. Lay the squares ½ inch apart on the baking sheet. Bake until the tops look dry and the nuts are browned, 8 to 10 minutes, rotating the sheet halfway through. Leave the cookies on the baking sheet until cool enough to handle (about 10 minutes), then transfer the cookies to a rack.
—*Joanne Chang*

PER SERVING: 40 CALORIES | 1G PROTEIN | 1G CARB | 2.5G TOTAL FAT | 1G SAT FAT | 4G MONO FAT | 0.5G POLY FAT | 5MG CHOL | 15MG SODIUM | 0G FIBER

chocolate-orange biscotti

**MAKES ABOUT 10 DOZEN
2½-INCH COOKIES**

FOR THE DOUGH

- 2½ cups whole skin-on hazelnuts
- 12 oz. high-quality bittersweet or semisweet chocolate
- 8 oz. (1 cup) unsalted butter, completely softened at room temperature
- 4 large eggs
- 1 cup firmly packed light brown sugar
- 1 cup granulated sugar
- 2 tsp. pure vanilla extract
- ½ tsp. pure almond extract
- 2 Tbs. instant espresso powder or finely ground coffee
- ¾ cup high-quality Dutch-processed cocoa powder, sifted
- 1 cup candied orange peel
- 18 oz. (4 cups) unbleached all-purpose flour
- 1 tsp. baking powder
- 1 tsp. kosher salt

FOR FINISHING

- 4 egg whites
- 1 tsp. best-quality pure orange extract (try Simply Organic® orange flavor)
- ¾ cup granulated sugar

These cookies are sparkly, festive, and full of delicious nuggets like hazelnuts, candied orange peel, and chocolate chunks, making them perfect for a holiday cookie tray. They are also sturdy enough to travel, so are lovely as a holiday gift.

MIX THE DOUGH

1. Position racks in the middle and top of the oven, and heat the oven to 350°F. Toast the hazelnuts on a baking sheet until they're well browned, about 10 minutes. Let cool. You won't need to skin them—the skins taste great—but if the nuts are bigger than ½ inch, chop them roughly. Chop the chocolate into slivers that are a scant 1 inch long and ⅛ inch wide.

2. With an electric mixer fitted with a paddle attachment, beat the butter on medium-high speed until light and creamy. Add the eggs one at a time. Add the brown and white sugars, vanilla extract, almond extract, espresso powder, and cocoa powder, scraping down the sides of the bowl as needed. Add the candied orange peel, flour, baking powder, and salt. Add the hazelnuts and chocolate slivers, mixing just to combine. The dough will be stiff and a bit sticky. Let the dough rest for 15 to 30 minutes before shaping.

SHAPE THE DOUGH AND DO THE INITIAL BAKING

Line two large baking sheets with parchment. Divide the dough into six equal pieces. Using as little flour as possible on the work surface, roll each piece into logs that are 12 to 14 inches long and 1¼ inches wide, working out the air pockets as you go. (If you're working ahead, wrap the logs in plastic wrap and refrigerate them overnight.) Transfer the logs to the lined baking sheets, setting the dough about 3 inches apart, patting the sides to smooth and straighten. In a small bowl, beat the egg whites with the orange extract until foamy. Brush the tops and sides of the logs with some of the whites. Sprinkle with ¼ cup of

variation

For a more intense chocolate flavor, replace the chocolate and cocoa with a 9.7-oz. bar of Scharffen Berger® 62% semi-sweet chocolate along with ¾ cup each Scharffen Berger nibs and cocoa.

the sugar. Bake until firm in the center, about 35 minutes, rotating the sheets to ensure even baking. Set the sheets on racks until the logs are cool enough to handle and so the dough won't compress when you cut it, about 30 minutes.

BAKE THE SECOND TIME
Reduce the oven to 300°F and line the baking sheets with fresh parchment, if needed. Using a serrated knife, saw the strips into ½-inch-thick slices, cutting crosswise. Lay the slices flat on the baking sheets. Brush the tops with the beaten egg white and sprinkle with another ¼ cup of the sugar. Bake for about 15 minutes, rotating the baking sheets as needed. Turn the biscotti over. Brush again with the egg white and sprinkle with the remaining ¼ cup sugar. Bake for another 10 to 15 minutes, watching carefully to make sure the chocolate doesn't burn. The centers will feel somewhat soft even when fully baked; they'll harden as the cookies cool. Set the baking sheets on racks, letting the cookies cool and crisp completely on the sheets. If stored airtight, the biscotti will keep for about 2 weeks.
—*Kathleen Weber*

chocolate-vanilla pinwheel cookies

MAKES ABOUT 10 DOZEN 2-INCH COOKIES

- 13½ oz. (3 cups) unbleached all-purpose flour
- ½ tsp. table salt
- ¼ tsp. baking soda
- 10 oz. (1¼ cups) unsalted butter, slightly softened
- 1¼ cups granulated sugar
- 1 large egg
- 1½ tsp. pure vanilla extract
- 1 tsp. instant espresso powder
- 3 Tbs. unsweetened Dutch processed cocoa powder
- 3 oz. bittersweet chocolate, melted and still warm

These pretty pinwheels look professionally made, but they're easily baked at home following the dough-layering technique outlined here. Once the layers of chocolate and vanilla dough get rolled together, these essentially become slice-and-bake cookies. Use a sharp knife and a ruler for even slices. You can freeze the logs for up to 3 months before baking them.

1. Sift together the flour, salt, and baking soda in a medium bowl. In the bowl of a stand mixer fitted with a paddle attachment, cream the butter on medium-low speed until smooth, about 2 minutes. Add the sugar in a steady stream and mix for another 2 minutes. Add the egg and vanilla and mix until well combined, scraping the bowl as needed. Reduce the speed to low and add the dry ingredients in two additions, mixing just until combined. Remove 2 cups less 2 Tbs. of the dough and set aside.

2. Dissolve the espresso powder in 2 Tbs. boiling water and set aside briefly to cool. Then mix the espresso and cocoa powders into the remaining dough. Reduce the mixer speed to low, add the warm melted chocolate, and mix just until thoroughly combined. Divide and shape the dough and roll it into pinwheel logs, following the photos and directions in the sidebar on p. 30.

3. Position racks in the upper and lower thirds of the oven. Heat the oven to 350°F. Line two rimmed baking sheets with parchment. Working with one log at a time, use a sharp, thin-bladed knife to slice the dough into ³⁄₁₆-inch-thick rounds. Lay the rounds about 1 inch apart on the prepared pans, and bake until the tops of the cookies feel set, 12 to 14 minutes (don't let the edges become too brown). To ensure even browning, rotate the sheets as needed during baking. Let the baked cookies stand for 1 minute on the pan. While they're still warm, use a thin metal spatula to transfer them to racks. When cool, store between sheets of waxed paper in an airtight container for up to 2 weeks or freeze for up to 3 months. —*Carol Walter*

How to Keep Pinwheel Logs Round

To keep your perfectly shaped round log from flattening out on the bottom while it chills, try these ideas:

• **Turn frequently.** Put the logs on a level shelf or flat baking sheet in the refrigerator or freezer, and turn each log every 15 minutes for the first hour. As the logs chill, the bottoms will flatten from the weight of the dough. To correct this, remold the logs by rolling them back and forth a few times on the countertop.

• **Use a cradle.** If you happen to have a baguette pan, it makes a perfect cradle for chilling logs of dough. If you don't, save a few empty paper towel rolls, cut each in half lengthwise to make two cardboard troughs with rounded bottoms, and then place a log in each half for chilling. For both of these methods, after the logs have chilled for 15 to 20 minutes, turn them over once and chill until firm.

continued on p. 30

making pinwheel cookies

For perfectly round cookies, chill the dough logs on a level surface and turn them every 15 minutes for the first hour to keep the bottoms from flattening. If the bottoms do flatten, give each log a quick roll before returning it to the refrigerator.

Portion each flavor of dough into three equal pieces (for accuracy, use a scale). Form each piece into a 5x5-inch square on a piece of plastic wrap and wrap well. The chocolate will be thicker than the vanilla. Refrigerate the dough for 30 minutes. (If the dough becomes too hard, let it stand at room temperature for a few minutes before rolling.)

While the dough is chilling, tear off twelve 12-inch squares of waxed paper. Roll each piece of dough into a 7x7-inch square between two sheets of the waxed paper. Without removing the waxed paper, layer the squares of dough on a baking sheet and refrigerate for 10 to 15 minutes. Have ready three 15-inch sheets of plastic wrap.

To shape the cookies, remove one square of the vanilla dough and one square of the chocolate dough from the refrigerator, and peel off the top sheet of waxed paper from each. Invert the chocolate square over the vanilla square (or vanilla can go on top of chocolate; try some of each for variety), taking care to align the two doughs as evenly as possible. Using your rolling pin, gently roll over the dough to seal the layers together. Peel off the top layer of waxed paper.

Starting with the edge of the dough closest to you, carefully curl the dough up and over with your fingertips so no space is visible in the center of the pinwheel.

Using the waxed paper as an aid, continue rolling the dough into a tight cylinder. After the cylinder is formed, roll it back and forth on the counter to slightly elongate and compact it. Transfer the log to the plastic wrap, centering it on the long edge closest to you. Roll tightly, twisting the ends of the plastic firmly to seal. With your hands on either end of the log, push firmly toward the center to compact the dough. The log should be about 9 inches long and 1½ inches thick. Repeat with the remaining dough. Refrigerate the logs until firm enough to slice, about 3 hours, or freeze for up to 3 months.

cocoa walnut butter cookies

**MAKES ABOUT 4 DOZEN
COOKIES**

4½ oz. (1 cup) unbleached all-purpose flour

½ cup natural or Dutch processed cocoa

½ tsp. baking soda

¼ tsp. baking powder

¼ tsp. table salt

3 oz. (6 Tbs.) unsalted butter, at room temperature

1 oz. (2 Tbs.) vegetable shortening

½ cup firmly packed brown sugar, sifted free of lumps

½ cup granulated sugar

1 large egg

1 tsp. pure vanilla extract

4 oz. (¾ cup) chopped walnuts

The texture of these simple-to-bake cookies is like the fudgiest brownie but a touch more delicate, and the flavor is seriously chocolate.

1. Position racks in the upper and lower thirds of the oven, and heat the oven to 350°F. Line two baking sheets with parchment or foil. In a medium mixing bowl, combine the flour, cocoa, baking soda, baking powder, and salt. Mix thoroughly with a wire whisk. Set aside.

2. In a stand mixer fitted with a paddle attachment (or in a large mixing bowl with a hand mixer), beat the butter and shortening on medium speed until creamy. Add the sugars, beating until well combined. Beat in the egg and vanilla extract. Turn the mixer to low speed and mix in the flour mixture just until incorporated. Mix in the nuts.

3. Drop heaping teaspoonfuls of batter about 1½ inches apart on the prepared baking sheets. Bake for 10 to 12 minutes. (After 5 minutes, swap the position of the baking sheets and rotate them 180 degrees for even baking.) The cookies will puff up and then settle down slightly when done. Cool on the baking sheets for a few minutes. With a metal spatula, transfer the cookies to a rack to cool completely.
—*Alice Medrich*

PER SERVING: 60 CALORIES | 1G PROTEIN | 7G CARB | 4G TOTAL FAT | 1G SAT FAT | 1.5G MONO FAT | 1.5G POLY FAT | 10MG CHOL | 30MG SODIUM | 0G FIBER

coconut chocolate almond biscotti

MAKES ABOUT 25 BISCOTTI

10⅛ oz. (2¼ cups) unbleached all-purpose flour

1½ tsp. baking powder

¼ tsp. table salt

4 oz. (½ cup) unsalted butter, softened

¾ cup firmly packed light brown sugar

2 large eggs, at room temperature

1 tsp. pure vanilla extract

½ cup firmly packed sweet-ened shredded coconut

1 cup chopped toasted almonds

1 cup semisweet mini chocolate chips

These biscotti are inspired by the Almond Joy® candy bar and the flavors of its almond, chocolate, and coconut combination.

1. In a medium bowl, whisk together the flour, baking powder, and salt. In a stand mixer fitted with a paddle attachment, beat the butter and sugar on medium speed until light and fluffy, 2 to 3 minutes. Add the eggs one at a time, mixing on medium speed after each addition until incorporated. Mix in the vanilla extract and then the coconut until well combined.

2. With the mixer on low speed, gradually add the flour mixture and mix just until combined. The dough will be sticky. With the mixer still on low, mix in the almonds and chocolate chips. Cover the bowl with plastic wrap and refrigerate for 30 minutes.

3. Position a rack in the center of the oven, and heat the oven to 350°F. Line a large cookie sheet with parchment. Divide the dough into equal halves and place on the cookie sheet. Working on the sheet, shape each half into a loaf about 10 inches long, 3 inches wide, and ¾ inch high. Bake until the tops are browned, cracked, and crusty and they spring back slightly when gently pressed, 30 to 35 minutes.

4. Cool for about 30 minutes on the cookie sheet. Reduce the oven temperature to 325°F.

5. Transfer each loaf to a cutting board. Using a sharp serrated bread knife, cut ½-inch-thick slices crosswise on the diagonal. When slic-ing, hold the sides of the loaf near each cut to keep the slices neat. Place the slices cut side down on the cookie sheet, and bake until the biscotti are dried and the cut surfaces are lightly browned, 15 to 20 minutes. Transfer the cookie sheet to a rack and let the biscotti cool completely. The biscotti may give slightly when pressed but will harden as they cool. —*Beth Kujawski*

PER SERVING: 170 CALORIES | 3G PROTEIN | 21G CARB | 8G TOTAL FAT | 4G SAT FAT | 3G MONO FAT | 1G POLY FAT | 25MG CHOL | 60MG SODIUM | 1G FIBER

double chocolate chunk fudge brownies

MAKES 12 BROWNIES

- 6 oz. (¾ cup) unsalted butter, cut into 6 pieces; more for the pan
- 2 oz. (⅔ cup) unsweetened cocoa powder (natural or Dutch processed)
- 1⅔ cups granulated sugar
- ¼ tsp. table salt
- 2 large eggs
- 1 tsp. pure vanilla extract
- 4½ oz. (1 cup) unbleached all-purpose flour
- 4 oz. very coarsely chopped semisweet or bittersweet chocolate (¾ cup)
- 2 oz. (½ cup) coarsely chopped walnuts or pecans (optional)

If you use a metal pan, the edges of these brownies will be flat and the texture will be even. If you use a Pyrex baking pan, your brownies will have puffier, drier edges, but it will be easier to get the brownies out of the pan.

1. Position a rack in the middle of the oven, and heat the oven to 350°F. Generously butter the bottom and sides of an 8-inch-square Pyrex or metal baking pan.

2. Melt the butter in a medium saucepan over medium heat, stirring occasionally. Remove the saucepan from the heat and add the cocoa. Whisk until smooth. Add the sugar and salt and whisk until blended. Add 1 egg and whisk until just blended. Whisk in the vanilla extract and the second egg until just blended. Sprinkle the flour over the mixture, and stir with a rubber spatula until just blended. Add the chopped chocolate and stir until combined.

3. Scrape the batter into the prepared baking pan and spread evenly. Scatter the nuts evenly over the batter, if using. Bake until a toothpick inserted in the center comes out with small, gooey clumps of brownie sticking to it, 33 to 38 minutes. Don't overbake or the brownies won't be fudgy. Transfer the baking dish to a rack and let cool completely.

4. Run a knife around the edges of the brownie and then pry it from the pan in one piece. Using a sharp knife, cut the cooled brownie into three equal strips and cut each strip into four equal pieces. Or, use a bench scraper to cut the brownie in the baking pan and then use a spatula to lift out the cut brownies. The cooler the brownie is, the cleaner the cutting will be, but these fudgy brownies will always leave some sticky crumbs on the knife. —*Abigail Johnson Dodge*

PER SERVING: 360 CALORIES | 4G PROTEIN | 45G CARB | 19G TOTAL FAT | 10G SAT FAT | 7G MONO FAT | 5G POLY FAT | 65MG CHOL | 65MG SODIUM | 2G FIBER

mexican-style pecan-chocolate squares

**MAKES SIXTEEN
2½-INCH SQUARES**

FOR THE COOKIE BASE

- **6 oz. (¾ cup) cold unsalted butter, cut into ½-inch pieces**
- **9 oz. (2 cups) unbleached all-purpose flour**
- **½ cup firmly packed light brown sugar**
- **2 tsp. ground cinnamon**
- **½ tsp. table salt**
- **2 oz. finely grated bittersweet chocolate (a scant ½ cup)**

FOR THE PECAN TOPPING

- **10 oz. (3 cups) pecans, toasted**
- **¼ lb. (½ cup) unsalted butter**
- **1 cup firmly packed dark brown sugar**
- **⅓ cup honey**
- **2 Tbs. heavy cream**
- **½ tsp. table salt**

Pecans add rich flavor to these bars. You can substitute walnuts if needed.

MAKE THE COOKIE BASE

Position a rack in the middle of the oven, and heat the oven to 350°F. Put the butter in a food processor, along with the flour, light brown sugar, cinnamon, and salt. Pulse until the mixture is well combined (about 20 pulses). Scatter the dough into a 9x9-inch baking pan, and press it evenly over the bottom. (Wipe out the processor bowl but don't bother washing it.) Bake the base until firm and lightly browned, about 25 minutes. When the cookie base comes out of the oven, sprinkle the grated chocolate evenly over the top. (Don't turn off the oven.) Set the pan aside.

MAKE THE PECAN TOPPING

As the cookie base bakes, pulse the pecans in the food processor until coarsely chopped. In a heavy-duty medium saucepan, melt the butter. Stir in the brown sugar, honey, cream, and salt. Simmer for 1 minute, stirring occasionally. Stir in the pecans. Pour the pecan mixture over the chocolate-sprinkled cookie base, spreading evenly. Bake until much of the filling is bubbling (not just the edges), 16 to 18 minutes. Let cool completely in the pan. When ready to serve, cut into 16 squares. Tightly covered, these bars will keep for about 5 days (though they never last that long).

—David Norman and Paula Disbrowe

PER SERVING: 430 CALORIES | 4G PROTEIN | 43G CARB | 30G TOTAL FAT | 11G SAT FAT | 11G MONO FAT | 5G POLY FAT | 40MG CHOL | 160MG SODIUM | 3G FIBER

kahlúa truffle triangles

**MAKES ABOUT 6 DOZEN
1½- TO 2-INCH TRIANGLES**

FOR THE CRUST

6¾ oz. (1 ½ cups) unbleached all-purpose flour

3 oz. (¾ cup) confectioners' sugar

¼ tsp. table salt

6 oz. (12 Tbs.) cold, unsalted butter, cut into 10 pieces; more for the pan

½ tsp. pure vanilla extract

FOR THE FILLING

1 lb. semisweet or bittersweet chocolate, broken into squares or very coarsely chopped

¾ cup whole or 2% milk

4 oz. (8 Tbs.) unsalted butter, cut into 6 pieces

4 large eggs

⅔ cup granulated sugar

2 Tbs. Kahlúa®

You can bake these up to 1 month ahead. Wrap the cooled baking pan in heavy-duty plastic wrap and freeze.

MAKE THE CRUST

1. Position a rack in the center of the oven, and heat the oven to 350°F. Line the bottom and sides of a 9x13-inch baking pan with foil, leaving some overhang on the long sides. Lightly butter the foil.

2. In a food processor, combine the flour, confectioners' sugar, and salt. Process the ingredients briefly to combine, about 15 seconds. Scatter the cold butter pieces and the vanilla extract over the flour mixture and process, using short pulses, until the dough forms small clumps, 1 to 1½ minutes. Turn the dough into the prepared pan. Using lightly floured fingertips, press the dough into the pan in an even layer. Bake until pale golden, especially around the edges, 22 to 25 minutes. Transfer the pan to a cooling rack, and lower the oven temperature to 325°F.

MAKE THE FILLING

1. In a medium bowl, melt the chocolate, milk, and butter together over a pot of barely simmering water or in the microwave. Whisk until smooth and set aside to cool slightly.

2. In a stand mixer fitted with a paddle attachment or in a large mixing bowl using a hand-held electric mixer, beat the eggs, sugar, and Kahlúa on medium-high speed until foamy and lighter in color, 2 minutes. Reduce the speed to low and gradually add the chocolate mixture. Stop the mixer and scrape down the bowl and beater. Beat on medium speed until well blended, about 30 seconds.

3. Pour the chocolate batter over the baked crust and spread evenly. Bake until the sides are slightly puffed and a toothpick inserted near the center comes out wet and gooey but not liquid, 30 to 35 minutes. Transfer the pan to a rack. As it cools, the center may sink a bit, leaving the edges slightly elevated. While the filling is still warm, use your fingertips to press the edges down to the level of the center, if necessary.

4. When completely cool, cover with plastic and refrigerate for at least 12 hours or up to 2 days. Using the foil handles, lift the rectangle from the pan and set it on a cutting board. Tipping the rectangle, carefully peel away the foil. Using a hot knife, cut 1½-inch-wide strips lengthwise, wiping the blade clean before each cut. Cut each strip on alternating diagonals to make small triangles. Let sit at room temperature for about 5 minutes before serving. *—Abigail Johnson Dodge*

PER SERVING: 90 CALORIES | 1G PROTEIN | 9G CARB | 6G TOTAL FAT | 3.5G SAT FAT | 1G MONO FAT | 0G POLY FAT | 20MG CHOL | 15MG SODIUM | 1G FIBER

thin and crisp chocolate chip cookies

**MAKES ABOUT 6 DOZEN
3-INCH COOKIES**

- **12 oz. (1½ cups) unsalted butter, at room temperature**
- **1 cup granulated sugar**
- **¾ cup firmly packed light brown sugar**
- **2 large eggs, at room temperature**
- **2 tsp. pure vanilla extract**
- **13½ oz. (3 cups) unbleached all-purpose flour**
- **1 tsp. table salt**
- **1 tsp. baking soda**
- **12 oz. semisweet chocolate chips**

Adding more white sugar than brown sugar increases the crispness. Be sure the butter and eggs are at room temperature before mixing to help the cookies spread thinner as they bake. Greased baking sheets encourage the cookies to spread even more.

1. Arrange racks in the upper and middle positions of the oven. Heat the oven to 375°F, and grease two baking sheets.

2. Using a mixer fitted with a paddle, beat together the butter, granulated sugar, and brown sugar on high until light and fluffy, about 1 minute. Scrape the bowl and beater. Add the eggs and vanilla extract, and beat on low until blended. Beat on high until light and fluffy, about 1 minute. Scrape the bowl and beater.

3. In a medium bowl, whisk together the flour, salt, and baking soda. Add this to the butter mixture, and beat on medium low until just blended. Stir in the chocolate chips with a wooden spoon.

4. Drop rounded measuring teaspoons of dough 2 inches apart onto the greased baking sheets. Bake until deep golden brown around the edges and golden in the center, 8 to 10 minutes, rotating the baking sheets halfway through for even results. Remove the sheets from the oven, let sit for 3 to 5 minutes, then transfer the cookies with a spatula to a wire rack to cool completely. Repeat until all the dough is baked.
—Bonnie Gorder-Hinchey

macadamia double-decker brownie bars

MAKES 4 DOZEN BARS

These gorgeous two-layer bars have a brownie base topped with a gooey nut-and-coconut-studded topping.

FOR THE BROWNIE LAYER

    Cooking spray

6 oz. (12 Tbs.) unsalted butter, cut into large chunks

1½ cups granulated sugar

2¼ oz. (¾ cup) unsweetened cocoa powder (natural or Dutch processed)

¼ tsp. table salt

2 large eggs

1 tsp. pure vanilla extract

3½ oz. (¾ cup) unbleached all-purpose flour

FOR THE MACADAMIA LAYER

½ cup firmly packed light brown sugar

1½ oz. (⅓ cup) unbleached all-purpose flour

⅔ cup light corn syrup

1½ oz. (3 Tbs.) unsalted butter, melted

1½ tsp. pure vanilla extract

2 large eggs

1½ cups roughly chopped salted macadamia nuts

⅓ cup sweetened coconut flakes

> **Dipping the knife in warm water and wiping it dry between cuts will keep the gooey topping from sticking to the knife.**

MAKE THE BROWNIE LAYER

1. Position a rack in the center of the oven, and heat the oven to 325°F. Line the bottom and sides of a 9x13-inch baking pan with foil, leaving some overhang on the sides, and spray with cooking spray.

2. In a medium saucepan over medium heat, whisk the butter until it is melted. Remove the pan from the heat, and add the sugar, cocoa powder, and salt. Whisk until well blended, about 1 minute. Add the eggs and vanilla extract and whisk until smooth. Add the flour and stir with a rubber spatula until blended. Scrape into the prepared pan and spread evenly. Bake until the top is shiny and dry looking and the brownie springs back slightly when pressed with a fingertip, about 20 minutes. (The brownie should not be completely baked.) Remove from the oven and place on a rack.

MAKE THE MACADAMIA TOPPING

1. While the brownie is baking, combine the brown sugar and flour in a large mixing bowl. Whisk until well blended, breaking up any large clumps. Add the corn syrup, melted butter, and vanilla extract. Whisk until blended, about 1 minute. Add the eggs and whisk just until combined, about 30 seconds. (Don't overmix or the batter will be foamy.) Add the nuts and coconut, and stir with a rubber spatula until evenly blended.

2. Pour the macadamia topping over the warm, partially baked brownie layer. Using a spatula, carefully spread the mixture into an even layer. Return the pan to the oven and bake until the top is golden brown, 37 to 40 minutes. Transfer the pan to a rack to cool completely. (At this point, the entire pan can be wrapped in plastic wrap, then foil, and frozen for up to 1 month.)

3. Using the foil as handles, lift the rectangle from the pan and invert onto a work surface. Carefully peel away the foil. Flip right side up. Using a sharp knife, cut into 2x2-inch squares and then cut each square into triangles. —*Abigail Johnson Dodge*

PER SERVING: 130 CALORIES | 1G PROTEIN | 16G CARB | 8G TOTAL FAT | 3G SAT FAT | 3.5G MONO FAT | 0G POLY FAT | 25MG CHOL | 35MG SODIUM | 1G FIBER

nutty butterscotch and chocolate bars

**MAKES 2 DOZEN
2-INCH BARS**

11¼ oz. (2½ cups) unbleached all-purpose flour

¾ tsp. baking soda

½ tsp. table salt

½ lb. (1 cup) unsalted butter, softened at room temperature; more for the pan

1¾ cups firmly packed light brown sugar

2 large eggs

1½ tsp. pure vanilla extract

7½ oz. (1¼ cups) semisweet chocolate chips

1¼ oz. (½ cup) sweetened coconut flakes

4½ oz. (1 cup) medium-finely chopped pecans or walnuts

This cookie goes by many aliases: blondie, golden brownie, congo bar. No matter what you call them, they're butterscotch-flavored, chewy, and loaded with texture.

1. Position a rack in the middle of the oven, and heat the oven to 325°F. Lightly grease the bottom and sides of a 9x13-inch baking pan.

2. In a medium bowl, whisk the flour, baking soda, and salt to blend. In a large bowl, combine the butter and brown sugar. With a hand-held mixer or a stand mixer fitted with a paddle attachment, beat the butter and brown sugar on medium until well blended and fluffy, about 2 minutes. Add the eggs and vanilla extract and continue to beat on medium until well blended, about another 1 minute. Add the flour mixture and mix on low until just blended, about 1 minute. Pour in the chocolate chips and coconut; mix on low until combined.

3. Scrape the dough into the prepared pan and spread evenly. Scatter the nuts evenly over the top. Bake until a toothpick inserted in the center comes out almost clean with a few moist crumbs clinging to it, about 40 minutes. Transfer the pan to a rack and let cool completely. Cut into bars, squares, or triangles. Cover with plastic and store at room temperature for up to 2 days or freeze for up to 1 month.
—Abigail Johnson Dodge

double dark chocolate thumbprints

MAKES ABOUT 4 DOZEN COOKIES

FOR THE COOKIES

- 6   oz. (1⅓ cups) unbleached all-purpose flour
- ½   tsp. table salt
- ½   tsp. baking powder
- ¼   tsp. baking soda
- 4   oz. (½ cup) unsalted butter, softened
- 1⅓ cups granulated sugar
- 1½ oz. (½ cup) natural, unsweetened cocoa powder, sifted if lumpy
- 3   large eggs
- ¾   tsp. pure vanilla extract
- 3   oz. bittersweet chocolate, melted and cooled slightly

FOR THE CHOCOLATE FILLING

- 3   oz. bittersweet chocolate, coarsely chopped (½ cup)
- 2   oz. (4 Tbs.) unsalted butter, cut into 3 pieces

These cookies are all about the chocolate. The dough has both cocoa and bittersweet chocolate, and the ganache filling is rich and dark.

MAKE THE COOKIES

1. Position a rack in the center of the oven, and heat the oven to 350°F. Line three cookie sheets with parchment or nonstick baking liners.

2. In a medium bowl, whisk together the flour, salt, baking powder, and baking soda.

3. In a stand mixer fitted with a paddle attachment, beat the butter, sugar, and cocoa powder on medium speed until well blended, about 2 minutes. Scrape down the bowl and the beater. Add the eggs one at a time, mixing until blended after each addition, about 30 seconds, and adding the vanilla extract along with the last egg. Continue mixing on medium speed until well blended, about 1 minute. Add the cooled, melted chocolate and mix until just blended, about 30 seconds. Add the flour mixture and mix on low speed until well blended, about 1 minute.

4. Using two tablespoons or a mini ice cream scoop, drop tablespoons of dough about 1½ inches apart on the prepared cookie sheets. Bake, one sheet at a time, until the cookies are puffed and the tops are cracked and look dry, 11 to 13 minutes. When the cookies are just out of the oven, use the rounded side of a half-teaspoon measure or the end of a thick-handled wooden spoon to make a small, deep well in the center of each cookie. Let the cookies sit on the cookie sheet for 5 minutes and then transfer them to a rack to cool completely. (At this point, you can fill the cookies immediately, or store in an airtight container at room temperature for up to 3 days or freeze for up to 1 month before filling.)

MAKE THE FILLING

Melt the chocolate and butter in the microwave or in a medium bowl set in a skillet of barely simmering water, stirring with a rubber spatula until smooth. Remove from the heat and set aside until cool and slightly thickened.

FILL THE COOKIES

Spoon the chocolate mixture into the wells of the cooled cookies. Set aside until the chocolate firms up, about 1 hour. Serve immediately or store in an airtight container at room temperature for up to 3 days.
—*Abigail Johnson Dodge*

PER SERVING: 90 CALORIES | 1G PROTEIN | 11G CARB | 4.5G TOTAL FAT | 2.5G SAT FAT | 1.5G MONO FAT | 0G POLY FAT | 20MG CHOL | 45MG SODIUM | 1G FIBER

mocha sandwich cookies

MAKES ABOUT 5 DOZEN COOKIES

FOR THE COOKIES

- 7½ oz. (1⅔ cups) unbleached all-purpose flour
- ¾ oz. (¼ cup) Dutch-processed cocoa
- ½ tsp. baking soda
- ¼ tsp. table salt
- 4 oz. (½ cup) unsalted butter, at room temperature
- ½ cup plus 2 Tbs. granulated sugar
- 6 Tbs. firmly packed light brown sugar
- 1 large egg
- 1 tsp. pure vanilla extract

Make Ahead

The filling can be made up to 3 days ahead and refrigerated. For the best texture, assemble the sandwiches as close to serving as possible.

Delicate chocolate cookies stack up with a mocha-cream-cheese filling in these sweet little sandwiches.

MAKE THE COOKIES

1. In a medium bowl, whisk the flour, cocoa, baking soda, and salt; set aside. With a hand mixer or a stand mixer fitted with a paddle attachment, cream the butter and sugars on medium speed until light and fluffy, about 2 minutes. Add the egg and vanilla extract, and continue beating until blended and smooth, about 30 seconds. Reduce the speed to low and slowly add the dry ingredients, mixing until the dough is just combined. Divide the dough in half. Wrap half of the dough in plastic and refrigerate.

2. Roll the other half of the dough between two sheets of parchment to an even ⅛-inch thickness. Slide the dough onto a cookie sheet and freeze until cold and firm, about 30 minutes. Repeat with the remaining dough.

3. Position a rack in the center of the oven, and heat the oven to 350°F. Line two cookie sheets with parchment.

4. Using 1½-inch round cookie cutters, cut out the dough and arrange the rounds 1 inch apart on the prepared sheets. If the dough gets too soft, return it to the freezer for a few minutes. Carefully press the scraps together, reroll, and cut. Repeat with the other half of the dough, then gather all the scraps together, reroll, and cut one more time.

5. Bake in batches, two sheets at a time, until the tops look dry, about 6 minutes. Let the cookies cool on their sheets for a minute and then let them cool completely on racks.

FOR THE MOCHA FILLING

- **1 Tbs. instant espresso**
- **2 oz. (4 Tbs.) unsalted butter, at room temperature**
- **2 oz. (4 Tbs.) cream cheese**
- **6 oz. (1½ cups) confectioners' sugar, sifted**
- **1 tsp. pure vanilla extract**
- **¾ oz. (¼ cup) Dutch-processed cocoa powder, sifted**

MAKE THE FILLING

1. In a small bowl, dissolve the espresso in 2 Tbs. hot water. Let cool slightly, 5 minutes.

2. With the mixer, cream the butter and cream cheese on medium speed until light and smooth, about 1 minute. Reduce the speed to low and slowly add half of the sugar, mixing until just combined. Add the espresso mixture and vanilla extract, and mix until just incorporated. Gradually mix in the remaining sugar and the cocoa. Increase the speed to medium and beat until the filling is light and fluffy, about 1 minute more.

ASSEMBLE THE COOKIES

Transfer the cooled cookies to a work surface, flipping half of them over. Using an offset spatula or butter knife, spread a thin layer of the filling onto each turned-over cookie. Set another cookie on top of each filled cookie, pressing gently to spread the filling. The cookies will keep at room temperature for up to 3 days or in the freezer for up to 1 month. *—David Crofton*

PER SERVING: 60 CALORIES I 1G PROTEIN I 9G CARB I 3G TOTAL FAT I 2G SAT FAT I 1G MONO FAT I 0G POLY FAT I 10MG CHOL I 25MG SODIUM I 0G FIBER

More about Dutch-processed cocoa powder

Dutch-processing cocoa involves washing the cocoa (before or after grinding) in an alkaline solution. The resulting cocoa is not only darker in color and mellower in flavor, but also is less acidic than the natural (non-alkalized) powder. Dutch-processed cocoa tends to produce moister and deeper-colored baked goods—an advantage that makes it a favorite of many pastry chefs.

nutty chocolate shortbread wedges

SERVES 12 TO 16

FOR THE SHORTBREAD

- ¼ lb. (½ cup) unsalted butter, at room temperature; more for the pan
- ½ cup granulated sugar
- ¾ oz. (¼ cup) unsweetened cocoa powder, preferably Dutch-processed
- ¼ tsp. table salt
- 1 large egg yolk
- ½ tsp. pure vanilla extract
- 4½ oz. (1 cup) unbleached all-purpose flour

FOR THE GLAZE

- 3 oz. bittersweet or semi-sweet chocolate, coarsely chopped (a generous ½ cup)
- 1 oz. (2 Tbs.) unsalted butter, cut into 2 pieces
- ½ cup (2 oz.) coarsely chopped pecans or walnuts, toasted and cooled, or chopped pistachios

This is a nontraditional shortbread because it contains an egg yolk, which gives the shortbread a softer, less sandy texture.

MAKE THE SHORTBREAD

1. Position a rack in the middle of the oven, and heat the oven to 350°F. Lightly butter the bottom and sides of a 9½-inch fluted tart pan with a removable bottom.

2. In a medium bowl, combine the butter, sugar, cocoa, and salt. Beat with an electric mixer on medium speed until well blended. Scrape the bowl. Add the egg yolk and vanilla extract and continue beating on medium speed until just combined. Add the flour and mix on low speed, scraping the bowl as needed, until the flour mixes in and the dough begins to clump together, about 1 minute. Scrape the dough into the pan, scattering the pieces of dough evenly. Using your finger-tips (lightly floured, if necessary), pat the dough onto the bottom (not up the sides) of the prepared pan to create an even layer. Bake until the top no longer looks wet and the dough just barely begins to pull away slightly from the sides of the pan, about 25 minutes.

MAKE THE GLAZE

Shortly before the shortbread is done, make the glaze. Melt the chocolate and butter in the top of a double boiler or in a microwave oven. Stir until smooth. When the shortbread is done, transfer the pan to a rack. Pour the warm glaze over the shortbread and, using an offset spatula, spread the glaze evenly to within ½ inch of the edge. Scatter the nuts evenly over the glaze and gently press them into the glaze. Let cool completely until the glaze is set, then remove the shortbread from the tart pan. Cut it into 12 or 16 wedges, and serve at room tem-perature. —*Abigail Johnson Dodge*

PER SERVING: 180 CALORIES | 2G PROTEIN | 16G CARB | 13G TOTAL FAT | 6G SAT FAT | 4G MONO FAT | 1.5G POLY FAT | 30MG CHOL | 40MG SODIUM | 1G FIBER

peanut butter and chocolate sandwiches

MAKES ABOUT 30
SANDWICH COOKIES
(OR 60 SINGLE COOKIES)

FOR THE PEANUT BUTTER COOKIES

- 2½ cups smooth peanut butter, at room temperature
- 1½ cups firmly packed light brown sugar
- 1 tsp. baking soda
- 2 large eggs
- 2 tsp. pure vanilla extract

FOR THE CHOCOLATE FILLING

- 10 oz. bittersweet chocolate, coarsely chopped (about 2 cups)
- 4 oz. (8 Tbs.) unsalted butter, cut into 4 pieces

These soft, flourless cookies house a bittersweet chocolate filling, for a taste combination that appeals to the kid in all of us. Substitute semi-sweet chocolate for the bittersweet in the filling for a sweeter kick.

MAKE THE COOKIES

1. Position a rack in the center of the oven, and heat the oven to 350°F. Line four cookie sheets with parchment or nonstick baking liners.

2. In the bowl of a stand mixer fitted with a paddle attachment (or in a large mixing bowl with a hand mixer), beat the peanut butter, brown sugar, and baking soda on medium speed until well blended, about 1 minute. Add the eggs and vanilla and mix on low speed until just blended, about 25 seconds.

3. Form level tablespoonfuls of the dough into balls about 1 inch in diameter. (The balls of dough may be frozen for 1 month. Thaw them overnight in the refrigerator before proceeding with the recipe.) Arrange the balls 1½ inches apart on the prepared baking sheets. Do not press down. Bake one sheet at a time until the cookies are puffed and crackled but still moist looking, about 11 minutes. Transfer the cookie sheet to a rack to cool about 10 minutes. Using a spatula, move the cookies to the rack and let cool completely. Repeat with the remaining cookies.

MAKE THE FILLING

Melt the chocolate and butter in a microwave or in a medium heat-proof bowl set in a skillet with 1 inch of barely simmering water, stirring with a rubber spatula until smooth. Remove from the heat and set aside until cool and slightly thickened, 20 to 30 minutes.

ASSEMBLE THE SANDWICHES

Turn half of the cooled cookies over so they are flat side up. Spoon 2 tsp. of the chocolate filling onto the center of each cookie. Top with the remaining cookies, flat side down. Press gently on each cookie to spread the filling almost to the edge. Set on the rack until the filling is firm, 20 to 30 minutes. —*Abigail Johnson Dodge*

PER SERVING: 250 CALORIES | 7G PROTEIN | 21G CARB | 17G TOTAL FAT | 6G SAT FAT | 7G MONO FAT | 3G POLY FAT | 20MG CHOL | 160MG SODIUM | 2G FIBER

peanut butter and chocolate shortbread bars

**MAKES 4 DOZEN
1½-INCH-SQUARE BARS**

FOR THE PEANUT SHORTBREAD

- 7 oz. (14 Tbs.) unsalted butter, melted and cooled to just warm
- ½ cup granulated sugar
- ½ tsp. table salt
- 9½ oz. (2 cups plus 2 Tbs.) unbleached all-purpose flour
- ½ cup unsalted peanuts, finely chopped

FOR THE PEANUT BUTTER FILLING

- 1 cup creamy peanut butter (not natural but an emulsified variety such as Jif®)
- 3 oz. (6 Tbs.) unsalted butter, at room temperature
- 6 oz. (1½ cups) confectioners' sugar
- 1 tsp. pure vanilla extract

FOR THE GANACHE

- 5 oz. good-quality bittersweet chocolate, such as Lindt® Excellence, chopped (about 1 heaping cup)
- ½ cup plus 2 Tbs. heavy cream

This classic bar cookie features a rich, buttery shortbread crust. The cookies will keep at room temperature for up to a week.

MAKE THE SHORTBREAD

1. Line a straight-sided 13x9-inch metal baking pan with foil, letting the ends overhang for easy removal of the shortbread later.

2. In a medium bowl, stir together the butter, sugar, and salt. Stir in the flour and peanuts to make a stiff dough. Press the mixture evenly into the bottom of the prepared pan. Prick the dough all over with a fork. Refrigerate the pan for 30 minutes (or freeze for 5 to 7 minutes), until the dough is firm.

3. Meanwhile, position a rack in the center of the oven, and heat the oven to 325°F.

4. Bake the dough for 20 minutes, then decrease the oven temperature to 300°F and bake until the crust is golden brown all over and completely set, 20 to 25 more minutes. Let the crust cool completely before topping.

MAKE THE FILLING

1. Put the peanut butter and butter in the bowl of a stand mixer fitted with a paddle attachment and beat on medium speed until smooth, about 1 minute. Add about half of the confectioners' sugar along with the vanilla extract and 1 Tbs. hot water. Beat on low speed until combined, then on medium speed until smooth and fluffy, about 1 more minute. Beat in the remaining sugar and mix until the mixture is smooth and thick, like frosting, about 1 more minute. If the filling seems too stiff, add another 1 Tbs. hot water and beat for another minute.

2. Using a knife or metal offset spatula, spread the filling over the fully cooled crust. The filling may not spread smoothly and evenly, but don't worry; the ganache will cover it.

MAKE THE GANACHE

1. Put the chocolate in a small heatproof bowl. In a small saucepan, bring the heavy cream to a boil. Remove from the heat and pour over the chocolate. Let sit for 3 minutes. Stir gently with a rubber spatula until combined and smooth.

2. Spread the ganache over the peanut butter filling using a metal off-set spatula to coat evenly. Let the bars sit for at least 3 hours to allow the ganache to set before cutting (or refrigerate for 1 hour).

3. Carefully lift the bars from the pan using the foil sides and transfer them to a cutting board. Separate the foil from the bars by sliding a spatula between them. Cut the bars into 1½-inch squares. They will keep at room temperature for 1 week. *—Nicole Rees*

PER SERVING: 150 CALORIES | 3G PROTEIN | 13G CARB | 11G TOTAL FAT | 5G SAT FAT | 3G MONO FAT | 1G POLY FAT | 15MG CHOL | 50MG SODIUM | 1G FIBER

pine nut and chocolate caramel bars

MAKES 2 DOZEN BARS

FOR THE CRUST

- **8 oz. (1 cup) unsalted butter, softened, cut into 6 pieces**
- **⅔ cup granulated sugar**
- **1 Tbs. finely grated orange zest**
- **¼ tsp. kosher salt**
- **11¼ oz. (2½ cups) unbleached all-purpose flour**
- **5 oz. bittersweet chocolate, chopped**

FOR THE TOPPING

- **1¼ cups granulated sugar**
- **¾ cup heavy cream**
- **1½ oz. (3 Tbs.) unsalted butter, cut into 6 pieces**
- **¼ tsp. kosher salt**
- **1½ cups pine nuts**

With an orange-scented short-bread crust, gooey caramel topping, and delicate choco-late drizzle, this addictive treat is a great riff on the classic chocolate turtle candy.

MAKE THE CRUST

1. Position a rack in the center of the oven, and heat the oven to 350°F. Line a straight-sided 13x9-inch metal baking pan with a large piece of heavy-duty foil, leaving a 2-inch overhang on two sides.

2. In a stand mixer fitted with a paddle attachment or in a large bowl using a hand mixer, beat the butter, sugar, orange zest, and salt on medium-high speed until light and fluffy, 1 to 3 minutes. Scrape the bowl. On low speed, mix in the flour until the dough is uniformly sandy, 1 to 2 minutes. Transfer the dough to the prepared pan and press evenly into the bottom. Bake until lightly golden, about 20 minutes. Let the crust cool completely on a wire rack.

3. Melt the chocolate in a medium heatproof bowl set in a skillet of barely simmering water, stirring frequently, until smooth (be careful not to get any water in the chocolate). With a small offset spatula, spread all but about 2 Tbs. of the melted chocolate evenly over the cooled crust. Return the bowl with the remaining chocolate to the skillet of warm water and set aside off the heat to keep warm.

MAKE THE TOPPING

Put 3 Tbs. of water in a heavy-duty 3-quart saucepan. Pour the sugar in the center of the pan and pat it down with a spatula just until evenly moistened. Cook over medium-high heat without stirring until the syrup turns amber, 6 to 8 minutes; swirl the pan as the sugar caramel-izes to help it cook evenly. Slowly whisk in the cream (be careful—it will bubble vigorously and produce a lot of steam). Whisk in the butter and salt and boil until the butter is combined, 1 minute more.

ASSEMBLE THE BARS

1. Pour the caramel evenly over the crust. Sprinkle the pine nuts over the caramel. Bake until the caramel is bubbling all over and jiggles only slightly in the center when the pan is nudged, 24 to 26 minutes.

2. If necessary, reheat the remaining chocolate until fluid. With a spoon, drizzle the chocolate over the top. Let cool completely before cutting into squares. —*Samantha Seneviratne*

PER SERVING: 310 CALORIES | 3G PROTEIN | 31G CARB | 20G TOTAL FAT | 9G SAT FAT | 5G MONO FAT | 3.5G POLY FAT | 35MG CHOL | 35MG SODIUM | 1G FIBER

rich, fudgy brownies

MAKES 16 BROWNIES

- 8 oz. (1 cup) unsalted butter; more softened butter for the pan
- 3 oz. (⅔ cup) unbleached all-purpose flour; more for the pan
- 2 cups granulated sugar
- 4 large eggs, at room temperature
- ½ tsp. pure vanilla extract
- 2½ oz. (¾ cup) unsweetened natural cocoa powder
- ½ tsp. baking powder
- ½ tsp. table salt
- 1 recipe Port-Soaked Dried Cherries (optional; recipe on p. 52)
- 1 recipe Port-Ganache Topping (optional; recipe on p. 52)

This brownie recipe gives you two options. For a picnic or a snack, make the brownies with the first eight ingredients. For an elegant dessert, add the Port-Soaked Dried Cherries to the batter and frost the cooled brownies with the Port-Ganache Topping.

1. Position a rack in the center of the oven, and heat the oven to 350°F. Butter and flour a 9-inch-square metal baking pan, tapping out the excess flour.

2. Melt the butter in a medium saucepan over medium heat. Remove the pan from the heat. Whisk or stir in the sugar, followed by the eggs and vanilla extract. Stir in the flour, cocoa, baking powder, and salt, starting slowly to keep the ingredients from flying out of the pan and stirring more vigorously as you go. Stir until the batter is smooth and uniform, about 1 minute. If you're using the Port-Soaked Cherries, stir them in at this time, along with any remaining liquid from the saucepan.

3. Spread the batter into the prepared baking pan, smoothing it so it fills the pan evenly. Bake until a toothpick or a skewer inserted ¾ inch into the center of the brownies comes out with just a few moist clumps clinging to it, about 40 minutes. Let the brownies cool completely in the pan on a rack.

4. If you're topping the brownies with the ganache, spread it evenly over the cooled brownies and give the ganache about 1 hour to set (it will still be quite soft and gooey). Cut into 16 squares. Keep the brownies well wrapped at room temperature. You can freeze them, too. *—Nicole Rees*

PER SERVING: 250 CALORIES I 3G PROTEIN I 32G CARB I 13G TOTAL FAT I 8G SAT FAT I 6G MONO FAT I 2.5G POLY FAT I 85MG CHOL I 105MG SODIUM I 1G FIBER

continued on p. 52

port-soaked dried cherries

MAKES ½ CUP

½ cup dried cherries, very coarsely chopped (or whole dried cranberries)

⅓ cup tawny port

In a small saucepan, bring the cherries and port to a boil over medium heat. Reduce the heat to low and cook for 2 minutes. Take the pan off the heat and let cool to room temperature.

port-ganache topping

MAKES 1 GENEROUS CUP

½ cup tawny port

½ cup heavy cream

6 oz. semisweet chocolate, finely chopped (about 1 cup)

1. In a small saucepan over medium heat, bring the port to a boil. Boil until the port is reduced to 2 Tbs., 3 to 6 minutes. Pour it into a small cup or bowl. Thoroughly rinse the pan. Bring the heavy cream to a boil in the pan over medium-high heat, stirring occasionally. Take the pan off the heat. Stir in the chopped chocolate and reduced port until the mixture is smooth and the chocolate is melted.

2. Pour the ganache into a bowl, and cover the surface with plastic wrap to prevent a skin from forming. Put the bowl in a cool part of the kitchen, and let the ganache cool to room temperature, stirring occasionally. When it's cool, spread it over the brownies as directed in the brownie recipe.

triple chocolate biscotti

**MAKES ABOUT 4 DOZEN
BISCOTTI**

- 9 oz. (1¾ cups) hazelnuts
- 10½ oz. (2⅔ cups) unbleached all-purpose flour
- 2 cups granulated sugar
- 3½ oz. (1 cup) Dutch-processed cocoa powder
- 1½ Tbs. finely ground dark-roast coffee beans or instant espresso powder
- 1½ tsp. baking soda
- ¼ tsp. salt
- 4 oz. (⅔ cup) chocolate chips
- 5 large eggs
- 1½ tsp. pure vanilla extract
- 12 oz. white chocolate

Covering one side of these chocolate biscotti with white chocolate gives them an elegant look and a moister texture.

1. Position a rack in the center of the oven, and heat the oven to 325°. Toast the hazelnuts on a baking sheet until they emit a nutty aroma but haven't turned dark brown inside, 10 to 15 minutes. If they still have skins, cover the nuts with a dishtowel or paper towels for a few minutes after you take them out of the oven, then rub the nuts with the towel to remove the skins. Set aside to cool.

2. Put the flour, sugar, cocoa powder, ground coffee beans, baking soda, and salt into the bowl of an electric mixer fitted with a paddle. Combine these ingredients on medium-low speed and then toss in the nuts and chocolate chips. In a separate bowl, lightly whisk together the eggs and vanilla extract. With the mixer running on low speed, slowly add the egg mixture to the mixing bowl and mix until the dough comes together. Remove the bowl from the mixer and mix in any remaining dry ingredients from the bottom by hand.

3. Line a cookie sheet with parchment. Divide the dough into quarters and place on the cookie sheet. Working on the sheet, shape each quarter into a loaf about 10 inches long and 2 inches in diameter. Place the logs 4 inches apart on the cookie sheet. Bake the logs at 325°F until the sides are firm, the tops are cracked, and the dough inside the cracks no longer looks wet, 30 to 35 minutes. Remove the baking sheet from the oven and reduce the oven temperature to 300°F. Let the logs cool on the baking sheet for at least 10 minutes before slicing. Cut the logs on a slight diagonal into ¾-inch-thick slices. Place the biscotti flat on the baking sheet and dry them in the oven until the biscotti offer resistance when pressed, about 25 minutes. Transfer the biscotti to a rack to cool.

4. While the biscotti are cooling, chop the white chocolate and melt it in a microwave on low or in a double boiler over simmering water. Using a knife, spread white chocolate on one cut side of each cooled biscotti. Put the biscotti, white chocolate side down, on a parchment-lined baking sheet. Allow the chocolate to harden. Peel the biscotti from the parchment and store in an airtight container.
—*Emily Luchetti*

ultimate fudgy brownies

MAKES 2 DOZEN

12 oz. (1½ cups) unsalted butter, cut into 9 pieces; more softened butter for the pan

3¾ oz. (1¼ cups) unsweetened natural cocoa powder, sifted if lumpy

2¾ cups granulated sugar

½ tsp. table salt

5 large eggs

2 tsp. pure vanilla extract

7½ oz. (1⅔ cups) unbleached all-purpose flour

> **The key to brownies with a moist, fudgy interior is to bake them just until a toothpick inserted in the center comes out with small bits of brownie attached. Baking any longer will result in dry, overcooked brownies.**

You won't find the secret to rich, fudgy chocolate brownies in a box: Make them from scratch for the best flavor and texture. This one-pot batter (fewer dishes to do!) comes together in minutes and requires no special equipment. And there's a good chance that the ingredients are already in your kitchen: cocoa powder, sugar, flour, butter, and eggs.

1. Position a rack in the center of the oven, and heat the oven to 325°F. Line the bottom and sides of a 9x13-inch straight-sided metal baking pan with heavy-duty aluminum foil, leaving about a 2-inch overhang on the short sides. Lightly butter the foil.

2. Put the butter in a large (4-quart) saucepan over medium-low heat and stir occasionally until melted, about 2 minutes. Off the heat, whisk in the cocoa powder until smooth, 1 minute. Add the sugar and salt, and whisk until well blended. Use your fingertip to check the temperature of the batter—it should be warm, not hot. If it's hot, set the pan aside for a minute or two before continuing.

3. Whisk in the eggs, two and then three at a time, until just blended. Whisk in the vanilla extract until the batter is well blended. Sprinkle the flour over the batter, and stir with a rubber spatula until just blended.

Tips for Success

• **Choose the right cocoa.** This recipe calls for natural unsweetened cocoa powder, which has a much stronger chocolate flavor than melted bittersweet chocolate. (Cocoa powder is chocolate with most of its cocoa butter pressed out, hence its big chocolate punch.) Don't substitute Dutch-processed cocoa; it has a milder flavor and so will your brownies.

• **Prep the pan.** For brownies with sharp, clean edges, use a straight-sided rectangular metal baking pan and line it with aluminum foil for easy brownie removal. The foil also helps with cleanup.

• **Check the batter temp.** Once you've combined the hot melted butter with the cocoa, sugar, and salt, check the batter with your fingertip before adding the eggs. It should be warm—not hot—or your eggs will cook and curdle. Set it aside to cool for a few minutes if necessary.

4. Scrape the batter into the prepared pan and spread evenly. Bake until a toothpick inserted in the center comes out with small bits of brownie sticking to it, 35 to 45 minutes. For fudgy brownies, do not overbake. Cool the brownies completely in the pan on a rack, about 3 hours.

5. When the brownies are cool, use the foil overhang to lift them from the pan. Invert onto a cutting board and carefully peel away the foil. Flip again and cut into 24 squares. Serve immediately or wrap in plastic and store at room temperature for up to 3 days. They can also be frozen in an airtight container or freezer bag for up to 1 month.
—*Abigail Johnson Dodge*

PER SERVING: 250 CALORIES | 3G PROTEIN | 32G CARB | 14G TOTAL FAT | 8G SAT FAT | 3.5G MONO FAT | 0.5G POLY FAT | 75MG CHOL | 65MG SODIUM | 2G FIBER

warm chocolate-stout brownie sundaes

SERVES 6;
MAKES ABOUT 1 CUP SAUCE

FOR THE BROWNIES

- 2 oz. (4 Tbs.) unsalted butter
- 3 oz. bittersweet chocolate (70% to 75% cacao), coarsely chopped (about ¾ cup)
- ½ tsp. instant espresso powder
- ¼ tsp. pure vanilla extract
- ⅛ tsp. table salt
- ½ cup firmly packed dark brown sugar
- 1 large egg, at room temperature
- ¼ cup chocolate stout, at room temperature
- 1⅛ oz. (¼ cup) unbleached all-purpose flour

FOR THE SAUCE

- ½ cup chocolate stout
- 3½ oz. bittersweet chocolate (70% to 75% cacao), chopped (generous ¾ cup)
- 2 Tbs. granulated sugar
- ¼ cup heavy cream

FOR SERVING

- 1 quart dulce de leche ice cream

Stout not only gives these brownies a moist texture but also serves as the base for an unusual chocolate sauce. If you can't find chocolate stout, regular stout is fine.

MAKE THE BROWNIES

1. Position a rack in the center of the oven, and heat the oven to 375°F. Line six standard-size muffin cups with cupcake liners.

2. In a 4-cup Pyrex measuring cup, microwave the butter on high until melted and very hot, 60 to 90 seconds. Add the chocolate to the melted butter and microwave on high for 30 seconds; let stand for 1 minute. Stir until the chocolate is completely melted and smooth, heating more, if necessary, in 15-second bursts.

3. Whisk the espresso powder, vanilla extract, and salt into the chocolate mixture. Whisk in the brown sugar until it begins to dissolve, about 30 seconds. Whisk in the egg until the mixture is thick and smooth, 30 to 45 seconds. Whisk in the stout and then the flour until the mixture is completely smooth, about 30 seconds.

4. Portion the batter evenly among the prepared muffin cups, filling each three-quarters full. Bake until the centers are barely set and a tester inserted in the center comes out with moist crumbs, 15 to 20 minutes. Transfer to a rack to cool slightly.

MAKE THE SAUCE

Meanwhile, in a heavy-duty 1-quart saucepan, boil the stout over high heat until reduced by half, 3 to 4 minutes. Remove from the heat. Add the chocolate and sugar; let stand for 1 minute. Add the cream and whisk until smooth.

SERVE THE SUNDAES

Remove the warm brownies from the liners and put them on small dessert plates. Top each with some of the ice cream and sauce and serve. —*Nicole Rees*

PER SERVING: 800 CALORIES | 11G PROTEIN | 79G CARB | 48G TOTAL FAT | 29G SAT FAT | 8G MONO FAT | 1G POLY FAT | 200MG CHOL | 220MG SODIUM | 3G FIBER

chocolate mousse layer cake
(recipe on p. 81)

cakes, breads & more

dark chocolate soufflé cakes with espresso-chocolate sauce

SERVES 6

Softened butter and granulated sugar for the ramekins

FOR THE ESPRESSO-CHOCOLATE SAUCE

- 1 tsp. instant espresso powder
- 8 oz. bittersweet or semisweet chocolate, coarsely chopped
- 3 oz. (6 Tbs.) unsalted butter, cut into 8 pieces

Table salt

FOR THE SOUFFLÉ CAKES

- 2 Tbs. unsweetened natural cocoa powder
- 3 large eggs, separated
- ⅛ tsp. cream of tartar
- 3 Tbs. granulated sugar

These soufflé cakes are pure chocolate goodness made practically foolproof. There's no tricky unmolding, and the superb bittersweet chocolate-sauce center doesn't need perfect timing to achieve. Don't worry about huge height for these soufflés, either, as they are even more flavorful after they have cooled and deflated slightly.

Put a metal or Pyrex pie plate or cake pan in the freezer to chill. Lightly butter six 6-oz. ramekins or custard cups. Coat with sugar and tap out the excess.

MAKE THE SAUCE

1. In a small bowl, combine the espresso powder with 2 Tbs. warm water and stir to dissolve.

2. In a medium heatproof bowl set in or over a skillet of barely simmering water, melt the chocolate and butter, stirring frequently until smooth. Add 2 pinches of salt, stir, and remove from the heat. Transfer 5 Tbs. of the chocolate mixture to the espresso and stir to blend. (Set the remaining melted chocolate aside.) Use a spatula to scrape the espresso mixture into a puddle on the chilled pie plate or cake pan, and return it to the freezer until firm, about 10 minutes. When the espresso-chocolate mixture is firm, use a teaspoon to scrape it into six rough balls. Keep the balls on the plate and refrigerate until ready to use.

MAKE THE SOUFFLÉ CAKES

1. Reheat the remaining chocolate mixture by setting its bowl in or over a skillet of hot water. When it's warm, remove it from the heat and whisk in the cocoa and 2 egg yolks.

2. In a clean, dry bowl, beat the 3 egg whites and cream of tartar on medium speed in a stand mixer (or on high speed with a hand-held mixer) until the whites mound gently. Gradually beat in the sugar and continue beating until the whites form medium-firm peaks when you lift the beaters; the tips should curl over but still look moist, glossy, and flexible.

3. With a rubber spatula, fold about one-quarter of the egg whites into the chocolate to lighten it. Scrape the remaining whites into the bowl and gently fold in until blended, taking care not to deflate the whites. Take the chocolate balls out of the refrigerator, and put one ball in the center of each ramekin. Divide the batter evenly among the ramekins, and level the tops gently with the back of a spoon. You can now heat the oven and bake right away or cover the ramekins with plastic wrap and refrigerate for up to 2 days.

BAKE THE SOUFFLÉ CAKES

Position a rack in the lower third of the oven, and heat the oven to 400°F. Remove the plastic from the ramekins, if necessary, and put the ramekins on a baking sheet. Bake until the soufflé cakes are puffed and possibly a little cracked on top (a toothpick inserted in the center will meet no resistance and will emerge mostly clean—the tip will be wet from the sauce at the bottom), 11 to 14 minutes (a minute or two longer if they were chilled overnight). Let cool for a few minutes before serving. —*Alice Medrich*

Make Ahead

The assembled, unbaked soufflé cakes can be wrapped in plastic and refrigerated for up to 2 days. They do not need to come to room temperature before baking, but will need to bake for 1 to 2 minutes longer.

german chocolate bombes

MAKES 10 INDIVIDUAL BOMBES

FOR THE CAKE

	Cooking spray
4	oz. unsweetened chocolate, chopped (about 1 cup)
1	oz. (¼ cup) natural cocoa powder
7	oz. (1½ cups) unbleached all-purpose flour
1	tsp. baking soda
¼	tsp. kosher salt
1½	cups firmly packed dark brown sugar
8	oz. (1 cup) unsalted butter, softened
4	large eggs, at room temperature
½	cup buttermilk, at room temperature
1	tsp. pure vanilla extract

FOR THE COCONUT-PECAN FILLING

3¼	oz. (about 1 cup) sweetened, shredded dried coconut, toasted and cooled
3	oz. (⅔ cup) pecans, toasted and cooled
⅔	cup granulated sugar
2½	oz. (5 Tbs.) unsalted butter, cut into chunks
6	large egg yolks
1	5-oz. can evaporated milk
½	tsp. pure vanilla extract

A riff on classic German chocolate cake, these showstopping desserts are the perfect ending for a dinner party because you can make them ahead. This recipe contains raw eggs; if that's a concern, buy pasteurized.

MAKE THE CAKE

1. Position a rack in the center of the oven, and heat the oven to 325°F. Coat a 13x18-inch rimmed baking sheet with cooking spray.

2. Put the chocolate and cocoa in a medium heatproof bowl, add 1½ cups boiling water, and whisk to combine and melt the chocolate. Set aside to cool slightly. In a small bowl, combine the flour, baking soda, and salt.

3. Beat the sugar and butter in a stand mixer fitted with a paddle attachment on medium speed until light and fluffy, 3 to 5 minutes, stopping to scrape the bowl halfway through. Add the eggs one at a time, beating well after each addition. Slowly add the buttermilk and vanilla extract—the batter will look curdled at this point. Reduce the mixer speed to low. Alternate adding the flour mixture (in three additions) with the chocolate mixture (in two additions), ending with the flour mixture. Scrape the batter into the prepared pan, and tap the pan on the counter to level the batter.

4. Bake until the cake springs back when poked in the center with a finger, about 20 minutes. Cool completely in the pan on a wire rack. (Well wrapped, the cake will keep for up to 2 days in the refrigerator or up to 1 month in the freezer.)

MAKE THE COCONUT-PECAN FILLING

1. Pulse the coconut and pecans in a food processor until they resemble coarse cornmeal.

2. Combine the sugar, butter, egg yolks, evaporated milk, and vanilla extract in a 3-quart saucepan. Cook over medium-low heat, stirring constantly with a spoon or spatula, until the mixture is thick enough to coat the spoon and hold a trail when a finger is drawn through it, 6 to 7 minutes. Transfer to a stand mixer fitted with a whisk attachment and whip on high speed until cooled, fluffy, and slightly lightened in color, 6 to 10 minutes. Add the coconut-pecan mixture, and beat on medium speed until combined, 1 minute more. Refrigerate until ready to use. (You can refrigerate the filling for up to 1 week.)

continued on p. 64

FOR THE CHOCOLATE MOUSSE

4 oz. bittersweet chocolate (preferably 70% cacao), chopped (about 1 cup)

3½ oz. (7 Tbs.) unsalted butter

2 large eggs, separated

1 Tbs. granulated sugar

¾ cup heavy cream

¼ tsp. pure vanilla extract

Pinch of kosher salt

FOR THE GLAZE

4 oz. bittersweet chocolate (preferably 70% cacao), finely chopped (about 1 cup)

2 Tbs. light corn syrup

1 cup heavy cream

MAKE THE CHOCOLATE MOUSSE

1. Melt the chocolate and butter in a large bowl set in a skillet of barely simmering water. Remove from the heat and stir with a spatula to combine. Set aside to cool slightly.

2. Whip the egg whites in a clean stand mixer fitted with a clean whisk attachment on medium-high speed until soft peaks form, 1 to 2 minutes. Slowly add the sugar and continue to whip to stiff peaks, 3 to 4 minutes.

3. In a medium bowl, whip the cream with a whisk or electric hand mixer to medium-stiff peaks.

4. In a small bowl, combine the egg yolks, vanilla extract, and salt. Mix the egg yolk mixture into the chocolate mixture with a spatula. Fold in the whipped egg whites, then fold in the whipped cream—there shouldn't be any visible streaks.

ASSEMBLE THE BOMBES

1. Set two silicone bombe molds that hold at least five bombes each (3¼-inch diameter and ½-cup capacity) on a 13x18-inch rimmed baking sheet.

2. Turn the cake out onto a cutting board. Use a 3⅛-inch round cutter to cut 10 circles from the chocolate cake. Reserve the remaining cake for another use.

3. Scoop about ¼ cup of the mousse into each mold, and smear it evenly all over the insides of the molds with the back of a small spoon. Refrigerate or freeze until set, 10 to 20 minutes. Evenly distribute the coconut-pecan filling among the molds (about 2½ Tbs. each), then gently press a cake circle into each mold. Cover with plastic wrap and freeze overnight.

4. Unmold the frozen bombes one at a time onto a wire rack set in a rimmed baking sheet. Let sit until nearly room temperature, 2 to 3 hours.

GLAZE THE BOMBES

1. Put the chopped chocolate and corn syrup in a medium stainless-steel bowl. In a small saucepan, heat the cream over medium-high heat until just boiling, then pour it over the chocolate mixture and let sit for 3 minutes. Whisk gently until smooth. Transfer to a liquid measuring cup for easy pouring.

2. Pour the glaze evenly over the bombes to coat them completely. Refrigerate until set, about 2 hours. (Glaze the bombes no more than 8 hours in advance.)

3. Let the bombes sit at room temperature for about 30 minutes before serving. *—Karen Hatfield*

PER SERVING: 850 CALORIES | 11G PROTEIN | 67G CARB | 63G TOTAL FAT | 36G SAT FAT | 20G MONO FAT | 4.5G POLY FAT | 310MG CHOL | 210MG SODIUM | 6G FIBER

how to make a bombe

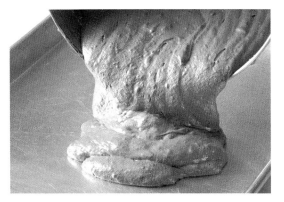

After pouring the cake batter into the pan, tap it on the counter to break any air pockets. This also spreads and levels the batter so the finished bombes are even.

Check the filling for doneness. It is fully cooked when it coats the back of a spoon and leaves a trail when you draw a finger through it. Any bits of cooked egg in the filling won't be noticeable when it's finished.

When melting the chocolate, adjust the heat under the skillet if the water gets too hot—it should be barely simmering so the chocolate doesn't scorch.

Use the back of a small spoon to smear the chocolate mousse evenly inside each mold. The more uniform the layers, the better the bombes will look.

Top each filled mold with a round of cake, gently pressing the cake into the coconut-pecan mixture to eliminate any air pockets and create a solid base for the bombes.

For even coating, slowly pour the glaze over the bombes in a steady circular motion, starting at the top and moving to the sides. Be sure the bombes are at cool room temperature so the glaze doesn't freeze on contact.

individual mocha soufflés

MAKES 6 SOUFFLÉS

3 oz. (6 Tbs.) unsalted butter, cut into pieces; more for the ramekins

Granulated sugar, for dusting

3 Tbs. dark rum, brandy, Grand Marnier®, or water

1½ tsp. instant coffee granules

6 oz. bittersweet chocolate, finely chopped

¼ tsp. table salt

3 large eggs, separated and at room temperature

3 oz. (¾ cup) confectioners' sugar

The great thing about these soufflés is that you must make them ahead so that they're chilled before they go in the oven. You can make and keep them in the refrigerator for up to 24 hours or you can freeze them for up to a month. If you plan to bake them the same day you make them, don't use the full 3 Tbs. of rum or brandy; rather, use only 1½ Tbs. of it plus 1½ Tbs. of water. Otherwise the alcohol flavor (which dissipates over time) will be too strong.

1. Lightly butter six 6-oz. ramekins and dust with granulated sugar, tapping out the excess. Set the ramekins on a small baking sheet.

2. In a small bowl, stir together the liquor or water and the instant coffee. Set aside and stir occasionally until the coffee is dissolved. Melt the chocolate and butter in a large metal bowl over a pan of simmering water or in a microwave. Remove from the heat and whisk until glossy and smooth. Stir in the coffee mixture and the salt. Whisk in the egg yolks, one at a time. Add about one-third of the confectioners' sugar, and whisk until well blended and smooth. Set aside.

3. In a medium bowl, beat the egg whites with an electric mixer on medium-high speed until they're very foamy and they're just beginning to hold soft peaks. Increase the speed to high and gradually sprinkle in the remaining confectioners' sugar. Continue beating until the peaks are firm and glossy. Spoon about one-quarter of the beaten whites into the chocolate mixture and whisk until blended. Add the remaining whites and gently fold them in until just blended. Pour evenly into prepared ramekins (the mixture will almost completely fill the ramekins). If you want to bake the soufflés within 24 hours, refrigerate them. (To refrigerate, chill for about 30 minutes, then cover in plastic and return to the refrigerator for up to 24 hours.) If you want to hold them for longer, freeze them according to the directions in the sidebar below.

Make Ahead

Put the filled ramekins in the freezer, uncovered, for 20 minutes. Then wrap each well in plastic and freeze for up to 2 weeks. To bake straight from the freezer, unwrap the ramekins and set on a small baking sheet or jellyroll pan. Let them sit for 20 minutes while heating the oven to 400°F. Bake on the baking sheet until they are puffed and have risen about 1 inch above the ramekin, 18 minutes. Remove from the oven and serve immediately.

4. To bake straight from the refrigerator: Position a rack in the center of the oven, and heat the oven to 400°F. Unwrap the ramekins, set them on a baking sheet, and bake until they're puffed and have risen about 1 inch above the ramekin, 15 minutes. The top will still be slightly sunken in the center; consider it a place to pop in a few berries or a dollop of whipped cream. Remove the soufflés from the oven and serve immediately. —*Abigail Johnson Dodge*

brown-butter banana cake with chocolate chips

MAKES 1 BUNDT CAKE; SERVES 12

- ½ lb. (1 cup) unsalted butter; more for the pan
- 1⅓ cups granulated sugar
- 3 large eggs
- 1 cup finely mashed ripe bananas (2 medium bananas)
- 1 tsp. pure vanilla extract
- ½ tsp. table salt
- 7½ oz. (1⅔ cups) unbleached all-purpose flour; more for the pan
- 1¼ tsp. baking soda
- ⅔ cup mini semisweet chocolate chips

Brown butter adds a wonderful nutty flavor to this super-moist snack cake.

1. Position a rack in the center of the oven, and heat the oven to 350°F. Butter and flour a 10-cup decorative tube or bundt pan. Tap out any excess flour.

2. Melt the butter in a medium saucepan over medium-low heat. Once the butter is melted, cook it slowly, letting it bubble, until it smells nutty or like butterscotch and turns a deep golden hue, 5 to 10 minutes. If the butter splatters, reduce the heat to low. Remove the pan from the heat, and pour the browned butter through a fine-mesh sieve into a medium bowl and discard the bits in the sieve. Let the butter cool until it's very warm rather than boiling hot, 5 to 10 minutes.

3. Using a whisk, stir the sugar and eggs into the butter. (Since the butter is quite warm, you can use cold eggs for this.) Whisk until the mixture is smooth (the sugar may still be somewhat grainy), 30 to 60 seconds. Whisk in the mashed bananas, vanilla extract, and salt. Sift the flour and baking soda directly onto the batter. Pour the chocolate chips over the flour. Using a rubber spatula, stir just until the batter is uniformly combined. Don't overmix.

4. Spoon the batter into the prepared pan, spreading it evenly with the rubber spatula. Bake until a skewer inserted in the center comes out with only moist crumbs clinging to it, 42 to 45 minutes. Set the pan on a rack to cool for 15 minutes. Invert the cake onto the rack and remove the pan. Let cool until just warm and then serve immediately or wrap well in plastic and store at room temperature for up to 5 days. —*Nicole Rees*

Tips for Speeding Up Baking Prep

- **Eggs at room temperature.** If you don't have time to wait for eggs to come to room temperature, soak them in warm water to speed them along.

- **Softened butter.** Soften butter by placing it on the range while the oven heats up. The microwave is great for softening butter, too, and also for bringing milk to room temperature and melting chocolate, as long as you keep a close watch to prevent overheating. Instead of using extra butter for greasing the pans, use what's left in the wrapper or a bit of whatever fat you're using in the recipe.

- **Sifting flour.** When it comes to sifting, use a strainer held over the bowl. If cocoa powder isn't involved (its lumps are small and stubborn) and you've measured your flour carefully on a scale, you can choose not to sift; instead, whisk the flour, salt, and leavens in a bowl until fluffy and well combined.

brownie cream cheese bites

MAKES 5 DOZEN BITES

FOR THE BROWNIES

4 oz. (½ cup) unsalted butter, cut into 3 pieces

4 oz. unsweetened chocolate, coarsely chopped

4 large eggs, at room temperature

¼ tsp. table salt

2 cups granulated sugar

1 tsp. pure vanilla extract

5¾ oz. (1¼ cups) unbleached all-purpose flour

FOR THE CREAM CHEESE TOPPING

6 oz. cream cheese, softened at room temperature

3 Tbs. granulated sugar

1 large egg yolk, at room temperature

½ cup semisweet mini chocolate chips

These mini cupcakes add a delicious burst of fudgy flavor and a playful element to the usual cookie assortment.

Position a rack in the center of the oven, and heat the oven to 350°F. Line three 1-dozen-capacity (five if you have them) mini muffin tins with foil or paper liners.

MAKE THE BROWNIE BATTER

1. Combine the butter and chocolate in a small heatproof bowl. Set the bowl over simmering water or in a microwave and heat, stirring frequently with a rubber spatula, until the butter and chocolate are melted and smooth. Set aside.

2. With a stand mixer (use the whisk attachment) or a hand mixer, beat the eggs and salt in a large bowl on medium speed until very foamy, about 2 minutes. Continue beating while gradually adding the sugar. Beat until thick and pale, about 3 minutes. With a large rubber spatula, scrape the chocolate mixture into the eggs, add the vanilla extract, and fold until the two mixtures are just barely incorporated. Add the flour and continue folding until just incorporated. Scrape the batter into a 1-gallon heavy-duty zip-top bag. Squeeze out as much air as possible and seal.

MAKE THE CREAM CHEESE TOPPING

In a medium bowl, beat the cream cheese and sugar with a wooden spoon until smooth and creamy. Add the egg yolk and mix until blended. Pour in the chips and mix until blended. Scrape into a 1-quart zip-top bag. Squeeze out as much air as possible and seal.

ASSEMBLE AND BAKE

1. Snip off ½ inch from one corner of each bag. Fill each lined muffin cup about two-thirds full with the brownie batter and then top with about 1 tsp. of the cream cheese mixture.

2. Bake the three trays in the center of the oven until the brownies are puffed and a pick inserted in the brownie comes out just barely clean, about 20 minutes. Let the brownies cool in trays on racks for 5 minutes before carefully lifting the liners out of the tins and transferring them to racks to cool completely. Be sure the tins are completely cool before lining and filling them with the remaining batters. Store at room temperature or freeze in an airtight container, separating the layers with waxed paper. *—Camilla Leonard*

chocolate cupcakes with dark chocolate frosting

MAKES 16 CUPCAKES

FOR THE FROSTING

- 4 oz. unsweetened chocolate
- ¾ cup evaporated milk
- 1 cup granulated sugar

  Pinch of salt

FOR THE CUPCAKES

- 4 oz. unsweetened chocolate
- 2 cups granulated sugar
- 6 oz. (1½ cups) unbleached all-purpose flour
- ¾ tsp. baking soda
- ½ tsp. salt
- 1 cup strong, hot coffee
- ½ cup sour cream
- ½ cup vegetable oil
- 2 eggs

These cupcakes become even more moist and fudgy the day after you make them.

MAKE THE FROSTING

In a double boiler, melt the chocolate carefully. In a blender, blend the evaporated milk, sugar, and salt until the sugar is dissolved. Add the chocolate and blend until the mixture is thick and glossy, about 3 minutes. Store at room temperature, covered with plastic, until ready to use. It will keep for up to 2 days.

BAKE THE CUPCAKES

1. Position a rack in the center of the oven, and heat the oven to 350°F. Grease your muffin tins.

2. Melt the chocolate carefully in a double boiler; set aside to cool. Sift the sugar, flour, baking soda, and salt into a medium bowl. In a large bowl, whisk together the coffee, sour cream, oil, and eggs; whisk in the chocolate. Add the dry ingredients, whisking until there are no lumps.

3. Pour the batter into the prepared muffin tins, dividing it evenly to make 16 cupcakes. Bake until a toothpick inserted into the middle of a cupcake comes out clean, 19 to 20 minutes. Allow the cupcakes to cool in the pan for 15 minutes, then remove them from the pan and let them cool further. Spread the frosting generously on the cupcakes.
—David Page and *Barbara Shinn*

PER SERVING: 360 CALORIES | 5G PROTEIN | 52G CARB | 18G TOTAL FAT | 7G SAT FAT | 5G MONO FAT | 4G POLY FAT | 35MG CHOL | 170MG SODIUM | 3G FIBER

chocolate layer cake
with mocha milk chocolate frosting

MAKES THREE 9-INCH CAKE
LAYERS AND ABOUT 4 CUPS
OF FROSTING

FOR THE CAKE

- 10½ oz. (3 cups) sifted unbleached cake flour
- 1½ tsp. baking soda
- ½ tsp. salt
- 2½ oz. (¾ cup plus 2 Tbs.) unsifted unsweetened natural (nonalkalized) cocoa
- ½ cup cold plain yogurt (regular or low fat)
- 1 Tbs. pure vanilla extract
- 6 oz. (12 Tbs.) unsalted butter, softened at room temperature
- 2⅔ cups granulated sugar
- 3 large eggs, at room temperature

FOR THE FROSTING

- 24 oz. milk chocolate, chopped into matchstick-size pieces
- 3 oz. (6 Tbs.) unsalted butter, cut into small pieces
- 4½ tsp. instant espresso powder
- Scant ⅛ tsp. salt
- 1 cup plus 2 Tbs. heavy cream
- 1½ tsp. pure vanilla extract

For best results in texture and flavor, this recipe needs natural (nonalkalized) cocoa, such as Hershey's, Nestlé, or Ghirardelli® rather than Dutch-processed (alkalized) cocoa.

BAKE THE CAKE

1. Position a rack in the lower third of the oven, and heat the oven to 350°F. Line the bottoms of three 9-inch cake pans with kitchen parchment (see the sidebar on p. 75) and lightly grease the sides. In a medium bowl, combine the flour, baking soda, and salt. Sift together three times and set aside. In a medium mixing bowl, pour 1 cup boiling water over the cocoa and stir to blend. Refrigerate to cool to lukewarm, stirring occasionally to speed cooling. Stir in ¾ cup cold water, the yogurt, and the vanilla extract. If necessary, refrigerate again to cool to room temperature before continuing.

2. In the bowl of an electric mixer, beat the butter and sugar until light in color and texture, 6 to 7 minutes at high speed with a hand-held mixer. If you're using a heavy-duty mixer, use the paddle attachment at medium speed (the whisk attachment will aerate the batter too much). The butter and sugar mixture will remain somewhat granular; this is fine. Whisk the eggs briefly and dribble them slowly into the butter mixture, 2 to 3 minutes, stopping as needed to scrape down the bowl and beaters.

3. Stop the mixer and spoon one-third of the flour mixture into the mixing bowl. Beat on low speed, scraping the bowl at least once, just until all traces of flour are incorporated. Stop the mixer and pour in half of the cocoa mixture. Beat on low to medium speed, scraping the bowl at least once, just until the mixture is blended. Stop mixing and spoon half of the remaining flour into the bowl. Beat as before. Stop mixing to add the remaining cocoa mixture and beat as before. Add the last of the flour mixture and beat it in. Divide the batter evenly among the prepared cake pans, spreading the batter to level it.

4. Bake, rotating the pans halfway through, until the cake just begins to shrink from the sides of the pan and a toothpick inserted in the center comes out clean, 30 to 35 minutes. Let the cakes cool on a rack for about 5 minutes. Invert the pans to unmold. Peel off the parchment liners and turn the layers right side up on the rack. Let cool completely before filling and frosting.

continued on p. 74

MAKE THE FROSTING

Put the chocolate, butter, espresso powder, and salt in a large bowl. In a small saucepan, bring the cream to a boil, then pour it over the chocolate mixture. Stir until the chocolate is completely melted and smooth. Stir in the vanilla extract. Refrigerate until the mixture is cold and feels quite firm when you touch it, at least 2 hours. When you're ready to frost the cake, beat the frosting with a hand-held electric mixer (it will seem a bit firm to beat at first), until the frosting lightens in color, has a spreadable but not-too-stiff consistency, and holds a nice shape. Frost the cake immediately using about ⅔ cup between each layer and the rest for the top and sides. —*Alice Medrich*

PER SERVING: 620 CALORIES I 7G PROTEIN I 77G CARB I 34G TOTAL FAT I 21G SAT FAT I 10G MONO FAT I 1G POLY FAT I 110MG CHOL I 270MG SODIUM I 3G FIBER

cake frosting tips

- Allow the cake layers to cool completely before frosting them so the frosting doesn't melt and make the cake slip and slide.

- Brush stray crumbs from all cake layers.

- Set the first layer, flat side down, on a serving plate or a piece of cardboard; cover the top evenly with ⅔ cup of the frosting.

- Set the second cake layer on top, flat side up; cover the top evenly with another ⅔ cup frosting.

- Set the third layer on top, flat side down.

- If the frosting is very soft and the cake layers start to slide, refrigerate the cake for about 20 minutes.

- Before frosting the sides, slide four wide strips of waxed paper under the sides to keep the serving platter clean.

- Spread a very thin layer of frosting all over the top and sides of the cake just to cover and smooth the cracks and secure loose cake crumbs. As you work, be sure to keep cake crumbs from getting into the frosting bowl.

- To spread the rest of the frosting lavishly over the cake, smooth it with a spatula, then create texture using a cake comb, a serrated knife, or the back of a spoon.

- If you like, dust lightly with confectioners' sugar or Dutch-processed cocoa or sprinkle with chocolate shavings.

making parchment pan liners

Lining cake pans with parchment makes it easier to remove the cake from the pan and speeds cleanup, too. Here's how to do it.

For a round pan: Cut a perfect circle by folding a square of parchment into quarters and then into eighths or sixteenths to make a triangle. Measure the size of the cake pan by holding the point of the triangle at the center of the inverted pan. Using scissors, snip the edges of the paper to match the size of the pan, giving it a slightly rounded shape. Unfold the paper and press it smoothly into the base of the lightly greased pan.

For a square pan: Hold the baking pan squarely in place on a piece of parchment with one hand and use the other to outline the base of the pan with a pencil. Take away the pan and cut just inside the pencil lines. Lightly grease the pan, lay the parchment in it, and smooth out any creases.

chocolate soufflés with brown sugar and rum whipped cream

SERVES 8

FOR THE SOUFFLÉS

- ½ oz. (1 Tbs.) unsalted butter, melted
- ½ cup plus 2 Tbs. granulated sugar
- ½ cup plus 1 Tbs. whole milk
- 6 oz. bittersweet chocolate, preferably 64% cacao, chopped
- 6 large egg whites, at room temperature
- 4 large egg yolks

FOR THE CREAM

- ½ cup heavy cream
- 1 Tbs. firmly packed light brown or demerara sugar
- 1 Tbs. dark rum
- ¼ tsp. pure vanilla extract

The anxiety of making soufflés is gone forever with this freezer-to-oven recipe. The whipped cream is delicious, but you can also serve pieces of English toffee and fresh, dried, or candied fruit with the soufflés so your guests can garnish as they please.

MAKE THE SOUFFLÉS

1. Brush eight 6-oz. straight-sided ramekins with the butter and coat evenly with 2 Tbs. of the sugar, tapping out the excess. Set aside.

2. In a 2- to 3-quart saucepan, heat the milk over medium-high heat until steaming hot. Add the chocolate and stir with a rubber spatula until melted. Transfer the chocolate mixture to a large bowl and set aside.

3. Combine the remaining ½ cup sugar and 2 Tbs. water in a 2-quart saucepan and set over medium heat, stirring frequently, until the sugar is completely dissolved. Let sit at room temperature while you whip the egg whites.

4. In a stand mixer fitted with a whisk attachment, whip the egg whites on medium speed until soft peaks form, about 3 minutes. With the mixer running, slowly pour the sugar syrup down the side of the bowl into the whites. Increase the speed to high, and beat until the whites hold medium peaks, about 1½ minutes.

5. Mix the egg yolks into the melted chocolate until combined. Fold one-third of the whites into the chocolate mixture until totally combined. Add the remaining two-thirds of the whites and fold in until no streaks remain. Divide the batter evenly among the prepared ramekins. Freeze until solid, at least 8 hours ahead, then wrap tightly with plastic wrap. (The soufflés may be made to this point up to 1 week ahead.)

BAKE THE SOUFFLÉS

When ready to serve, position a rack in the top third of the oven, and heat the oven to 375°F. Remove the ramekins from the freezer, and bake until the tops are puffed and cracked (either at the edges or on top) and the soufflés are barely set in the middle, 18 to 20 minutes.

MAKE THE WHIPPED CREAM

While the soufflés are baking, in a medium bowl, whip the cream using a hand mixer on medium speed until thickened enough to hold very soft peaks. Add the brown sugar, rum, and vanilla extract, and continue to mix until soft peaks form.

Serve the soufflés, topped with dollops of whipped cream, immediately after baking. —*Bruce Aidells* and *Nancy Oakes*

PER SERVING: 300 CALORIES | 7G PROTEIN | 32G CARB | 16G TOTAL FAT | 10G SAT FAT | 5G MONO FAT | 1G POLY FAT | 130MG CHOL | 80MG SODIUM | 2G FIBER

chocolate-beet layer cake

SERVES 10

FOR THE CAKE

2	medium beets, trimmed
½	Tbs. vegetable oil
6	oz. (¾ cup) unsalted butter, softened; more for the pans
9	oz. (2 cups) unbleached all-purpose flour; more for the pans
2	oz. (⅔ cup) natural cocoa powder, such as Scharffen Berger
1	tsp. baking soda
1	tsp. kosher salt
1¾	cups granulated sugar
2	large eggs, at room temperature
1	tsp. pure vanilla extract

FOR THE FROSTING

5	oz. (10 Tbs.) unsalted butter
1	cup granulated sugar
2¼	oz. (¾ cup) natural cocoa powder, such as Scharffen Berger
¾	cup heavy cream
1	tsp. instant espresso powder
1	tsp. pure vanilla extract
½	tsp. kosher salt

Make Ahead

The beets can be roasted up to 3 days ahead and refrigerated. The cake can be assembled up to 2 days ahead. Cover with a cake dome and store at room temperature.

Roasted beets make this cake moist, dense, and rich. There's no earthy flavor, and without the beets, this cake would be nowhere near as delicious.

PREPARE THE BEETS

Position a rack in the center of the oven, and heat the oven to 375°F. Put the beets on a piece of foil large enough to wrap them. Coat well in oil. Wrap the beets in foil and roast until tender when pierced with a knife, 1 hour. Let cool.

MAKE THE CAKE

1. Reduce the oven temperature to 350°F. Coat two 9-inch round cake pans generously with butter. Line the bottoms with parchment and butter the parchment. Dust the pans with flour; tap out any excess.

2. Peel and finely grate enough of the beets to yield ¾ cup. Sift the flour, cocoa powder, baking soda, and salt into a medium bowl.

3. Using a stand mixer fitted with a paddle attachment or an electric hand mixer, beat the butter and sugar on medium-low speed until fluffy, about 3 minutes. Beat in the eggs one at a time. Mix in the beets and the vanilla extract. Reduce the speed to low, and add half of the flour mixture; mix until fully incorporated. Add 1¼ cups hot water and the remaining flour mixture; mix on medium until smooth, about 2 minutes. Divide the batter evenly between the prepared pans, smoothing the tops.

4. Bake the cakes, rotating halfway through baking, until a toothpick inserted in the center of the cakes comes out clean, 25 minutes. Let the cakes cool in their pans on a rack for 10 minutes, then turn them out onto racks and peel off the parchment. Allow them to cool completely.

MAKE THE FROSTING

Melt the butter in a 3-quart saucepan over medium heat. Add the sugar and cocoa powder and mix until combined. Stir in the cream, espresso powder, vanilla extract, and salt. Bring the mixture to a simmer and cook, stirring constantly, until smooth. Pour the mixture into a bowl and let it cool slightly. Refrigerate, stirring every 10 minutes, until soft peaks form and the frosting is completely cool, about 1 hour.

ASSEMBLE THE CAKE

Place one cake on a plate and spread a generous ½ cup frosting evenly over the top. Top with the second cake and spread a generous ½ cup frosting over it. Frost the sides with the remaining frosting.

—*Jeanne Kelley*

PER SERVING: 690 CALORIES I 7G PROTEIN I 82G CARB I 37G TOTAL FAT I 22G SAT FAT I 9G MONO FAT I 2G POLY FAT I 130MG CHOL I 330MG SODIUM I 3G FIBER

chocolate-espresso mousse torte

SERVES 12

- **1 Tbs. softened unsalted butter for the pan**
- **1 recipe Basic Ganache (recipe on the facing page)**
- **1 Tbs. instant espresso granules**
- **6 large eggs, at room temperature**
- **½ cup granulated sugar**
- **1⅛ oz. (¼ cup) unbleached all-purpose flour**
- **1 Tbs. confectioners' sugar**
- **¼ tsp. ground cinnamon**

Be sure to wrap your springform pan with heavy-duty aluminum foil (or two layers of regular foil); even the best pans can let water in. This torte is delicious alone or with lightly sweetened whipped cream.

1. Position a rack in the center of the oven, and heat the oven to 400°F. Generously butter a 10-inch springform pan and wrap the bottom and sides in heavy-duty aluminum foil. Have ready a roasting pan just big enough to accommodate the springform, and put a kettle of water on to boil.

2. Make the Basic Ganache. Dissolve the espresso powder in 1 Tbs. hot water, and add it to the warm ganache still in the food processor. Process until fully incorporated, about 10 seconds. Transfer the espresso-flavored ganache to a large bowl.

3. In the bowl of a stand mixer fitted with a whisk attachment, whip the eggs, sugar, and flour at just under high speed until pale, light, and fluffy and at least doubled in volume (if not tripled), about 6 minutes. Add about one-third of the egg mixture to the ganache, and mix with a rubber spatula until combined. Add the remaining egg mixture, and gently fold together until just combined and no obvious streaks of egg remain.

4. Pour the batter into the prepared springform pan. Set the pan inside the roasting pan and fill the roasting pan with 1 to 1½ inches of boiling water. Bake until a dry crust forms on the top of the torte and the edges seem set but the center is still a bit wobbly when you jiggle it, 15 to 20 minutes. Remove the torte from the water bath and its foil wrap. Let the torte cool on a wire rack to room temperature and then refrigerate until cold and completely set, at least 3 hours or overnight.

5. To unmold, carefully remove the springform ring. Put a piece of plastic wrap over the top of the torte. Invert the torte onto a baking sheet and remove the pan bottom; use a thin-bladed knife to help

separate the torte and pan bottom if necessary. Invert the torte again onto a serving plate and remove the plastic wrap. Just before serving, put the confectioners' sugar and cinnamon in a small, fine-mesh strainer and sift over the top of the torte.

6. To cut the torte as cleanly as possible, dip your knife in hot water to heat the blade and wipe dry before each cut. Or for a cleaner cut, use unwaxed dental floss. —*Greg Case and Keri Fisher*

PER SERVING: 290 CALORIES | 5G PROTEIN | 30G CARB | 19G TOTAL FAT | 11G SAT FAT | 6G MONO FAT | 0.9G POLY FAT | 135MG CHOL | 45MG SODIUM | 2G FIBER

basic ganache

MAKES ABOUT 2 CUPS

12 oz. semisweet chocolate (55% to 60% cacao), coarsely chopped or broken into pieces (2 slightly heaping cups)

1 cup heavy cream

1. Grind the chocolate in a food processor until it reaches the consistency of coarse meal, about 30 seconds. Bring the cream to a boil in a small saucepan over medium heat. Add the cream to the food processor and process until smooth, about 10 seconds.

2. If not using right away, transfer the ganache to a bowl, cover, and refrigerate. To reheat, warm it gently in a double boiler or in the microwave.

Choosing Chocolate for Ganache

Since chocolate is one of only two ingredients in ganache, the flavor of the ganache will depend largely on the flavor of the chocolate.

This ganache is made with semisweet chocolate, which is loosely defined by the Food and Drug Administration as having at least 35% total cacao bean content. Most semisweet chocolates, however, have anywhere from 55% to 70% cacao, and some go even higher. But higher cacao content doesn't necessarily mean better chocolate. The best way to learn what type of chocolate you prefer is to try several kinds. Expensive, high-percentage brands tend to be bitter and complex, traits that are appealing to some people. Chocolates with lower cacao content tend to be sweeter. So if you like the taste of milk chocolate, you might like these chocolates better. A chocolate that's between 55% and 60%, however, is rich and moderately sweet without a strong, bitter edge, and it produces consistent results when making ganache. Ganache made with higher-percentage chocolate may be less stable and prone to seizing.

Don't cut corners by using chocolate chips. They usually contain added ingredients that help them hold their shape when baked but can translate into an overly thick, viscous ganache.

chocolate french toast

SERVES 2 TO 4

⅔ cup granulated sugar

1 oz. (⅓ cup) unsweetened cocoa powder (natural or Dutch processed)

⅛ tsp. baking powder

¼ tsp. table salt

1 cup whole milk

4 large eggs

1 tsp. pure vanilla extract

Four 1-inch-thick slices challah bread (stale is fine)

2 oz. (¼ cup) unsalted butter

Confectioners' sugar, for garnish (optional)

Fresh raspberries, strawberries, or sliced bananas, for garnish (optional)

This recipe calls for challah bread, which isn't a conventional baking staple but is convenient to have on hand. Keep thick slices of this braided egg bread in the freezer so you can turn out this snack at any time.

1. In a medium bowl, combine the sugar, cocoa powder, baking powder, and salt. Whisk until well blended and no cocoa lumps remain. Pour in about half of the milk, and whisk until the mixture is a lump-free paste. Add the remaining milk, the eggs, and the vanilla extract. Whisk until well blended.

2. Arrange the bread in a single layer in a 9x13-inch baking dish (or similar vessel) and pour the cocoa mixture over the bread. Turn the bread once to get both sides nicely coated. Poke each bread slice repeatedly with the tines of a fork to encourage the bread to absorb the batter. Let soak, turning every 10 minutes, until the bread is well saturated, 20 to 30 minutes.

3. Set a griddle or large nonstick skillet over medium heat. When the pan is hot, add the butter and spread to cover the pan. (If using a skillet, you'll need to cook the French toast in two batches, using 2 Tbs. butter for each batch.) Using your fingers and a large rubber spatula, carefully transfer the bread slices, one at a time, from the batter to the griddle. Cook until the underside looks browned and lightly crisp, 3 to 4 minutes. (Reduce the temperature if the slices are browning too fast.) Flip and continue cooking until the slices are slightly puffed in the center and are bouncy to the touch, another 3 to 4 minutes. Transfer the French toast to plates and serve immediately, dusted with confectioners' sugar and fruit, if you like. *—Abigail Johnson Dodge*

PER SERVING: 490 CALORIES | 14G PROTEIN | 60G CARB | 22G TOTAL FAT | 11G SAT FAT | 10G MONO FAT | 4.5G POLY FAT | 270MG CHOL | 450MG SODIUM | 2G FIBER

chocolate mousse layer cake

MAKES ONE 9-INCH CAKE;
SERVES 12

Vegetable oil or pan spray for
the pan

Unbleached all-purpose
flour for the pans

6 oz. (1½ cups) unbleached
cake flour

1 oz. (6 Tbs.) unsweetened
natural cocoa powder

2 tsp. baking powder

¼ tsp. baking soda

¼ tsp. table salt

1 cup granulated sugar

¼ cup vegetable oil

1 large egg

2 tsp. pure vanilla extract

1 recipe Chocolate Mousse
(recipe on p. 83)

Decoration (see the sidebar
on p. 82)

To cut layers for the cake,
use two toothpicks to
divide the cake into three
equal layers. Do this at
four points around the
cake. Cut the cake as
explained in the recipe,
using the picks as guides.

*This drop-dead delicious—and gorgeous (see p. 58)—mousse cake
doesn't require any special equipment, and you can bake, assemble,
and decorate it over the course of several days. Depending on
your skill level, choose one of the options in the sidebar on p. 82 for
dressing it up.*

MAKE THE CAKE

1. Position a rack in the center of the oven, and heat the oven to 325°F.
Lightly grease a 9x2-inch round cake pan, line the bottom with parchment, and flour the sides (but not the bottom).

2. Sift the cake flour, cocoa powder, baking powder, baking soda,
and salt into a large bowl. Add the sugar and whisk until well blended.
Measure the oil into a 1-cup liquid measure, add the egg and vanilla
extract, and mix with a fork to blend. Add the egg-oil mixture to the dry
ingredients and then add 1 cup water. Whisk until the dry ingredients
are just moist, about 1 minute, scraping down the sides of the bowl.
Pour the batter into the prepared pan.

3. Bake until a pick inserted into the center of the cake comes out
clean, 32 to 34 minutes. Let cool on a rack for 20 minutes. Lightly
grease a wire rack, invert the cake onto it, lift off the pan, peel off the
paper, and let the cake cool completely.

ASSEMBLE THE CAKE

1. Set the ring of a 9-inch springform pan on a large, flat cake plate. To
cut the cake into layers, it helps if the cake is slightly chilled. Set the
cake bottom side up on a parchment-lined work surface. Cut into
three equal layers. Set aside without separating the layers.

2. Gently flip the top cake layer (really the bottom) upside down and
center it in the springform ring so the mousse can flow over the edge
to frost the sides; handle the cake carefully (if it breaks, just piece it
together). Scoop about one-third of the mousse (a heaping 2 cups)
onto the cake layer in the ring and gently spread to cover.

3. Flip the next cake layer (the center) on top of the mousse and press
gently to level it, if necessary. Scoop half of the remaining mousse
over the layer and spread gently. Flip the remaining cake layer upside
down and set it on top of the mousse. Press gently to level it. Spread
on the remaining mousse and smooth the top; the cake should fill the
ring (don't worry if a little mousse leaks out of the bottom). Put the
cake in the fridge for at least 6 hours and up to 24.

continued on p. 82

DECORATE THE CAKE

1. Take the cake from the fridge. Run a long, thin knife or metal spatula under hot water and dry it well. Slide the warm knife between the cake and the ring, pressing the knife against the ring, to loosen the cake. Carefully release the springform clasp; gently pry it all the way open. Lift off the ring and clean the plate edge. If you're decorating the cake with nuts or chocolate shavings, mold strips of foil around the cake plate to keep it clean.

2. If the cake's sides have bare patches, use a small metal spatula to touch them up with some of the reserved mousse. Chill the cake.

3. Follow the decorating instructions below. Once decorated, keep the cake refrigerated and serve it within 8 hours. Remove from the fridge 10 to 15 minutes before serving. —*Abigail Johnson Dodge*

Decorating the Cake

Make shavings or curls to decorate the cake for a fancy presentation. Or, leave the top of the cake plain and add chopped nuts around the side.

To make shavings or curls, you'll need a 10- to 12-oz. thick block of bittersweet, semisweet, milk, or white chocolate. Set out two large (11x17-inch) sheets of parchment or waxed paper.

Start with shavings. Rub the chocolate with your palm to warm it. Wrap plastic wrap around half of the chocolate block so it's easier to grip. Drag a vegetable peeler across the side of the block, letting the shavings fall on the paper. As your hand warms the chocolate, turn the block around. You'll get larger shavings from the warmer side. Stop when you have 1½ to 2 cups.

Next, make curls using the same technique as for shavings. The chocolate must be a bit warmer, though. Microwave the chocolate block briefly, using 5-second jolts on high, until it feels just slightly warm. One or two 5-second bursts should be sufficient; white chocolate needs even less time. Use the peeler as for shavings, but apply a bit more pressure. If the chocolate still makes shavings or won't give big curls, it isn't warm enough, so heat it again for 5 seconds. If it melts against the peeler, it's too warm, so let it cool. Let the curls fall in an even, single layer on the other sheet of paper until the curls cover the paper.

To add shavings to the side of the cake, use a soupspoon to scoop up some shavings. Starting at the bottom of the cake and using light pressure, gently drag the spoon up the side so the shavings stick; continue until the cake is covered. Arrange curls on the top.

To decorate with nuts, chop 1½ cups of toasted walnuts into medium-fine pieces. Scoop up a handful and pat them onto the side of the cake. Repeat until all the sides are covered.

chocolate mousse

MAKES 8 CUPS

2	**cups heavy cream**
¾	**oz. (¼ cup) unsweetened natural cocoa powder**
13	**oz. bittersweet chocolate, chopped**
4	**oz. (½ cup) unsalted butter, at room temperature and cut into small pieces**
2	**tsp. pure vanilla extract or 1 to 2 Tbs. brandy or Cointreau®**
	Pinch of table salt
7	**large egg whites, at room temperature**
½	**cup granulated sugar**

Before you start the mousse, have the three layers of cake ready.

1. Set up an ice bath by partially filling a large bowl with cold water and some ice.

2. Combine the cream and cocoa powder in a large saucepan set over medium heat. Bring to a full boil, whisking occasionally to blend in the cocoa. Slide the pan off the heat and immediately add the chopped chocolate and butter; whisk slowly until melted and smooth.

3. Scrape the chocolate mixture into a large bowl. Add the vanilla extract or brandy and the salt. Set over the ice bath and stir constantly with a rubber spatula, scraping the sides frequently, until the chocolate cools to room temperature (don't stop stirring or lumps will form). Remove the bowl from the ice bath.

4. Put the egg whites in a large clean bowl. Whip with an electric mixer on medium-low speed until very foamy. Increase the speed to medium high, and beat until the whites form very loose, soft peaks. Slowly add the sugar. Continue beating until the whites are shiny and form floppy peaks.

5. Working quickly, scoop about one-third of the whites into the cooled chocolate mixture and fold together with a rubber spatula or a whisk until blended. Scrape the remaining whites into the chocolate and fold together gently but thoroughly. Scoop out about 1 cup of the mousse into a bowl, cover, and refrigerate for finishing touchups. Use the rest of the mousse to assemble the cake.

tips for making the mousse

When cooling the chocolate over the ice bath, stir constantly for a smooth consistency. Scrape the sides frequently with a rubber spatula, as the chocolate there is quick to set and can cause lumps.

Before beating the whites, be sure your beater and bowl are super clean; the slightest hint of grease can ruin beaten egg whites. The whites are perfectly beaten when the tips of the peaks flop over loosely onto themselves. For this mousse, slightly underwhipped whites are better than slightly over-whipped ones.

Lighten the chocolate with some of the whites to make folding easier. Then fold in the remaining whites, aiming to incorporate them into the chocolate without deflating too much of the foam. Work gently but quickly—as the whites sit, they lose their softness and become lumpy.

chocolate-orange roulade

SERVES 12

**FOR THE CHOCOLATE
SPONGE CAKE**

3   oz. bittersweet chocolate,
    chopped

    Softened butter for the pan

    Unbleached all-purpose
    flour for the pan

9   large eggs, separated

1   cup granulated sugar

1⅛ oz. (6 Tbs.) Dutch-
    processed cocoa powder,
    sifted; more for dusting

⅛   tsp. table salt

FOR THE ORANGE FILLING

2   large egg whites

½   cup granulated sugar

    Generous pinch of table salt

5   oz. (10 Tbs.) unsalted but-
    ter, completely softened at
    room temperature

1   vanilla bean, seeds scraped,
    pod saved for another use

½   tsp. pure vanilla extract

    Finely grated zest of
    1 orange (about 2 Tbs.)

*An easy-to-handle chocolate sponge cake and a step-by-step guide
guarantees impressive—and delicious—results.*

MAKE THE SPONGE CAKE

1. Position a rack in the center of the oven, and heat the oven to 350°F.
In a double boiler, melt the chocolate with 2 Tbs. warm water. Let cool
to room temperature.

2. Grease the bottom of an 18x13-inch rimmed baking sheet (a
standard half sheet pan) with the softened butter. Line the pan with
parchment; butter and then flour the parchment.

3. With an electric mixer, whip the egg yolks in a large bowl on medium-
high speed until light in color and beginning to thicken, 2 to 3 minutes
in a stand mixer or 3 to 5 minutes with a hand mixer. Add ½ cup of the
sugar, and whip until very thick and pale yellow, about 2 minutes.
Reduce the speed to low and mix in the melted chocolate. With a
rubber spatula, stir in the cocoa powder and salt until blended.

4. In a clean, dry bowl with clean, dry beaters (any grease will keep the
whites from whipping), whip the egg whites with an electric mixer at
medium speed until they're frothy and begin to increase in volume,
about 30 seconds. In a steady stream, add the remaining ½ cup sugar.
Increase the speed to medium high, and whip until soft peaks form,
2 to 3 minutes in a stand mixer or 4 to 6 minutes with a hand mixer.

5. With a rubber spatula, fold the whites into the chocolate mixture in
two equal additions. You can fold in the first half vigorously to lighten
the yolks, but fold in the second half gently, mixing just until the batter
is evenly colored with no streaks of white. Don't overmix. Scrape the
batter into the baking pan, gently spreading and smoothing it to make
sure it's level. Bake until the top springs back lightly when touched,
22 to 25 minutes.

6. Meanwhile, spread a clean dishtowel (at least as big as the cake
pan) on the counter. Using a sieve, dust the towel with cocoa powder,
completely covering it (this will keep the cake from sticking to the
towel as it cools).

7. Immediately after taking the cake from the oven, run a small knife
around the inside edge to loosen it from the pan. Invert the cake pan
onto the towel in one quick motion. Remove the pan. Carefully peel
off the parchment. Using both hands and starting from one of the
short ends, roll up the cake and the towel together. Let cool to room
temperature.

FOR THE CHOCOLATE GLAZE

3 Tbs. heavy cream

¾ cup granulated sugar

1½ oz. (½ cup) Dutch-processed cocoa powder

1½ tsp. unflavored powdered gelatin

1 recipe Whipped Cream (recipe on p. 87)

½ cup candied orange zest, for garnish

MAKE THE FILLING

Fill a wide pot or straight-sided skillet with 1 to 2 inches of very hot water. In the bowl of an electric mixer, whisk the egg whites, sugar, and salt until blended. Set the bowl in the pot of hot water; make sure the water comes up to at least the level of the mixture in the bowl. Whisk until the mixture is almost hot (about 120°F), about 90 seconds. Take the bowl out of the water. With an electric mixer on medium-high speed, whip the whites until cool and thick, 2 to 3 minutes. Reduce to medium speed, add the butter, a tablespoon at a time, and mix until the butter is completely incorporated. The filling should be soft and loose; it will firm up as the cake chills. (If it seems very runny, refrigerate it for up to 20 minutes.) With the mixer on low speed, blend in the vanilla bean, vanilla extract, and orange zest.

FILL AND ROLL THE ROULADE

Carefully unroll the cooled, towel-wrapped cake. Spread the filling over the cake, covering it evenly to within 2 inches of the edges. Reroll the cake, without the towel this time. The filling may squish out of the ends a bit; this is fine. Line a rimmed baking sheet with foil and set a wire rack on the foil. Slide two large metal spatulas (or a spatula and your hand) under the roulade and transfer it to the rack. (Or, if working ahead, transfer it to a large sheet of plastic, wrap it snugly, and refrigerate for up to a day; transfer to the rack before glazing.)

GLAZE THE ROULADE

1. In a large saucepan, combine the cream, sugar, ½ cup of water, and the cocoa powder. Bring the mixture to a boil and then reduce the heat to a simmer, whisking often, until very thick, like hot fudge sauce, 8 to 10 minutes from when the mixture began simmering. Pay close attention: This mixture boils over easily. Remove the pan from the heat. While the mixture is cooling, bloom the gelatin in 1½ Tbs. of water (see the sidebar on p. 87). Melt the bloomed gelatin over very hot water or in the microwave. Whisk the gelatin into the chocolate mixture and strain the glaze through a medium sieve into a metal bowl. Let the glaze cool at room temperature until thick but still pourable, 5 to 10 minutes; the glaze should be about 110°F to 120°F. (If you've made the cake ahead, unwrap it and put it on a rack set over a foil-lined baking sheet.)

2. Pour the glaze over the roulade, using an offset spatula to help the glaze cover the top and sides evenly. Don't worry about covering the ends; they'll be trimmed later. Refrigerate uncovered for at least 30 minutes or up to 4 hours.

continued on p. 87

GARNISH AND SERVE

1. Prepare the Whipped Cream as directed below.

2. The glaze will have "glued" the roulade to the rack, so slide a metal spatula between it and the rack to release it. Transfer the roulade to a serving platter, using two large offset spatulas to get underneath and pressing the spatulas against the rack as you go. Trim the ends of the roulade. Fill a tall container with hot water and have a dishtowel handy so that you can clean and dry the knife after cutting each slice. Using a long, sharp knife, cut ¾-inch-thick straight slices, or cut pieces on an angle, rinsing and drying the knife after each slice. Put a dollop of the Whipped Cream next to each slice. Garnish with the candied orange zest and serve. *—Emily Luchetti*

whipped cream

MAKES ENOUGH TO GARNISH 12 SLICES

- ¾ **cup heavy cream**
- 2 **tsp. granulated sugar**
- ½ **tsp. pure vanilla extract**

With a whisk or hand mixer, whip together the cream, sugar, and vanilla extract until soft peaks form.

Blooming Gelatin

Although gelatin isn't an everyday ingredient, learning to work with it can give you spectacular-looking desserts. Gelatin is a stabilizer derived from animal collagen, and working with it isn't difficult. However, before adding it to a recipe, it must be softened and then melted. For powdered gelatin, the softening process is also known as "blooming."

To bloom gelatin, sprinkle powdered gelatin evenly over its softening liquid to keep lumps from forming. Then set the gelatin aside for a few minutes until it swells or "blooms" as it absorbs the liquid. Finally, melt the gelatin either in a hot water bath or in a microwave for about 10 seconds on high until it becomes translucent. Use your fingers to check that all the granules have totally dissolved.

continued on p. 88

how to make a roulade

Spread the batter in the pan using a light touch so the spatula just skims the surface.

After inverting the baked cake onto a cocoa-dusted dishtowel, peel away the parchment. A light film of cake may stick to the parchment, but that's fine.

Roll up the cake and the towel together. Rolled like this, the cake will hold its finished shape better. Let it cool completely.

Mix in the flavoring to finish making the filling.

With the filling spread out on the cake, gently roll the cake. The filling may squish out the edges a bit as you roll, but don't worry; it will set as it chills in the refrigerator.

Strain the glaze through a medium sieve to get the perfect texture.

Pour on the glaze to completely cover the roulade; you might need to coax it a little with a spatula.

After chilling, use two large spatulas to transfer the roulade to a flat serving platter.

chocolate stout cake

MAKES 1 LARGE BUNDT CAKE OR 12 MINIATURE BUNDT CAKES

10 oz. (1 ¼ cups) unsalted butter, softened at room temperature; more for the pan

2¼ oz. (¾ cup) unsweetened natural cocoa powder (not Dutch processed); more for the pan

1¼ cups stout, such as Guinness® (don't include the foam when measuring)

⅓ cup dark molasses (not blackstrap)

7½ oz. (1 ⅔ cups) unbleached all-purpose flour

1½ tsp. baking powder

½ tsp. baking soda

½ tsp. table salt

1½ cups firmly packed light brown sugar

3 large eggs, at room temperature

6 oz. semisweet chocolate, very finely chopped

1 recipe Chocolate Glaze (optional; recipe on p. 90)

Rich, dark, and toasty stout beer plus deeply flavored molasses give the chocolate flavor of this cake some wonderful nuance.

1. Position a rack in the center of the oven, and heat the oven to 350°F. Butter a 10- or 12-cup bundt pan (or twelve 1-cup mini bundt pans) and then lightly coat with sifted cocoa powder. Tap out any excess cocoa.

2. In a small saucepan over high heat, bring the stout and molasses to a simmer. Remove the pan from the heat and let stand while preparing the cake batter.

3. Sift together the flour, cocoa powder, baking powder, baking soda, and salt. With a stand mixer (use a paddle attachment) or a hand mixer, cream the butter in a large bowl on medium speed until smooth, about 1 minute. Add the brown sugar and beat on medium speed until light and fluffy, about 3 minutes. Stop to scrape the sides of the bowl as needed. Beat in the eggs one at a time, stopping to scrape the bowl after each addition. With the mixer on low speed, alternate adding the flour and stout mixtures, beginning and ending with the flour. Stop the mixer at least one last time to scrape the bowl and then beat at medium speed until the batter is smooth, about 20 seconds. Stir in the chopped chocolate.

continued on p. 90

4. Spoon the batter into the prepared pan (or pans), spreading it evenly with a rubber spatula. Run a knife through the batter to eliminate any air pockets. Bake until a wooden skewer inserted in the center comes out with only a few moist crumbs clinging to it, 45 to 50 minutes (about 35 minutes for mini cakes). Set the pan on a rack to cool for 20 minutes. Invert the cake onto the rack and remove the pan. Let cool until just barely warm. Drizzle with the glaze (if using) and then let cool to room temperature before serving. If you're making the cake ahead, wrap it while still barely warm without the glaze. If you plan to freeze the cake, don't glaze it until you're ready to serve it or give it away. *—Nicole Rees*

chocolate glaze

¾ **cup heavy cream**

6   **oz. semisweet chocolate, chopped**

Bring the cream to a boil in a small saucepan over high heat. Remove the pan from the heat and add the chocolate. Let stand for 1 minute and then whisk until the chocolate is melted and smooth. Let cool for 5 minutes before drizzling over the barely warm cake.

chocolate strawberry shortcakes

FOR THE CHOCOLATE BISCUITS

10	oz. (about 2 ¼ cups) unbleached all-purpose flour
1½	oz. (about ¼ cup plus 3 Tbs.) Dutch-processed cocoa powder, such as Droste®
¼	cup granulated sugar; plus about 3 Tbs. for sprinkling
1½	Tbs. baking powder
¾	tsp. table salt
4½	oz. (9 Tbs.) cold unsalted butter, cut into small pieces
6½	oz. semisweet chocolate, grated or finely chopped (the food processor works well); more for garnish
1¼	cups heavy cream; plus about 3 Tbs. for brushing
1½	tsp. pure vanilla extract

FOR THE STRAWBERRIES

5	cups ⅛-inch-thick strawberry slices (from about 3 pints)
1	to 3 Tbs. granulated sugar, depending on the sweetness of the berries

FOR THE WHIPPED CREAM

1½	cups heavy cream
2	Tbs. granulated sugar
¾	tsp. pure vanilla extract

Tender and rich, the chocolate biscuits are the perfect partner for seasonal berries; try a mix of strawberries, raspberries, and black-berries for a variation.

MAKE THE BISCUITS

1. Line a heavy baking sheet with parchment. Sift the flour, cocoa powder, sugar, baking powder, and salt into a large bowl. Toss with a fork to combine. Cut the butter into the dry ingredients with a pastry cutter or a fork until the largest pieces of butter are the size of peas. Add the grated chocolate and toss to combine. Combine the cream and vanilla extract in a liquid measure. Make a well in the center of the flour mixture and pour the cream into the well. Mix with a fork until the dough is evenly moistened and just combined; it should look shaggy and still feel a little dry. Gently knead by hand five or six times to pick up any dry ingredients remaining in the bottom of the bowl and to create a loose ball.

2. Turn the dough out onto a lightly floured work surface and pat it into an 8-inch square, ¾ to 1 inch thick. Transfer the dough to the parchment-lined baking sheet, cover with plastic wrap, and chill for 20 minutes. Meanwhile, position a rack in the center of the oven, and heat the oven to 425°F. Remove the dough from the refrigerator and trim about ¼ inch from each side to create a neat, sharp edge (a bench knife or a pastry scraper works well, or use a large chef's knife, being sure to cut straight down). Cut the dough into nine even squares (about 2½ inches square) and spread them about 2 inches apart on the baking sheet. With a pastry brush or the back of a spoon, brush each biscuit with a thin layer of cream and sprinkle generously with sugar. Bake until the biscuits look a little dry and are mostly firm to the touch (they should spring back slightly when gently pressed), 18 to 20 minutes.

PREPARE THE STRAWBERRIES

Toss the strawberries with 1 Tbs. sugar and taste. If they're still tart, sprinkle with another 1 to 2 Tbs. sugar. Let sit at room temperature until the sugar dissolves and the berries begin to release their juices, at least 30 minutes but no more than 2 hours.

WHIP THE CREAM

Pour the cream into a cold mixing bowl, and beat with a hand mixer until it begins to thicken. Add the sugar and vanilla extract and, using a whisk, continue to beat by hand until the cream is softly whipped or until the whisk leaves distinct marks in the cream; it should be soft and billowy but still hold its shape.

continued on p. 92

ASSEMBLE THE SHORTCAKES

While the biscuits are still warm, split them in half horizontally with a serrated knife. For each serving, set the bottom half of a biscuit on a plate. Scoop about ½ cup of the berries and their juices over the biscuit. Add a generous dollop of whipped cream, and cover with the top half of the biscuit. Top with a small dollop of cream, a sprinkling of grated chocolate, and a berry or two and serve.

—*Katherine Eastman Seeley*

PER SERVING: 660 CALORIES | 8G PROTEIN | 61G CARB | 46G TOTAL FAT | 28G SAT FAT | 14G MONO FAT | 2G POLY FAT | 130MG CHOL | 470MG SODIUM | 7G FIBER

4 steps to tender biscuits

Cut the butter into the flour mixture with a pastry cutter or a fork until the largest pieces of butter are the size of peas. The butter will melt and create steam when baked, making a flaky biscuit.

Make a well and pour in the cream. Mix just until the ingredients start to come together. If your dough is too dry to combine, add more cream, a tablespoon at a time.

Work the dough gently until just combined. Knead gently to bring the dough together into a loose ball.

Gently pat the dough into a square about 1 inch thick and refrigerate for 20 minutes. This gives the flour a chance to relax and also helps the biscuits hold their shape when baked.

cinnamon-caramel-ganache layer cake

SERVES 12 TO 16

FOR THE FILLING

- 2 **cups heavy cream**
- 1 **3-inch cinnamon stick, lightly crushed**
- ¼ **tsp. table salt**
- 4½ **oz. semisweet chocolate (up to 62% cacao), coarsely chopped**
- ½ **cup granulated sugar**

FOR THE FROSTING

- 6 **oz. bittersweet chocolate (70% or 72% cacao), chopped medium fine**
- 2 **oz. (4 Tbs.) unsalted butter, cut into 4 pieces**
- 1 **Tbs. light corn syrup**
-    **Pinch of table salt**

FOR THE CAKE

- 1½ **oz. (½ cup) unsweetened natural cocoa powder**
- ½ **cup buttermilk, at room temperature**
- 6 **oz. (1½ cups) unbleached cake flour**
- ¾ **tsp. baking soda**
- ¼ **tsp. table salt**
- 4 **oz. (8 Tbs.) slightly softened unsalted butter, cut into 4 pieces**
- 1 **cup granulated sugar**
- ½ **cup firmly packed light brown sugar**
- 2 **large eggs, lightly beaten and at room temperature**

  Bittersweet chocolate shards, for garnish (optional; see the sidebar on p. 97)

Make the filling and the frosting first, letting the former chill and the latter thicken slightly at room temperature while the cake is baking and cooling.

MAKE THE FILLING

1. In a medium saucepan, bring the cream, cinnamon, salt, and 2 Tbs. water to a simmer over medium-high heat. Off the heat, cover and steep for 15 minutes. Meanwhile, put the chocolate in a medium bowl and set a fine-mesh strainer over it.

2. Pour ¼ cup water into a heavy-duty 3-quart saucepan. Pour the sugar in the center of the pan and pat it down until evenly moistened (there should be clear water all around the sugar). Cover the pan and cook over medium-high heat until the sugar dissolves, 2 to 4 minutes. Uncover and cook without stirring until the syrup begins to color slightly, about 1 minute. Reduce the heat to medium and continue to cook, swirling the pot gently if the syrup colors unevenly.

3. When the caramel turns reddish amber, 1 to 2 minutes longer, take the pan off the heat and immediately stir in the cream mixture. Simmer over low heat, stirring constantly, until the caramel is completely dissolved, 1 to 3 minutes.

4. Pour the caramel cream through the strainer onto the chocolate and discard the cinnamon. Whisk until the chocolate melts and the mixture is smooth. Scrape into a wide, shallow bowl, cover loosely, and refrigerate until thoroughly chilled, at least 4 hours and up to 3 days.

MAKE THE FROSTING

Put the chocolate, butter, corn syrup, and salt in a heatproof bowl set in a skillet of barely simmering water. Stir gently until the chocolate melts and the mixture is perfectly smooth. Off the heat, stir in 6 Tbs. cool water. Let cool and thicken at room temperature without stirring for at least 3 hours. The consistency should be like chocolate pudding.

MAKE THE CAKE

1. Line the bottoms of three 9x2-inch round cake pans with parchment.

2. Position a rack in the lower third of the oven if the three pans will fit on it. Otherwise, position racks in the upper and lower thirds of the oven. Heat the oven to 350°F.

3. In a small bowl, whisk the cocoa powder and ½ cup lukewarm water. In a liquid measuring cup, mix the buttermilk with ½ cup cool water.

4. In a medium bowl, whisk the flour, baking soda, and salt, and sift them three times onto a sheet of parchment.

continued on p. 96

5. In a stand mixer fitted with a paddle attachment, beat the butter on medium speed until creamy, about 15 seconds. Add the sugars gradually, beating until the mixture lightens in color and appears sandy but fluffy, about 5 minutes total. Dribble the eggs in a little at a time, taking a full minute to add them. Continue to beat for a few seconds until the mixture is smooth and fluffy.

6. Stop the mixer and add the cocoa mixture. Beat on medium speed just until combined. Stop the mixer and, using the parchment as a chute, add about one-quarter of the flour. Mix on low speed just until incorporated. Stop the mixer and add one-third of the buttermilk. Mix just until blended. Repeat, stopping the mixer between additions and scraping the bowl as necessary, until the remaining flour and buttermilk are mixed in.

7. Divide the batter evenly among the pans. Bake until a toothpick inserted in the center of each cake comes out clean, 17 to 20 minutes (if baking on two levels, rotate the upper and lower pans halfway through baking). Let the cakes cool on racks for 5 minutes and then turn onto the racks, remove the parchment, and cool completely.

ASSEMBLE THE CAKE

1. Beat the chilled filling in a stand mixer fitted with a paddle attachment at medium speed until it's very thick and stiff enough to hold a shape but still spreadable, 1 to 2 minutes. Don't overbeat.

2. Put a cake layer upside down on a cardboard cake circle or tart pan bottom. Spread half of the filling evenly all the way to the edge of the layer. Top with a second upside-down layer and gently press in place. Spread with the remaining filling. Top with the third layer, again upside down. Smooth any filling protruding from the sides.

FROST THE CAKE

Using an offset spatula, spread a very thin layer (about ½ cup) of frosting evenly over the top and sides of the assembled cake to smooth the surface, glue on crumbs, and fill cracks. (Stirring the frosting more than necessary dulls the finish and makes it set up too hard.) Spread the remaining frosting all over the top and sides of the cake, swirling the surface with the spatula if desired. Top with the chocolate shards (if using), and serve at room temperature. —*Alice Medrich*

PER SERVING: 430 CALORIES | 4G PROTEIN | 49G CARB | 26G TOTAL FAT | 16G SAT FAT | 8G MONO FAT | 1G POLY FAT | 90MG CHOL | 190MG SODIUM | 3G FIBER

how to make bittersweet chocolate shards

Melt 4 oz. chopped bittersweet chocolate in a clean, dry heatproof bowl set in a wide pan of nearly simmering water, stirring frequently with a dry spatula until smooth. Remove the bowl from the water and wipe the bottom dry.

Tear off two 16-inch-long sheets of waxed paper. Scrape the melted chocolate onto one sheet and spread with an offset metal spatula in a thin, even layer to within about ⅓ inch from each edge. Cover the chocolate with the second sheet of waxed paper.

Starting at one short edge, roll the paper and chocolate into a narrow tube about 1 inch in diameter. Refrigerate the tube seam side down on a baking sheet for at least 2 hours.

Remove the tube from the fridge and quickly unroll it while the chocolate is still cold and brittle to crack it into long, curved shards. Peel back the top sheet of waxed paper.

Immediately slide a metal spatula under the chocolate to release it from the waxed paper, and then slide the shards onto a rimmed baking sheet. Refrigerate until ready to use. Warm fingers will melt the shards, so handle them with a spatula or tongs.

coffee-cocoa snack cake

MAKES ONE 9-INCH-SQUARE CAKE; SERVES 16

- 5 oz. (10 Tbs.) very soft unsalted butter; more for the pan
- 7¼ oz. (1½ cups plus 2 Tbs.) unbleached all-purpose flour; more for the pan
- 1⅔ cups granulated sugar
- 2 large eggs, at room temperature
- 1 tsp. pure vanilla extract
- ½ tsp. table salt
- 2½ oz. (½ cup plus ⅓ cup) unsweetened natural cocoa powder (not Dutch processed)
- 1 tsp. baking soda
- 1 tsp. baking powder
- 1½ cups good-quality brewed coffee, cooled to warm

The coffee in this recipe intensifies the chocolate flavor of this supermoist cake. Use a freshly ground, medium-bodied variety, such as Colombian.

1. Position a rack in the center of the oven, and heat the oven to 350°F. Generously butter a 9-inch-square baking pan. Line the bottom of the pan with a square of parchment, butter the parchment, and then flour the bottom and sides of the pan. Tap out any excess flour.

2. If mixing by hand, put the softened butter and sugar in a medium bowl. Using a wooden spoon, cream them until smooth, about 1 minute. Switch to a whisk and blend in the eggs one at a time. Stir for another 30 seconds, until the batter is smooth and the sugar begins to dissolve. (If using a stand mixer, put the butter and sugar in the bowl and, using a paddle attachment, cream until smooth, about 1 minute. Blend in the eggs one at a time, mixing just until incorporated, about 20 seconds. Then switch to a whisk and blend in the rest of the ingredients by hand.) Mix in the vanilla extract and salt. Sift the flour, cocoa powder, baking soda, and baking powder directly onto the batter. Pour in the coffee. Gently whisk the ingredients until the mixture is smooth and mostly free of lumps.

3. Pour the batter into the prepared pan, spreading it evenly with a rubber spatula. Bake until a skewer inserted in the center comes out with only moist crumbs clinging to it, 40 to 43 minutes. Set the pan on a rack to cool for 20 minutes. Carefully run a knife around the edges of the pan, invert the cake onto the rack, and remove the pan. Invert again onto another rack and let cool right side up until just warm. Serve immediately or wrap in plastic and store at room temperature for up to 5 days. —*Nicole Rees*

chocolate-pomegranate torte

SERVES 12 TO 14

FOR THE CAKE

- 2 oz. (4 Tbs.) softened unsalted butter, cut into 4 pieces; more for the pan
- 6 oz. bittersweet chocolate (70% or 72% cacao)
- 3 large eggs, separated
- ¾ cup granulated sugar
- ¼ tsp. table salt
- ⅛ tsp. cream of tartar
- 2¼ oz. (½ cup) unbleached all-purpose flour

FOR THE POMEGRANATE JELLY

- 1 medium Pink Lady or Braeburn apple
- 1½ cups pure unsweetened pomegranate juice
- ¼ cup plus 2 Tbs. granulated sugar
- 12 fresh or frozen cranberries

For the best flavor and texture, make the cake and spread it with the jelly a day or two before serving. Glaze it on the day you serve it.

MAKE THE CAKE

1. Position a rack in the center of the oven, and heat the oven to 350°F. Lightly grease the sides of a 9x2-inch round cake pan and line the bottom with parchment.

2. Finely grate 2 oz. of the chocolate and set aside. Coarsely chop the remaining chocolate and combine with the butter and 3 Tbs. water in a heatproof bowl. Set the bowl in a skillet of barely simmering water, and stir frequently until the mixture is melted and smooth. Set aside.

3. In a large bowl, whisk the egg yolks with ½ cup of the sugar and the salt until thick and lightened in color.

4. In a stand mixer fitted with a whisk attachment, beat the egg whites and cream of tartar at medium-high speed to soft peaks, about 2 minutes. With the motor running, gradually add the remaining ¼ cup sugar, beating to stiff peaks, 1 to 2 minutes more.

5. Whisk the warm chocolate and the flour into the yolk mixture. With a rubber spatula, fold one-quarter of the whites into the chocolate batter. Scrape the remaining whites into the chocolate mixture and sprinkle the grated chocolate on top. Fold together. Pour the batter into the prepared pan and spread it evenly.

6. Bake until a toothpick inserted in the center of the cake comes out smudged with a few moist crumbs, about 25 minutes. Let cool in the pan on a rack for 10 minutes. Run a knife around the edge of the cake and invert it onto another rack. Remove the pan and parchment and invert the cake onto the first rack (it's normal for the cake to have a crusty exterior that may crack with handling). Let cool completely.

continued on p. 100

FOR THE GLAZE

6 oz. bittersweet chocolate (70% or 72% cacao), chopped medium fine

3 oz. (6 Tbs.) unsalted butter, cut into 6 pieces

1 Tbs. honey or light corn syrup

Pinch of table salt

Fresh pomegranate seeds, for garnish (optional)

MAKE THE POMEGRANATE JELLY

1. Grate enough of the apple (including the peel) to yield ¾ cup. In a medium saucepan, bring the grated apple, pomegranate juice, sugar, and cranberries to a simmer over medium heat. Simmer, covered, until the apple is softened and the mixture has thickened a little, about 10 minutes. Uncover and continue to simmer, stirring occasionally at first and then constantly toward the end, until the liquid has evaporated and the mixture is reduced to ¾ cup, about 5 minutes.

2. With a rubber spatula, press the pulp through a medium-mesh strainer into a bowl until you can't get any more juice out of the pulp. Scrape all of the juice clinging to the bottom of the strainer into the bowl and discard the pulp in the strainer.

3. Brush away any loose crumbs and easily detachable crusty pieces from the sides and top of the cake. Transfer the cake to a cardboard circle or tart pan bottom.

4. Stir the jelly to blend it, scrape it onto the cake, and spread it evenly over the top. Let the jelly cool until it's set, about 1 hour. At this point, the cake may be covered with an inverted cake pan, wrapped in plastic (the pan keeps the plastic from touching the cake), and stored at room temperature for up to 2 days.

MAKE THE GLAZE

1. Put the chocolate, butter, honey, and salt in a heatproof bowl set in a skillet of barely simmering water. Stir gently until the chocolate melts and the mixture is perfectly smooth. Remove from the heat and stir in 2 Tbs. cool water. Let cool to room temperature without stirring. If not using right away, cover and store at room temperature. Set the cake on a rack set over a baking sheet. With an offset spatula, spread ⅓ cup of the glaze around the sides of the cake and on top of the gel (be careful not to disturb the gel) to smooth the surfaces and glue on any crumbs. Rewarm the remaining glaze gently to 90°F in a skillet of barely simmering water—the glaze should have the consistency of thick, pourable cream.

2. Scrape all of the glaze onto the top of the cake. Spread the glaze over the top and all around the sides. For the shiniest glaze, work quickly and use as few strokes as possible. Scoop up any excess glaze from the baking sheet and use it to cover bare spots.

3. Garnish with pomegranate seeds (if using) and let the cake rest on the rack for 10 minutes. Transfer to a cake plate and let sit at room temperature until set, 15 to 30 minutes, or up to several hours before serving. —*Alice Medrich*

PER SERVING: 350 CALORIES | 5G PROTEIN | 41G CARB | 20G TOTAL FAT | 11G SAT FAT | 6G MONO FAT | 2.5G POLY FAT | 70MG CHOL | 105MG SODIUM | 3G FIBER

coffee and cream icebox cake

SERVES 8

1¾ cups heavy cream

1 Tbs. instant espresso powder

1 Tbs. granulated sugar

44 Nabisco FAMOUS® Chocolate Wafers

¼ cup finely chopped, toasted hazelnuts, for garnish

¼ cup crushed chocolate wafer cookie crumbs, for garnish

Coffee and hazelnuts give this cake—a variation on Nabisco's Famous Wafer Roll recipe—a more sophisticated flavor. To be safe, buy two boxes of cookies, as some may break. This cake slices best after 2 days in the refrigerator.

1. Lightly grease a 6-cup loaf pan. Line the pan with two pieces of overlapping plastic wrap, allowing the excess to hang over the edges of the pan.

2. In a medium bowl, combine the cream, espresso powder, and sugar. Whisk until the cream holds firm peaks. Spoon about two-thirds of the whipped cream into the prepared pan. Tap the pan firmly on the counter to even the cream and eliminate any air bubbles.

3. Starting at a short side of the pan, arrange 11 cookies in the cream, standing them on their edge in a row like dominoes. Gently squeeze the cookies together as you go. Do the same with a second row of cookies, slightly overlapping the cookies from the second row with the cookies in the first row. Continue with two more rows for a total of four rows.

4. Press down on the cookies gently. Cover them with the remaining cream. Smooth the cream with a spatula, gently pressing to make sure any gaps between the cookies are filled. Tap the pan on the counter several times to eliminate any air pockets.

5. Cover the cake with the excess plastic wrap and refrigerate for at least 24 hours, preferably 2 days. When ready to serve, peel the plastic wrap from the top and gently tug on the plastic to loosen the cake from the sides of the pan. Set a cutting board on top of the pan and invert the cake onto the board. Lift the pan off and gently peel away the plastic wrap. Mix the hazelnuts with the cookie crumbs and sprinkle over the top of the cake. Slice carefully with a warm knife. —*Heather Ho*

PER SERVING: 380 CALORIES | 4G PROTEIN | 33G CARB | 26G TOTAL FAT | 14G SAT FAT | 9G MONO FAT | 2G POLY FAT | 75MG CHOL | 300MG SODIUM | 1G FIBER

Line up the cookies in slightly overlapping rows. Gently squeeze the cookies together as you go, bringing the bottom layer of whipped cream up between them.

Spread the remaining coffee cream over and in between the cookies. Gently press down with the spatula to be sure the cream is filling any hard-to-reach pockets.

flourless chocolate cake with chocolate glaze

MAKES ONE 9-INCH CAKE; SERVES 12 GENEROUSLY

FOR THE CAKE

- **6 oz. (¾ cup) unsalted butter, cut into 6 pieces; more for the pan**
- **¾ oz. (¼ cup) unsweetened natural cocoa powder, sifted if lumpy; more for the pan**
- **12 oz. bittersweet chocolate, coarsely chopped (2¼ cups)**
- **5 large eggs**
- **1 cup granulated sugar**
- **1½ tsp. pure vanilla extract**
- **¼ tsp. table salt**

FOR THE GLAZE

- **4 oz. bittersweet chocolate, coarsely chopped (¾ cup)**
- **1½ oz. (3 Tbs.) unsalted butter**

This cake comes together quickly and easily, but it does need time to chill, so make it early in the day if you're serving it the same night.

MAKE THE CAKE

1. Position a rack in the center of the oven, and heat the oven to 300°F. Lightly butter the bottom of a 9x2-inch round cake pan and line it with a round of parchment. Lightly butter the parchment and the sides of the pan and dust with cocoa powder. Tap out any excess.

2. Melt the butter and bittersweet chocolate in the microwave or in a medium metal bowl set in a skillet of barely simmering water, stirring with a rubber spatula until smooth. Remove the bowl from the water bath and set aside to cool slightly. In the bowl of a stand mixer fitted with a whisk attachment, combine the eggs, sugar, vanilla extract, salt, and 2 Tbs. water. Beat on medium-high speed until the mixture is very foamy, pale in color, and doubled in volume, 2 minutes. Reduce the mixer speed to low and gradually pour in the chocolate mixture. Increase the speed to medium high and continue beating until well blended, about 30 seconds. Add the cocoa powder and mix on medium low just until blended, about 30 seconds.

3. Pour the batter into the prepared pan. Bake until a pick inserted in the center comes out looking wet with small, gooey clumps, 40 to 45 minutes. Don't overcook. Let cool in the pan on a rack for 30 minutes. If necessary, gently push the edges down with your fingertips until the layer is even. Run a small knife around the edge of the pan to loosen the cake. Cover the cake pan with a wire rack and invert. Remove the pan and parchment and let the cake cool completely. The cake may look cinched in around its sides, which is fine. Transfer to a cake plate. Cover and refrigerate the cake until it's very cold, at least 6 hours or overnight.

GLAZE THE CAKE

Melt the chocolate and butter in the microwave or in a medium metal bowl set in a skillet of barely simmering water, stirring with a rubber spatula until smooth. Pour the warm glaze over the chilled cake and, using an offset spatula, spread the glaze evenly to within ¼ inch of the edge. Refrigerate the cake until the glaze is set, 20 to 40 minutes. Before serving, remove the cake from the refrigerator and let it come to room temperature, 20 to 30 minutes. To serve, cut the cake into small, if not tiny, slices using a hot knife. *—Abigail Johnson Dodge*

PER SERVING: 420 CALORIES | 6G PROTEIN | 37G CARB | 33G TOTAL FAT | 18G SAT FAT | 5G MONO FAT | 1.5G POLY FAT | 125MG CHOL | 80MG SODIUM | 3G FIBER

german chocolate cake

SERVES 16

FOR THE CAKES

- 4 oz. (½ cup) unsalted butter, softened; more for the pans

- 4 oz. semisweet or bittersweet chocolate (up to 70% cacao), coarsely chopped (about 1 cup)

- 9 oz. (2 cups) unbleached all-purpose flour

- 1 tsp. baking soda

- ½ tsp. table salt

- 4 large eggs, at room temperature

- 2 cups granulated sugar

- 1 tsp. pure vanilla extract

- 1 cup buttermilk, at room temperature

FOR THE COCONUT-PECAN FILLING

- 7 oz. (about 2 cups) sweetened, shredded dried coconut

- 4 large egg yolks

- 1 12-oz. can evaporated milk

- 1½ cups granulated sugar

- 2 tsp. pure vanilla extract

- ¾ tsp. table salt

- 6 oz. (¾ cup) unsalted butter, cut into chunks

- 1½ cups pecan halves, toasted and coarsely chopped

You can use any semisweet or bittersweet chocolate you like for this cake, as long as it contains 70% cacao or less. Any more than that could adversely affect the cake's moist, tender texture.

MAKE THE CAKES

1. Position racks in the upper and lower thirds of the oven, and heat the oven to 350°F. Grease the sides of three 9x2-inch round cake pans with butter and line the bottoms with parchment circles.

2. Put the chocolate in a small bowl and pour ½ cup boiling water over it. Let stand for several seconds and then whisk until the chocolate is dissolved. Set aside until cool to the touch before mixing the batter.

3. Sift the flour, baking soda, and salt onto a sheet of waxed paper. Whisk the eggs in a small measuring cup.

4. Beat the butter for a few seconds in a stand mixer fitted with a paddle attachment on medium-low speed. Add the sugar in a steady stream and then beat on medium speed, scraping the bowl as necessary, until the mixture is lightened in color and fluffy, 4 to 5 minutes. Still on medium speed, add the eggs a little at a time, taking a full 1½ minutes to add them all. Add the melted chocolate and vanilla extract and beat just until blended. With the mixer turned off, add one-quarter of the flour mixture. Mix on medium-low speed just until incorporated. Add one-third of the buttermilk and mix until blended. Repeat, each time adding another quarter of the flour, then a third of the buttermilk, until the last of the flour is added. Scrape the bowl as necessary and mix each addition only until it is incorporated.

5. Divide the batter among the pans and spread it evenly. Bake, rotating the pans and swapping their positions, until the cakes just start to pull away from the sides of the pans and spring back when very gently pressed with a finger, 20 to 25 minutes. Let the cakes cool in their pans on a rack for 10 minutes.

6. Run a knife or small spatula around the edges to separate the cakes from the pans. Turn the cakes out onto the rack and peel off the parchment. Cool completely.

MAKE THE FILLING

1. Spread the coconut on a rimmed baking sheet. Bake at 350°F, stirring every 2 minutes, until golden brown, about 10 minutes. Scrape the toasted coconut onto a sheet of waxed paper and let cool completely.

2. Whisk the egg yolks with the evaporated milk, sugar, vanilla extract, and salt in a heavy-duty, nonreactive 4-quart saucepan. Add the butter. Set over medium heat and stir constantly with a heatproof spatula, scraping the bottom and corners of the pot. When the mixture starts to boil, adjust the heat so that it boils actively but not furiously, and cook, stirring constantly, until golden and thickened, 3 to 4 minutes. Off the heat, stir in the coconut and pecans. Let cool completely.

ASSEMBLE THE CAKE

Put one cake layer on a cake plate. Spread one-third of the filling over the top of the cake, leaving a ¼-inch border. Top with a second cake layer. Spread with half of the remaining filling. Put the third cake layer on top and cover it with the remaining filling. Leave the sides of the cake exposed. Serve at room temperature. The cake will keep in the refrigerator for up to 2 days. Let it come to cool room temperature before serving.   *—Alice Medrich*

PER SERVING: 590 CALORIES | 8G PROTEIN | 72G CARB | 31G TOTAL FAT | 16G SAT FAT | 10G MONO FAT | 3.5G POLY FAT | 170MG CHOL | 360MG SODIUM | 3G FIBER

tips for making the cake

| Mix the beaten eggs into the batter a little at a time over the course of 1½ minutes to properly aerate the batter. This gives the finished cakes a light, tender crumb. | Stir the coconut every couple of minutes so it toasts evenly, and watch carefully, as it can go from toasted to burnt in seconds. | The key to this filling is to cook it, stirring constantly to avoid burning, until golden and thick. This gives it a delicious caramelized flavor and a dense consistency. | Leave a ¼-inch border around each cake layer as you spread the filling so it doesn't overflow under the weight of the next layer. |

hot chocolate layer cake with homemade marshmallows

SERVES 16

FOR THE CAKE

6 oz. (¾ cup) unsalted butter; more for the pans

13½ oz. (3 cups) unbleached all-purpose flour; more for the pans

¾ cup canola oil

4½ oz. bittersweet chocolate, finely chopped

3 cups granulated sugar

2¼ oz. (¾ cup) natural unsweetened cocoa powder

3 large eggs, at room temperature

¾ cup buttermilk, at room temperature

2 Tbs. pure vanilla extract

2½ tsp. baking soda

½ tsp. kosher salt

FOR THE FROSTING

2½ cups heavy cream

3 oz. (6 Tbs.) unsalted butter

1 vanilla bean, split lengthwise and seeds scraped out

6 oz. bittersweet chocolate, finely chopped

2 cups granulated sugar

6 oz. (2 cups) natural unsweetened cocoa powder; more for decorating

½ cup Lyle's Golden Syrup

¼ tsp. kosher salt

All the rich flavor of hot chocolate—in cake form. Homemade marshmallows piled on top seal the deal.

MAKE THE CAKE

1. Position racks in the bottom and top thirds of the oven, and heat the oven to 350°F.

2. Butter three 9x2-inch round cake pans and line each with a parchment round. Butter the parchment, then dust with flour and knock out the excess.

3. In a 3-quart saucepan, combine the butter, oil, chopped chocolate, and 1 cup water. Heat over medium heat until melted.

4. In a large bowl, whisk the flour, sugar, and cocoa powder. Pour the hot chocolate mixture into the sugar mixture and whisk until combined.

5. Whisk in the eggs, one at a time, then whisk in the buttermilk, vanilla extract, baking soda, and salt. Divide the batter evenly among the prepared pans.

6. Set two pans on the top rack and the third on the lower rack. Stagger the pans on the oven racks so that no pan is directly over another. Bake, swapping and rotating the pans' positions after 20 minutes, until a toothpick inserted in the center of each cake comes out clean, 35 to 40 minutes. Let cool on racks for 10 minutes. Invert the cakes onto the racks, remove the parchment, and let cool completely.

MAKE THE FROSTING

In a 4-quart saucepan over low heat, combine the cream, butter, and vanilla bean and seeds, and stir until the butter is melted. Remove the vanilla bean and whisk in the chopped chocolate until melted. Whisk in the sugar, cocoa powder, syrup, and salt until smooth—be sure the cocoa powder dissolves completely. Pour into a 9x13-inch pan and freeze until firm, about 2 hours, or refrigerate overnight.

MAKE THE MARSHMALLOWS

1. Pour ¾ cup cold water into the bowl of a stand mixer. Sprinkle the gelatin over the water. Attach the bowl to the mixer and fit it with a whisk attachment.

2. Clip a candy thermometer to a 3-quart saucepan; don't let the tip of the thermometer touch the bottom of the pan. In the saucepan, boil the granulated sugar, corn syrup, salt, and ¾ cup water over medium heat without stirring until it reaches 234°F to 235°F, about 10 minutes. With the mixer on low speed, pour the hot sugar mixture into the gelatin in a slow, thin stream.

continued on p. 108

3 ¼-oz. envelopes unflavored powdered gelatin

2 cups granulated sugar

1 cup light corn syrup

¼ tsp. kosher salt

1 tsp. pure vanilla extract

1 cup plus 2 Tbs. confectioners' sugar; more as needed

Make Ahead

You can bake, cool, wrap, and store the cake layers at room temperature for up to 1 day or freeze for up to 1 month. You can refrigerate the frosting for up to 3 days. The assembled cake can be refrigerated for up to 4 hours (return to room temperature before serving). Wrapped well, leftover marshmallows keep at room temperature for up to 1 month.

3. Add the vanilla extract, carefully increase the speed to high, and beat until the mixture has thickened and cooled, about 5 minutes (the bottom of the bowl should be just warm to the touch). Line a 9x13-inch pan with foil, leaving an overhang on two sides. Sift 1 Tbs. of the confectioners' sugar into the bottom of the pan, then pour the marshmallow mixture into the pan and sift another 1 Tbs. confectioners' sugar on top. Let sit at room temperature until set, at least 2 hours.

ASSEMBLE THE CAKE

1. Remove the frosting from the freezer or refrigerator. Transfer to the bowl of a stand mixer fitted with a paddle attachment and beat on medium speed for 2 minutes to soften. Change to a whisk attachment and beat at medium-high speed until light and fluffy, about 3 minutes.

2. Put a cake layer on a flat serving platter or a cake stand lined with strips of waxed paper to keep it clean while icing. Top the layer with 1½ cups of the frosting, spreading it evenly with an offset spatula to the cake's edge. Repeat with another cake layer and 1½ cups frosting. Top with the last cake layer.

3. Put 1½ cups of the frosting in a small bowl. With an offset spatula, spread this frosting in a thin layer over the top and sides of the cake. Refrigerate the cake until the frosting firms enough to seal in the crumbs, 20 to 30 minutes.

4. Spread the remaining frosting in a smooth layer over the top and sides of the cake. If necessary, you can rewhip the remaining frosting to loosen and lighten it. Remove the waxed paper strips.

5. Use the foil overhang to lift the marshmallow from the pan. Using a knife that has been dipped in cold water, cut along the edge of the marshmallow to release it from the foil. Transfer to a cutting board and remove the foil. Put the remaining 1 cup confectioners' sugar in a medium bowl. Cut the marshmallow into cubes of different sizes, from ¼ to ¾ inch (you will need to continue to dip the knife in cold water as you cut the marshmallows). The marshmallows will be very sticky—dip the cut edges in the confectioners' sugar to make them easier to handle. As you work, toss a few cubes at a time in the sugar to coat, then shake in a strainer to remove the excess. Mound the marshmallows on top of the cake (you'll need only a third to half of them). Sift some cocoa powder over the marshmallows. *—Rebecca Rather*

PER SERVING: 1,080 CALORIES | 14G PROTEIN | 161G CARB | 47G TOTAL FAT | 23G SAT FAT | 17G MONO FAT | 4.5G POLY FAT | 130MG CHOL | 350MG SODIUM | 8G FIBER

mocha chip cupcakes

MAKES 12 CUPCAKES

- 3 oz. unsweetened chocolate, chopped
- 4½ oz. (1 cup) unbleached all-purpose flour
- ½ tsp. baking soda
- ¼ tsp. table salt
- 4 oz. (½ cup) unsalted butter, at room temperature
- 1 cup granulated sugar
- 2 large eggs
- 1½ tsp. pure vanilla extract
- 2 tsp. instant espresso powder, dissolved in ½ cup cool water
- 4 oz. (⅔ cup) semisweet chocolate chips
- 1 recipe Chocolate-Sour Cream Frosting (recipe on p. 110)

These cupcakes look—and taste—spectacular on their own, but you can also dress them up with a decorative garnish or festive liner. If desired, finish with chocolate curls, shiny dragées, or a smattering of chocolate or colored sprinkles.

1. Position a rack in the lower third of the oven, and heat the oven to 350°F. Line 12 standard-size muffin cups with paper liners.

2. Put the unsweetened chocolate in the top of a double boiler or in a metal bowl set over a small saucepan of barely simmering water. Stir occasionally until the chocolate is melted and smooth. Set aside to cool slightly.

3. Sift the flour, baking soda, and salt into a small bowl. In a large bowl, beat the butter with a stand mixer fitted with a paddle attachment (or a hand mixer) on medium speed until the butter is smooth, 30 to 60 seconds. With the mixer running, slowly pour in the sugar. Stop the mixer, scrape the bowl and beaters, then beat on medium-high speed until the mixture is light and fluffy, 2 to 3 minutes. Beat in the eggs, one at a time, on medium speed, beating until the batter is smooth after each addition (about 30 seconds). Scrape the bowl after each addition. Add the vanilla extract and melted chocolate (which may be slightly warm) and beat until smooth and blended. On low speed, add the dry ingredients in three installments, alternating with the espresso in two additions, mixing after each addition only until the batter is smooth. Stir in the chocolate chips by hand.

continued on p. 110

4. Divide the batter evenly among the prepared muffin cups. (Use two rounded soupspoons: one to pick up the batter, one to push it off.) Don't smooth the batter. Bake until the cupcakes spring back when gently pressed in the center, 20 to 22 minutes. Let them cool in the tin for 5 minutes on a wire rack. Carefully remove the cupcakes from the tin, set them on the rack, and let cool completely.

5. Put a generous spoonful of the frosting on top of each cupcake and use the back of the spoon to spread and swirl it. Let the frosting set for about 30 minutes before serving.   —*Greg Patent*

PER SERVING: 280 CALORIES | 4G PROTEIN | 34G CARB | 15G TOTAL FAT | 9G SAT FAT | 4G MONO FAT | 1G POLY FAT | 55MG CHOL | 135MG SODIUM | 2G FIBER

chocolate-sour cream frosting

MAKES ABOUT 1¼ CUPS

2 oz. unsweetened chocolate, chopped

1 Tbs. unsalted butter

⅓ cup sour cream (not low fat)

¾ tsp. pure vanilla extract

Pinch of salt

6 oz. confectioners' sugar (1½ cups, spooned and leveled)

Milk, if necessary

1. Put the chocolate and butter in the top of a double boiler or in a metal bowl set over a small saucepan of barely simmering water. Stir occasionally until the chocolate mixture is melted and smooth. Set aside to cool until barely warm.

2. In a medium bowl, whisk the sour cream, vanilla, and salt to blend. Gradually whisk in the confectioners' sugar until smooth. Add the chocolate mixture and beat it in with the whisk until the frosting is smooth and creamy. The frosting must be thick and spreadable. If it's too thick, thin it with droplets of milk. If it's too thin, chill it briefly, stirring occasionally, until adequately thickened.

flourless chocolate and vanilla marble cake

MAKES ONE 9½-INCH CAKE; SERVES 16

Softened butter for the pan

FOR THE VANILLA BATTER

8 oz. cream cheese, softened at room temperature

⅔ cup granulated sugar

1 large egg

1 tsp. pure vanilla extract

FOR THE CHOCOLATE BATTER

10 oz. bittersweet chocolate, finely chopped

5 oz. (10 Tbs.) unsalted butter, cut into 6 pieces

3 large eggs

⅓ cup granulated sugar

1 Tbs. dark rum or espresso

1 tsp. pure vanilla extract

Pinch of table salt

Cocoa powder, for dusting

> Sprinkle cocoa on the bottom of the cake before inverting it onto another plate; the cocoa will keep the cake from sticking when you slice and serve it.

This dense, luscious cake has a texture a little like fudge and a little like cheesecake. Use a hot knife (run under hot water and dry it) to slice the cake. Wipe the blade clean between slices.

Position a rack in the center of the oven, and heat the oven to 300°F. Grease a 9x2-inch round cake pan and line the bottom with parchment.

MAKE THE VANILLA BATTER
In a medium bowl, beat the softened cream cheese with an electric mixer until smooth. Add the sugar and continue beating until well blended and no lumps remain. Add the egg and vanilla extract and beat just until blended. Set aside.

MAKE THE CHOCOLATE BATTER
In a medium bowl, melt the chocolate and butter in a large metal bowl over a pan of simmering water or in the microwave. Whisk until smooth and set aside to cool slightly. With a stand mixer fitted with a whip attachment (or with a hand mixer), beat the eggs, sugar, rum or espresso, vanilla extract, and salt on medium high until the mixture is pale and thick, 3 to 4 minutes. With the mixer on low, gradually pour in the chocolate mixture and continue beating until well blended.

COMBINE AND BAKE
1. Spread about half of the chocolate batter in the bottom of the pan. Alternately add large scoopfuls of each of the remaining batters to the cake pan. Using a knife or the tip of a rubber spatula, gently swirl the two batters together so they're mixed but not completely blended. Rap the pan against the countertop several times to settle the batters.

2. Bake until a pick inserted about 2 inches from the edge comes out gooey but not liquid, 40 to 42 minutes. The top will be puffed and slightly cracked, especially around the edges. It will sink as it cools. Let cool on a rack until just slightly warm, about 1½ hours. Loosen the cake from the pan by holding the pan almost perpendicular to the counter; tap the pan on the counter while rotating it clockwise. Invert onto a large flat plate. Remove the pan and carefully peel off the parchment. Sift some cocoa powder over the cake (this will make it easier to remove the slices when serving). Invert again onto a similar plate so that the top side is up. Let cool completely. Cover and refrigerate for at least 4 hours or overnight, or freeze. *—Abigail Johnson Dodge*

molten chocolate cakes with raspberries

SERVES 6

4 oz. (½ cup) unsalted butter, cut into 6 pieces; more for the ramekins

7 oz. bittersweet chocolate (60% to 65% cacao), chopped (about 1¾ cups)

½ cup granulated sugar

¼ tsp. table salt

3 large eggs, at room temperature

3 Tbs. tawny port

½ tsp. pure vanilla extract

1 Tbs. unbleached all-purpose flour

Confectioners' sugar, for dusting

Raspberries, for garnish

These cakes, which come together in a single saucepan, will please even the most serious dark-chocolate aficionados. Tawny port, with its fruit and caramel notes, bolsters the flavor of the intense bittersweet chocolate.

1. Position a rack in the center of the oven, and heat the oven to 425°F. Generously butter six 4-oz. ramekins. Put the ramekins in a baking pan with sides that are at least 2 inches high. Bring a kettle of water to boil and keep at a simmer until needed.

2. Heat the butter and chocolate in a heavy-duty 3-quart saucepan over low heat, stirring frequently, until completely melted, 2 to 3 minutes. Remove from the heat.

3. Whisk in the sugar and salt until dissolved, about 30 seconds. Whisk in the eggs until smooth, about 1 minute. Whisk in the port and vanilla extract until combined, 15 to 20 seconds. Sprinkle the flour over the top and whisk until incorporated, about 30 seconds.

4. Divide the batter evenly among the ramekins, filling each about two-thirds full. Carefully pour the boiling water into the pan so that it reaches at least halfway up the sides of the ramekins. Bake until the tops are just set and dry, 14 to 16 minutes. Remove the cakes from the oven and water bath, and let cool for 2 minutes. Dust with confectioners' sugar, top with a few raspberries, and serve warm. —*Nicole Rees*

PER SERVING: 430 CALORIES | 6G PROTEIN | 38G CARB | 28G TOTAL FAT | 17G SAT FAT | 9G MONO FAT | 1G POLY FAT | 135MG CHOL | 170MG SODIUM | 4G FIBER

Secrets to Sweet Success

Here's what you need to know about working with chocolate and cocoa powder.

Chocolate

• If a recipe specifies a cacao percentage, stick to it. If not, don't choose one higher than 75% cacao; otherwise, there may not be enough sugar in the recipe to produce the ideal finished texture.

• To chop a small amount of chocolate, a chef's knife does the trick; for a large quantity, use a food processor. Chop as finely as possible for quick, even melting.

• For speed, skip the double boiler and melt chocolate over the lowest possible flame or at half-power in your microwave. Stir often and monitor the melting—overheated chocolate becomes grainy and unusable.

• Store chocolate in a cool, dry place. A warm or humid kitchen can cause the fat or sugar or both to rise to the chocolate's surface, resulting in a grayish-white coating called bloom. Though harmless and fine to eat or bake with, it's not pretty.

• If you live in a hot, humid climate, store chocolate in the refrigerator to prevent bloom. Before using, let it come to room temperature in its wrapper to avoid condensation, which can cause the chocolate to seize if melted alone.

• Stored in a cool, dry cupboard, dark bar chocolate will last a year (6 months for milk chocolate).

Cocoa Powder

• Keep both natural and Dutch-processed cocoa in the pantry.

• Use the type of cocoa your recipe requires. Natural cocoa is slightly acidic, so it's usually paired with baking soda to neutralize the acidity and deepen the color. Dutch-processed cocoa has been treated with an alkaline solution to darken its color and mellow its flavor. It's neutral to slightly alkaline, so it's typically paired with neutral baking powder. If your recipe doesn't call for baking powder, baking soda, or acidic ingredients like sour cream or buttermilk, you can use either cocoa.

• If your cocoa powder is lumpy, sift it through a sieve before using. This is usually necessary only with cocoa that has been stored for a few months; lumps in fresh cocoa will disappear with gentle whisking.

• Whisk cocoa in with dry ingredients or with the smallest amount of liquid before adding it to wet ingredients; otherwise, it's harder to break up any lumps.

• Stored in a cool, dry cupboard, cocoa powder will last for up to a year and a half.

southern devil's food cake

SERVES 8 TO 10

FOR THE GANACHE

- 1 lb. semisweet chocolate (preferably 58% cacao), finely chopped
- 2 cups heavy cream
- 1 oz. (2 Tbs.) unsalted butter, softened

FOR THE CAKE

- 6 oz. (¾ cup) unsalted butter, softened; more for the pans
- 8 oz. (1¾ cups) unbleached all-purpose flour; more for the pans
- 2 cups firmly packed dark brown sugar
- 2 tsp. pure vanilla extract
- 3 large eggs, at room temperature
- 2¼ oz. (¾ cup) unsweetened Dutch-processed cocoa powder
- 1¼ tsp. baking soda
- 1 tsp. baking powder
- 1 tsp. kosher salt
- 1½ cups buttermilk, preferably low fat, at room temperature
- ¼ cup mayonnaise

The secret ingredient in this sinful chocolate classic? A bit of mayonnaise in the batter—a southern touch of goodness that makes the cake extra moist.

MAKE THE GANACHE

Put the chopped chocolate in a medium bowl. Bring the cream to a boil in a 2-quart saucepan over medium-high heat. Pour the hot cream directly over the chocolate and let it sit without stirring for 5 minutes. Using a whisk, stir in the center of the mixture in a small, tight circular motion until fully combined. Add the butter and stir until it is fully incorporated. Put a piece of plastic wrap directly onto the surface of the ganache and set aside at room temperature for at least 8 hours or overnight.

MAKE THE CAKE

1. Position a rack in the center of the oven, and heat the oven to 350°F.

2. Butter two 8x2-inch round cake pans and line each with a parchment round. Butter the parchment, dust with flour, and tap out any excess.

3. In a stand mixer fitted with a paddle attachment, beat the butter, brown sugar, and vanilla extract on medium-high speed until lighter in color and slightly increased in volume, 3 to 5 minutes. Lower the speed to medium and add the eggs, one at a time, mixing until each is fully incorporated before adding the next.

continued on p. 116

4. Sift the flour, cocoa powder, baking soda, and baking powder onto a piece of parchment. Add the salt to the dry ingredients after sifting.

5. Using the parchment as a chute, add one-quarter of the dry ingredients to the batter, and mix on low speed until incorporated. Add about ½ cup of the buttermilk and mix on low speed until incorporated. Continue to alternate dry ingredients and buttermilk, mixing until incorporated after each addition and stopping to scrape the bowl and beater as necessary. Using a whisk, fold the mayonnaise into the batter.

6. Divide the batter evenly between the prepared pans, and bake until a toothpick inserted in the center of the cakes comes out clean and the sides of the cake have begun to pull away from the pan slightly, 40 to 45 minutes. Remove the pans from the oven and let cool on a rack for 15 minutes. Invert the cakes onto the rack and remove the pans and parchment. Let the cakes cool completely. (The cakes may be made 1 day ahead; wrap well and store at room temperature.)

ASSEMBLE THE CAKE

Using a serrated knife, cut each cake in half horizontally. Put one of the base layers on a cake plate and tuck strips of waxed paper under the cake to keep the plate clean while icing the cake. Top the cake with about ⅓ cup of the ganache, spreading it evenly over the top. Add another cake layer, top with ganache, and repeat until the last layer is in place. Spread a thin layer of ganache over the top and sides of the cake and refrigerate for 15 minutes to seal in any crumbs. Spread the remaining ganache over the top and sides. Remove the waxed paper. The cake may be refrigerated, covered, for up to 2 days. Return to room temperature 2 hours before serving. *—David Guas*

PER SERVING: 890 CALORIES | 11G PROTEIN | 98G CARB | 53G TOTAL FAT | 30G SAT FAT | 15G MONO FAT | 4.5G POLY FAT | 175MG CHOL | 440MG SODIUM | 10G FIBER

triple chocolate cheesecake

MAKES ONE 9-INCH CAKE; SERVES 16

An intense creamy filling and three layers of chocolate flavor will satisfy both cheesecake and chocolate fans alike.

FOR THE CRUST

- 1½ **cups very finely crushed chocolate cookie crumbs (about 30 Nabisco FAMOUS Chocolate Wafers)**
- 3 **Tbs. granulated sugar**
- ⅛ **tsp. ground cinnamon (optional)**
- ¼ **cup unsalted butter, melted**

FOR THE FILLING

- ½ **cup sour cream**
- 2 **tsp. pure vanilla extract**
- 1 **tsp. instant coffee granules or espresso powder**
- 8 **oz. bittersweet chocolate, finely chopped**
- 3 **8-oz. packages cream cheese, at room temperature**
- 3 **Tbs. natural, unsweetened cocoa powder, sifted if lumpy**
- ¼ **tsp. table salt**
- 1¼ **cups granulated sugar**
- 3 **large eggs, at room temperature**

MAKE THE CRUST

Position a rack in the center of the oven, and heat the oven to 400°F. In a medium bowl, stir together the cookie crumbs, sugar, and cinnamon (if using) until blended. Drizzle with the melted butter and mix until well blended and the crumbs are evenly moist. Dump the mixture into a 9-inch springform pan, and press evenly onto the bottom and about 1 inch up the sides of the pan (to press, use plastic wrap, a straight-sided, flat-based coffee mug, or a tart tamper). Bake for 10 minutes, then set on a wire rack to cool. Reduce the oven temperature to 300°F.

MAKE THE FILLING AND BAKE

1. Mix the sour cream, vanilla extract, and coffee granules in a small bowl. Set aside and stir occasionally until the coffee dissolves.

2. Melt the chocolate in a double boiler over medium heat (or in a microwave; see the sidebar on p. 118). Stir until smooth. Set aside to cool slightly.

3. In a stand mixer fitted with a paddle attachment, beat the cream cheese, cocoa powder, and salt until very smooth and fluffy, scraping down the sides of the bowl and paddle frequently (and with each subsequent addition). Add the sugar and continue beating until well blended and smooth. Scrape the cooled chocolate into the bowl;

continued on p. 118

beat until blended. Beat in the sour cream mixture until well blended. Add the eggs, one at a time, and beat until just blended. (Don't over-beat the filling once the eggs have been added or the cheesecake will puff too much.) Pour the filling over the cooled crust, spread evenly, and smooth the top.

4. Bake at 300°F until the center barely jiggles when nudged, 50 to 60 minutes. The cake will be slightly puffed, with a few little cracks around the edge. Let cool to room temperature on a rack and then refrigerate until well chilled, at least a few hours, or overnight for the best texture and flavor. (This cake freezes well, too: Put the unmolded cake in the freezer, uncovered, until the top is cold and firm, then wrap it in two layers of plastic and one layer of foil.)

SERVE
Unclasp the pan's ring, remove it, and run a long, thin metal spatula under the bottom crust. Carefully slide the cake onto a flat serving plate. Run a thin knife under hot water, wipe it dry, and cut the cake into slices, heating and wiping the knife as needed.
—*Abigail Johnson Dodge*

PER SERVING: 390 CALORIES | 7G PROTEIN | 35G CARB | 27G TOTAL FAT | 16G SAT FAT | 8G MONO FAT | 3G POLY FAT | 100MG CHOL | 240MG SODIUM | 1G FIBER

Melting Chocolate in a Microwave

This shortcut is a great alternative to the traditional method of melting chocolate in a double boiler. Microwaves vary greatly, so you may need to adjust the timing to suit your machine.

Put the finely chopped chocolate in a wide, shallow bowl and heat it in the microwave on high or medium high until it just starts to melt, about a minute. Give the chocolate a good stir and microwave it again until it's almost completely melted, another 15 to 30 seconds. Remove the bowl and continue stirring until the chocolate is completely melted.

white chocolate macadamia cake with raspberries and white chocolate buttercream

SERVES 16

FOR THE CAKE

- 12 oz. (1½ cups) unsalted butter, softened; more for the pans
- 14 oz. (3½ cups) unbleached cake flour
- 1½ tsp. baking powder
- ¾ tsp. baking soda
- ¾ tsp. kosher salt
- 2⅓ cups granulated sugar
- 2 tsp. pure vanilla extract
- 3 large eggs, at room temperature
- 1½ cups buttermilk, at room temperature
- 6½ oz. white chocolate, chopped (1⅓ cups)
- 4 oz. (1 cup) chopped toasted macadamia nuts

FOR THE WHITE CHOCOLATE LEAVES

- 9 to 12 organic lemon leaves, preferably different sizes
- 6 oz. white chocolate, coarsely chopped (1¼ cups)

FOR THE BUTTERCREAM

- 4 large eggs
- 4 large egg yolks
- 2 cups granulated sugar
- 1½ lb. (3 cups) unsalted butter, softened
- ½ tsp. kosher salt
- 8 oz. white chocolate, melted and cooled to room temperature

White chocolate leaves and a sleek coat of buttercream give this three-layer stunner a dressed-up look.

MAKE THE CAKE

1. Position racks in the bottom and top thirds of the oven, and heat the oven to 350°F.

2. Butter three 9x2-inch round cake pans and line each with a parchment round. Butter the parchment.

3. Combine the flour, baking powder, baking soda, and salt in a medium bowl.

4. In a stand mixer fitted with a paddle attachment, beat the butter and sugar on medium speed until light and fluffy, 3 to 5 minutes. Scrape down the bowl. Add the vanilla extract and then the eggs one at a time, beating well after each addition.

5. Add about one-third of the flour mixture and mix on low speed until incorporated. Add half of the buttermilk and mix until incorporated. Continue adding the flour mixture and the buttermilk, alternating between the two and ending with the flour. The batter will be thick and glossy. Fold in the white chocolate and macadamia nuts.

6. Divide the cake batter evenly among the prepared cake pans. Level the batter with a spatula. Set two pans on the top rack and the third on the lower rack. Stagger the pans on the oven racks so that no pan is directly over another. Bake, swapping and rotating the pans' positions after 15 minutes, until a toothpick inserted in the center of each cake comes out clean, 28 to 35 minutes total. Let cool on racks for 10 minutes. Invert the cakes onto the racks, remove the parchment, and let cool completely.

MAKE THE WHITE CHOCOLATE LEAVES

1. Wash the lemon leaves and dry them with paper towels. Line two rimmed baking sheets with parchment.

2. Put the white chocolate in a metal bowl over a saucepan of barely simmering water and whisk until melted and smooth.

3. Using a small pastry brush, paint a thick coat of chocolate on the underside of each leaf. Don't let chocolate drip over the sides of the leaves, or they will be difficult to peel off later.

continued on p. 120

FOR THE FILLING

2 cups raspberry jam

2 cups (8 oz.) fresh
raspberries

**FOR THE DECORATION
(OPTIONAL)**

¼ to ⅓ cup fresh raspberries

3 to 6 small sprigs fresh mint

making white chocolate leaves

To make the white choco-
late leaves, paint the un-
dersides of organic lemon
leaves (look for them at a
flower shop) with melted
white chocolate, and then
peel the leaves away once
the chocolate has set.
Make sure no chocolate
drips over the sides of
the leaves, or they'll be
difficult to peel off.

4. Place the leaves chocolate side up on the prepared baking sheet
and leave in a cool, dry place or refrigerate until the chocolate has set.

5. Hold the leaf stem and peel the leaf carefully away from the chocolate. Transfer the chocolate leaves to the other prepared baking sheet
and refrigerate until ready to use.

MAKE THE BUTTERCREAM

1. In a stand mixer fitted with a whisk attachment, whip the eggs and
egg yolks on high speed until thick and lightened, about 5 minutes.

2. Meanwhile, clip a candy thermometer to a 3-quart saucepan; don't
let the tip touch the bottom of the pan. Combine the sugar with ½ cup
water in the pan and simmer over medium heat until it reaches 234°F
to 235°F. Transfer the sugar mixture to a heatproof measuring cup.
With the mixer running on low speed, pour the sugar mixture down the
side of the bowl into the egg mixture in a slow, thin stream. Increase
the speed to medium and beat until the mixture has cooled (the bowl
should be barely warm to the touch), 6 to 8 minutes. Add the butter
4 Tbs. at a time, beating on medium speed until incorporated, about
20 seconds for each addition. (Don't worry if the mixture looks thin at
first; it'll thicken as you add more butter.) After all the butter has been
added, add the salt, raise the speed to medium high, and beat until
thick and glossy, about 1 minute. Fold the white chocolate into the
buttercream.

ASSEMBLE THE CAKE

1. Put a cake layer on a flat serving platter or a cake stand lined with
strips of waxed paper to keep it clean while icing. Top the layer with
1 cup of the jam, spreading it evenly with an offset spatula to the
cake's edge. Scatter 1 cup of the raspberries evenly over the jam.
Repeat with a second cake layer, the remaining 1 cup jam, and the
remaining 1 cup raspberries. Top with the last cake layer.

2. Put 2 cups of the buttercream in a small bowl. With an offset spatula,
spread this buttercream in a thin layer over the top and sides of the
cake. Refrigerate the cake until the buttercream firms enough to seal
in the crumbs, 20 to 30 minutes. Spread the remaining buttercream
in a thick, smooth layer over the entire cake. Remove the waxed
paper strips.

3. Decorate with the white chocolate leaves, fresh raspberries, and
mint leaves, if using. Before serving, let sit at room temperature until the
chocolate leaves soften slightly, about 30 minutes. *—Rebecca Rather*

PER SERVING: 1180 CALORIES | 10G PROTEIN | 130G CARB | 72G TOTAL FAT |
44G SAT FAT | 22G MONO FAT | 3G POLY FAT | 290MG CHOL | 290MG SODIUM | 2G FIBER

white chocolate raspberry cheesecake

SERVES 10 TO 12

FOR THE CRUST

8	oz. vanilla wafers, finely crushed (2 cups of crumbs)
3	Tbs. granulated sugar
7	Tbs. unsalted butter, melted

FOR THE FILLING

3	8-oz. packages cream cheese, at room temperature
8	oz. white chocolate, melted and cooled
2	Tbs. unbleached all-purpose flour
	Table salt
1¼	cups granulated sugar
3	Tbs. Chambord
1	Tbs. pure vanilla extract
4	large eggs, at room temperature

FOR THE TOPPING

4	cups fresh raspberries
¼	cup seedless raspberry or red currant jam

Make Ahead

To freeze, put the un-molded, cooled cake on a rimmed baking sheet in the freezer, uncovered, until the top is cold and firm. Then wrap it in two layers of plastic and one layer of foil. Thaw overnight in the refrigerator.

This showstopping cheese-cake is topped with a pile of jewel-like glazed raspberries, a tart contrast to the sweet white chocolate filling.

MAKE THE CRUST

Position a rack in the center of the oven, and heat the oven to 375°F. In a medium bowl, stir together the vanilla wafer crumbs and sugar. Mix in the melted butter until the crumbs are evenly moist and clump together slightly. Transfer the mixture to a 9-inch springform pan, and press evenly onto the bottom and about 2 inches up the sides of the pan (to press, use plastic wrap or a flat-bottom measuring cup). Bake until the crust is fragrant and slightly darkened, 9 to 12 minutes. Let the pan cool on a rack. Lower the oven temperature to 300°F.

FILL AND BAKE THE CHEESECAKE

In a stand mixer fitted with a paddle attachment, beat the cream cheese, melted white chocolate, flour, and a pinch of table salt on medium speed, scraping down the sides of the bowl and the paddle frequently, until very smooth and fluffy, about 5 minutes. Make sure the cheese has no lumps. Add the sugar and continue beating until well blended and smooth. Add the Chambord and vanilla extract, and beat until blended, about 30 seconds. Add the eggs one at a time, beating just until blended. (Don't overbeat once the eggs have been added or the cheesecake will puff too much and crack as it cools.) Pour the filling into the cooled crust and smooth the top. Bake at 300°F until the center jiggles when nudged, 55 to 65 minutes. The cake will be slightly puffed around the edges, and the center will still look moist. Set on a rack and let cool completely. Cover and refriger-ate until well chilled, at least 8 hours and up to 3 days. The cake can also be frozen at this point for up to 1 month.

TOP AND SERVE

Unclasp and remove the side of the springform pan and run a long, thin metal spatula under the bottom crust. Carefully slide the cake onto a flat serving plate. Arrange the raspberries on top of the cake. To glaze the berries, heat the jam in a small saucepan with 1 Tbs. water, stirring frequently, until melted and smooth; strain. Brush the rasp-berries with the melted jam mixture. To cut, run a thin knife under hot water, wipe it dry, and cut the cake into slices, heating and wiping the knife after every slice. *—Abigail Johnson Dodge*

yogurt cake with chocolate ganache frosting

SERVES 12

FOR THE CAKE

- 4 oz. (½ cup) unsalted butter, softened; more for the pan
- 9 oz. (2 cups) unbleached all-purpose flour
- 1 tsp. baking powder
- 1 tsp. baking soda
- ¼ tsp. table salt
- 1 cup granulated sugar
- 3 large eggs
- 1½ cups plain yogurt (low fat or full fat)
- 2 tsp. pure vanilla extract

FOR THE GANACHE FROSTING

- ¾ cup heavy cream
- 8 oz. semisweet chocolate, broken into small pieces
- 1 Tbs. light corn syrup

Yogurt adds moisture to this dense cake's crumb and a light tartness that breaks up the richness of the ganache frosting. Dairy tends to dull the flavor of cocoa, so this cake is vanilla instead of chocolate, but chocolate lovers can still get their fix from the cake's heavenly chocolate ganache icing.

MAKE THE CAKE

1. Position a rack in the center of the oven, and heat the oven to 350°F. Butter a 9-inch cake pan. Line the pan with a piece of parchment paper cut to size.

2. In a medium bowl, whisk together the flour, baking powder, baking soda, and salt. In a stand mixer fitted with a paddle attachment or in a large bowl with an electric hand mixer, cream the butter and sugar on medium speed until smooth and fluffy. Reduce the speed to low, add the eggs, and then add the yogurt and vanilla extract, scraping down the sides of the bowl as needed. Add the dry ingredients and mix until just incorporated.

3. Transfer the batter to the prepared pan and bake until a toothpick inserted into the center comes out clean, about 45 minutes. Let cool completely on a rack before turning the cake out of the pan.

MAKE THE FROSTING

Bring the cream to a simmer in a small saucepan over medium heat. Reduce the heat to low, add the chocolate and corn syrup, and whisk until the chocolate is completely melted. Remove from the heat and let cool for 15 minutes. Transfer to a large bowl and refrigerate uncovered, stirring every 30 minutes or so, until it firms to a spreadable texture, about 45 minutes.

FROST THE CAKE AND SERVE

Transfer the cake to a cake plate. Frost the cake and serve right away, or refrigerate for up to 5 days in an airtight cake container (return to room temperature before serving). *—Tony Rosenfeld*

> **Yogurt is a lower-fat substitution for richer ingredients like butter or oil. And like buttermilk and sour cream, yogurt not only adds tang to cakes but also helps to create a moist texture.**

chocolate pavlova with tangerine whipped cream

SERVES 10

- 4 large egg whites, at room temperature
- ⅛ tsp. cream of tartar
- ⅛ tsp. table salt
- 1 cup plus 2 Tbs. granulated sugar
- 1½ tsp. cornstarch
- 1 Tbs. red-wine vinegar
- ¾ oz. (¼ cup) unsweetened Dutch-processed cocoa powder, sifted
- 1 cup heavy cream

  Finely grated zest of 1 tangerine (about 1¼ tsp.)
- 1½ cups fresh fruit, such as raspberries, sliced straw-berries, peeled and sliced mango, or a mix
- 3 kiwi, peeled and sliced into half moons

The meringue base has a chewy, brownielike interior and a crackly crust; it's topped with whipped cream and fresh fruit.

Position a rack in the center of the oven, and heat the oven to 350°F. Cut a piece of parchment so that it fits flat on a baking sheet. With a pencil, draw a 9-inch circle in the center of the parchment (tracing a 9-inch cake pan works fine). Line the baking sheet with the parchment, pencil side facing down (you should still be able to see the circle).

MAKE THE MERINGUE

With an electric hand mixer or stand mixer (use the whisk attach-ment), whip the egg whites, cream of tartar, and salt in a large, dry bowl on medium speed until foamy, about 30 seconds. Gradually add 1 cup of the sugar and then the cornstarch and vinegar; whip on medium high until the whites hold stiff peaks and look glossy, another 3 to 5 minutes. Add the sifted cocoa powder and mix on low speed until mostly combined, 20 to 30 seconds, scraping the bowl as needed. Finish mixing the cocoa into the meringue by hand with a rubber spatula until well combined and no streaks of white remain.

SHAPE AND BAKE

1. Pile the meringue inside the circle on the parchment. Using the spatula, spread the meringue to even it out slightly—it doesn't need to align perfectly with the circle, and it shouldn't be perfectly smooth or overworked. The natural swirls and ridges give the finished meringue character.

2. Bake for 10 minutes, then reduce the heat to 300°F and bake until the meringue has puffed and cracked around its edges, another 45 to 50 minutes. Turn off the oven, prop the oven door open, and leave the meringue in the oven to cool to room temperature, at least 30 minutes. The delicate meringue won't collapse as much if it cools gradually.

ASSEMBLE AND SERVE

Just before serving, put the meringue on a serving platter. In a chilled medium stainless-steel bowl, beat the cream with the remaining 2 Tbs. sugar until it holds soft peaks. Whip in the tangerine zest, mak-ing sure it's evenly distributed. Pile the whipped cream on the meringue, spreading it almost out to the edge, and then top with the fruit. To serve, slice into wedges with a serrated knife. —*Gale Gand*

PER SERVING: 200 CALORIES | 3G PROTEIN | 30G CARB | 9G TOTAL FAT | 6G SAT FAT | 3G MONO FAT | 0G POLY FAT | 35MG CHOL | 60MG SODIUM | 2G FIBER

making the pavlova

Whip the egg white mixture on medium high until the whites hold stiff peaks and look glossy, 3 to 5 minutes.

With the meringue on the parchment, use the spatula to spread it and even it out.

Swirls and ridges stay in place as the meringue cools.

rich chocolate muffins

MAKES ABOUT 20 MEDIUM MUFFINS

- **10** oz. bittersweet chocolate
- **8** oz. unsweetened chocolate
- **1¼** lb. (2 ½ cups) unsalted butter
- **1** lb. (3 ½ cups) unbleached all-purpose flour
- **4½** cups granulated sugar
- **12** eggs, cracked into a bowl

These deeply chocolate muffins benefit from a good chocolate like Callebaut®.

1. In a saucepan, melt the two chocolates with the butter. Let cool slightly. In a large bowl, mix the flour and sugar. Whisk the eggs into the dry ingredients. Pour the chocolate into the egg mixture and stir until well blended; chill for at least 3 hours.

2. Position a rack in the center of the oven, and heat the oven to 350°F. Line a muffin tin with muffin papers. Scoop about ½ cup batter into each tin so that the curve of the batter is even with the rim of the cup (refrigerate extra batter in an airtight container for up to a week). Bake the muffins until the tops puff and crackle and are slightly soft to the touch and a toothpick stuck in the center has moist but not wet crumbs clinging to it, about 30 minutes. —*Kathleen Stewart*

PER SERVING: 630 CALORIES | 9G PROTEIN | 73G CARB | 38G TOTAL FAT | 22G SAT FAT | 10G MONO FAT | 2G POLY FAT | 190MG CHOL | 45MG SODIUM | 3G FIBER

white chocolate soufflé cakes with raspberry-chocolate sauce

SERVES 6

Softened butter and granulated sugar for the ramekins

**FOR THE RASPBERRY-CHOCOLATE
SAUCE**

½ cup fresh raspberries, rinsed,
or ¾ cup thawed frozen
raspberries

3 oz. bittersweet or semisweet
chocolate, chopped

1 oz. (2 Tbs.) unsalted butter

1 Tbs. granulated sugar

FOR THE SOUFFLÉ CAKES

3 large eggs, separated, at
room temperature

3 Tbs. unbleached all-purpose
flour

⅛ tsp. table salt

¾ cup whole milk

6 oz. white chocolate (El Rey or
Callebaut are great), finely
chopped

¼ tsp. pure vanilla extract

Scant ¼ tsp. cream of tartar

2 Tbs. granulated sugar

*Dip into these light, delicate
cakes and discover a warm
chocolate sauce.*

Put a metal or Pyrex pie plate or
cake pan in the freezer to chill.
Lightly butter six 6-oz. ramekins
or custard cups. Coat with sugar
and tap out the excess.

MAKE THE SAUCE

1. Purée the raspberries in a food processor. Transfer the purée to a
fine-mesh sieve set over a small bowl. Strain the purée by pressing
and scraping with a rubber spatula. Discard the seeds.

2. In a medium heatproof bowl set in or over a skillet of barely simmering water, combine the chocolate, butter, sugar, and 2 Tbs. of the
raspberry purée (save any extra for another use). Stir frequently with
a rubber spatula until melted and smooth. Scrape into a puddle on
the chilled plate and return to the freezer until firm, 20 to 30 minutes.
When the raspberry-chocolate mixture is firm, use a teaspoon to
scrape it into six rough balls. Keep the balls on the plate and refrigerate until ready to use.

MAKE THE SOUFFLÉ CAKES

1. Put the 3 egg yolks in a medium bowl near the stove and have
another large, clean bowl at hand. Combine the flour and salt in a
small, heavy saucepan. Whisk in just enough of the milk to make a
smooth paste. Whisk in the remaining milk. Set the pan over medium
heat and cook, whisking constantly, until the mixture has the consistency of a thick cream sauce, 2 to 3 minutes. Whisk about 2 Tbs. of
the hot sauce into the yolks to warm them up gently. Scrape the yolks
back into the saucepan and cook for 1 to 2 minutes, whisking constantly, until the mixture becomes a thick pastry cream; it should be
about as thick as store-bought mayonnaise. Use a rubber spatula to
scrape the pastry cream into the clean bowl. Add the white chocolate
and whisk until it's fully melted and incorporated into the warm pastry
cream. Stir in the vanilla extract. Set aside for a few minutes until tepid.

2. In a clean, dry bowl, beat the egg whites and cream of tartar on
medium speed in a stand mixer (or on high with a hand-held mixer)
until the whites mound gently. Gradually beat in the sugar and continue beating until the whites form medium-stiff peaks when you lift

continued on p. 128

making the chocolate ball centers

Start by pouring a mixture of melted chocolate and butter into a puddle on a pie plate. Freeze until firm and then scoop into six rough balls.

Put one chocolate ball in the center of each ramekin and spoon the batter on top. As the cakes bake, the chocolate melts into a warm, sumptuous sauce.

the beaters; the tips should curl over but still look moist, glossy, and flexible. With a rubber spatula, fold about one-quarter of the whites into the white chocolate pastry cream to lighten it. Scrape the remaining whites into the bowl and gently fold in until blended, taking care not to deflate the whites. Take the chocolate balls out of the refrigerator and put one ball in the center of each ramekin. Divide the batter evenly among the ramekins and level the tops gently with the back of a spoon. You can now heat the oven and bake right away or cover the ramekins with plastic and refrigerate for up to 2 days.

3. When you're ready to bake, position a rack in the lower third of the oven, and heat the oven to 375°F. Remove the plastic and put the ramekins on a baking sheet. Bake until the cakes are puffed and golden brown on top—they'll quiver when tapped and seem soft in the center, 16 to 18 minutes. Let cool for a few minutes before serving.
—*Alice Medrich*

Reviving Overbeaten Egg Whites

If you've beaten your egg whites properly, they should have medium-stiff peaks whose tips curl when the beaters are lifted. But if you overbeat your egg whites—to the point that they clump instead of blend when you fold them—there is a fix. Here's how it works: First, use a clean spatula to scoop a quarter of the whites into the batter (as directed in the recipe). If the whites clump badly instead of blend as you fold, beat a fresh egg white into the remaining whites for a few seconds to remoisten them—they won't be perfect, but they should soften up. You can now fold the revived whites into your batter.

chocolate chip muffins

MAKES 12 MUFFINS

FOR THE MUFFINS

- **1** lb. (3½ cups) unbleached all-purpose flour
- **4** tsp. baking powder
- **½** tsp. baking soda
- **½** tsp. table salt
- **1⅓** cups granulated sugar
- **5** oz. (10 Tbs.) unsalted butter, melted and cooled slightly
- **1** cup whole milk, at room temperature
- **1** cup crème fraîche or sour cream, at room temperature
- **2** large eggs, at room temperature
- **1** large egg yolk, at room temperature
- **1** tsp. pure vanilla extract
- **1½** cups chocolate chips
- **¾** cup coarsely chopped, toasted pecans or walnuts (optional)

FOR THE GLAZE

- **12½** oz. (3 cups) confectioners' sugar
- **¼** tsp. ground cinnamon (optional)

These muffins are a perfect morning snack. Serve them plain or, for a sweeter treat, dress them up with an easy-to-make glaze. They'll keep for a day or two in an airtight container, but their first day is the best.

MAKE THE MUFFINS

1. Position a rack in the center of the oven, and heat the oven to 350°F. Lightly oil (or spray with nonstick cooking spray) the top of a standard 12-cup muffin tin and then line with paper or foil baking cups. (Spraying the pan keeps the muffin tops from sticking to the pan's surface.)

2. In a large bowl, sift together the flour, baking powder, baking soda, and salt; mix well. In a medium bowl, whisk the sugar, butter, milk, crème fraîche or sour cream, eggs, egg yolk, and vanilla extract until well combined. Pour the wet ingredients into the dry, and fold gently with a rubber spatula just until the dry ingredients are mostly moistened; the batter will be lumpy, and there should still be quite a few streaks of dry flour. Fold in the chocolate chips and the nuts, if using, until just combined. Don't overmix; the batter will still be lumpy.

3. If you have an ice cream scoop with a "sweeper," use it to fill the muffin cups. Otherwise, use two spoons to spoon in the batter, distributing all of the batter evenly. The batter should mound higher than the rim of the cups by about ¾ inch or more, especially if using nuts (overfilling gives you those great big bakery-style muffin tops).

4. Bake until the muffins are golden brown and spring back lightly when you press the middle, 30 to 35 minutes. (The muffin tops will probably meld together.) Let the muffin tin cool on a rack for 15 to 20 minutes. Use a table knife to separate the tops and then invert the pan and pop out the muffins. Serve the muffins as is or glaze them.

MAKE THE GLAZE

1. Combine the confectioners' sugar, 6 Tbs. water, and cinnamon, if using, and whisk until smooth. The glaze should be thin enough that it will drip off of a spoon; if it's more like a spreadable icing, thin it with more water, 1 Tbs. at a time. The glaze can be made up to 2 days in advance; store in an airtight container at room temperature.

2. When the muffins have cooled down but are still slightly warm, put them on a rack over foil to catch any glaze that drips off. Dab the glaze on the muffins with a pastry brush, or spoon the glaze on and let it drip over the sides. It should leave a smooth, somewhat translucent coating. You may not need all of the glaze. Wait 20 to 30 minutes for the glaze to set—it won't dry completely—before serving.
—Joanne Chang

chocolate banana swirl coffee cake

SERVES 10 TO 12

FOR THE PAN

2	Tbs. granulated sugar
⅓	cup medium-finely chopped walnuts
	Softened unsalted butter

FOR THE CAKE

9	oz. (2 cups) unbleached all-purpose flour
2	tsp. baking powder
¼	tsp. baking soda
¼	tsp. table salt
6	oz. (¾ cup) unsalted butter, completely softened at room temperature
1¼	cups granulated sugar
3	very ripe medium bananas (unpeeled, about 14 oz. total), peeled
2	tsp. pure vanilla extract
3	large eggs
3	oz. (6 Tbs.) buttermilk
4	oz. bittersweet chocolate, melted and cooled

This cake puts very ripe bananas to good use. Be sure to follow the time guidelines for unmolding the cake. If you wait too long, it will stick to the pan; take it out too early and it might break into chunks.

PREPARE THE PAN

Position a rack in the middle of the oven and heat the oven to 350°F. In a small bowl, mix the sugar with the chopped walnuts. Generously butter a large bundt pan and coat with the nuts and sugar, pressing the nuts with your fingers to help them stick. The pan sides will be coated and some of the nuts will fall to the bottom—that's fine.

MIX THE BATTER

1. In a medium bowl, whisk the flour, baking powder, baking soda, and salt until well blended. With an electric mixer, beat the butter, sugar, bananas, and vanilla extract until well blended and the bananas are almost smooth, scraping down the sides of the bowl as needed. Add the eggs one at a time, beating until just incorporated.

2. Remove the bowl from the mixer. With a rubber spatula, alternately add half the flour mixture, all the buttermilk, and then the rest of the flour mixture, stirring until each addition is just blended. Spoon half the batter into a medium bowl and gently stir in the melted chocolate until just combined. With a large spoon, alternately add a scoopful of each

Coffee Cake Basics

• **Keep ingredients at room temperature.** It's easier to blend them this way, with less risk of overmixing and ending up with a tough cake.

• **Make sure the butter is softened,** so it's easier to beat in air. Along with baking powder, the air bubbles help leaven the cake and create a light texture.

• **Measure your ingredients carefully,** and weigh the dry ingredients. A common reason cake recipes don't turn out is because of imprecise measuring.

• **Go easy on the mixing.** Follow the recipe directions: "Mix until just incorporated" is meant to ensure a tender crumb.

• **Let all cakes cool on a rack.** This helps air circulate and will keep the cake from getting soggy on the bottom.

batter to the prepared pan, working around the pan until all the batter is used. Gently run a knife or the tip of a rubber spatula through the batter, once clockwise and once counterclockwise, to slightly swirl the batters. Gently tap the pan on the counter to settle the ingredients.

BAKE THE CAKE

Bake until a pick inserted in the center comes out with just a few crumbs sticking to it, about 40 minutes. Let the cake cool in the pan on a wire rack for 15 minutes. Gently tap the sides of the pan on the counter to loosen the cake. Invert the pan onto the rack, lift off the pan, and let the cake cool completely. —*Abigail Johnson Dodge*

chocolate chunk scones

MAKES 8 LARGE SCONES

- 9 oz. (2 cups) unbleached all-purpose flour
- ⅓ cup granulated sugar
- 1 Tbs. baking powder
- ½ tsp. table salt
- 5½ oz. bittersweet or semi-sweet chocolate, coarsely chopped (1 cup)
- 3 oz. (6 Tbs.) cold unsalted butter, cut into cubes
- ¾ cup heavy cream
- 2 large egg yolks, lightly beaten

FOR FINISHING

- 1 large egg lightly beaten with 1 Tbs. milk, for glazing
- 1 to 1½ tsp. granulated sugar

Choose a good-quality bittersweet or semisweet chocolate. The better the chocolate, the better the scones will taste.

1. Position a rack in the lower third of the oven, and heat the oven to 400°F. Line a heavy baking sheet with parchment. In a large bowl, whisk together the flour, sugar, baking powder, and salt. Add the chopped chocolate, tossing until the pieces are evenly distributed and coated with flour. Cut in the butter with a pastry blender or two table knives until the largest pieces of butter are about the size of peas.

2. In a small bowl, stir the cream and egg yolks just to blend. Add this all at once to the flour mixture. Stir with a fork to begin combining the wet and dry ingredients, and then use your hands to gently knead the mixture together until all the dry ingredients are absorbed into the dough and it can be gathered into a moist, shaggy ball. Don't overknead: This dough is sticky but benefits from minimal handling. Set the rough ball in the center of the prepared baking sheet, and pat it gently into a round about 1 inch thick and 7 inches in diameter. Don't be tempted to make the round any flatter.

3. Using a sharp knife or a pastry scraper, cut the round into eight wedges; separate the wedges. Brush the scones with the egg-milk glaze (you won't need to use all of it) and sprinkle with the sugar. Bake until the scones are deep golden and a toothpick inserted into the center of a wedge comes out clean, 18 to 22 minutes. Slide the parchment onto a rack and let the scones cool for 10 to 15 minutes before serving. *—Regan Daley*

mixing and shaping tips

Cut the butter into the flour until the largest chunks are the size of peas. Two table knives can stand in for a pastry cutter.

Knead just until you can gather the dough into a shaggy ball.

Pat the shaggy ball into a manageable round.

Section the round into eighths with a dough scraper or a knife.

chocolate-hazelnut waffles with frangelico-brown-butter syrup

MAKES FOUR 8-INCH BELGIAN WAFFLES AND 1 GENEROUS CUP SYRUP

FOR THE WAFFLES

- 6 oz. (1⅓ cups) unbleached all-purpose flour
- 2 oz. (⅔ cup) natural cocoa powder
- 1½ oz. (⅓ cup) toasted, peeled hazelnuts
- 1½ tsp. baking powder
- ½ tsp. baking soda
- ½ tsp. table salt
- ¾ cup granulated sugar
- 2 large eggs, at room temperature
- 3 oz. (6 Tbs.) unsalted butter, melted
- ⅓ cup sour cream
- ½ tsp. pure vanilla extract

FOR THE SYRUP

- 3 oz. (6 Tbs.) unsalted butter
- ¾ cup firmly packed dark brown sugar
- 6 tbs. hazelnut liqueur, such as Frangelico®
- Pinch of table salt

If you can't find peeled hazelnuts, spread skin-on hazelnuts on a rimmed baking sheet and toast them in a moderately hot oven until the skins dry and crack, 5 to 6 minutes. Wrap the toasted nuts in a clean kitchen towel and rub off the skins.

MAKE THE WAFFLES

1. Heat a waffle maker.

2. Put the flour, cocoa powder, hazelnuts, baking powder, baking soda, and salt in a food processor and process until the nuts are finely chopped, about 30 seconds.

3. In a large bowl, whisk the sugar and eggs until thick and the sugar begins to dissolve, about 1 minute. Whisk in the butter, sour cream, and vanilla extract until smooth. Whisk in ¾ cup warm water until smooth. Add the flour mixture and whisk to combine. The batter will be a little lumpy.

4. Cook the batter in the waffle maker according to the manufacturer's instructions. For crisper waffles, heat the oven to 200°F and set the waffles in a single layer directly on the oven rack.

MAKE THE SYRUP

1. While you cook the waffles, cook the butter in a heavy-duty 1-quart saucepan over medium-high heat until melted and lightly browned, 2 to 3 minutes. Remove the pan from the heat, and whisk in the brown sugar, hazelnut liqueur, and salt until smooth. Return the pan to medium-high heat and bring to a boil. Cook until the mixture begins to foam slightly, about 30 seconds.

2. Serve the waffles with the syrup. *—Nicole Rees*

PER SERVING: 1,010 CALORIES | 13G PROTEIN | 132G CARB | 46G TOTAL FAT | 26G SAT FAT | 16G MONO FAT | 3G POLY FAT | 195MG CHOL | 700MG SODIUM | 7G FIBER

russian chocolate braid

MAKES 1 LOAF

- **1 recipe Sour Cream and Potato Sweet Dough (recipe on the facing page)**
- **1 cup Pastry Cream, chilled (recipe below)**
- **½ cup mini chocolate chips or chopped semisweet or bittersweet chocolate**
- **1 large egg, beaten**

This old-fashioned sweet bread is similar to a Jewish babka. The dough is super tender as well as flavorful because of the addition of sour cream and potato—it can't get any more Russian than this.

1. Line a heavy baking sheet (or an insulated sheet or two sheets sandwiched together) with parchment or butter it. Roll the dough into a rectangle about 13x16 inches and about ⅛ inch thick. Stir the chilled pastry cream to soften it and then spread it over the dough in a thin layer. Scatter the chocolate chips evenly over the surface. Roll the rectangle into a cylinder from the wider side and pinch the long edge to seal. Put the cylinder on the baking sheet. Cut the cylinder in half lengthwise, splitting it into two thin half-cylindrical strips. Arrange the strips parallel to one another so that the filling is facing up, push them together, and wrap them around each other to form a twist, working from the center.

2. Position a rack in the center of the oven, and heat the oven to 350°F. Cover the shaped dough and proof until it's large, puffy, and remains indented when lightly pressed with your fingertip, about 45 minutes.

3. Brush the braid with the beaten egg, taking care not to smear the filling or dislodge the chocolate bits. Bake until golden brown, about 35 minutes, rotating the pan halfway through baking. Let cool on a rack for 1 hour before slicing. —*Maggie Glezer*

PER SERVING: 220 CALORIES I 5G PROTEIN I 30G CARB I 9G TOTAL FAT I 5G SAT FAT I 3G MONO FAT I 1G POLY FAT I 100MG CHOL I 170MG SODIUM I 1G FIBER

pastry cream

MAKES 1 CUP

- **1 cup whole milk**
- **One 2-inch piece vanilla bean, slashed lengthwise and seeds scraped out, or ½ tsp. pure vanilla extract**
- **¼ cup granulated sugar**
- **3 Tbs. unbleached all-purpose flour**
- **¼ tsp. table salt**
- **2 large egg yolks**

Make the pastry cream just after you make the dough to allow it enough time to cool.

In a medium saucepan, warm the milk over medium heat (if you're using a vanilla bean, add it now) just until a skin forms. Take the pan off the heat. In a medium mixing bowl, combine the sugar, flour, and salt. Add the yolks, beating with a wooden spoon. Whisk in the warm milk in a thin stream, whisking constantly. Return the milk mixture to the saucepan. Cook over medium heat, whisking constantly, until the mixture is extremely thick and gluey (you'll need to switch to a wooden spoon), about 5 minutes. If you're using vanilla extract, stir it in now. Immediately force the pastry cream through a sieve. Gently press a piece of plastic onto the surface of the hot pastry cream to prevent a skin from forming. Let cool, then refrigerate until ready to use it.

sour cream and potato sweet dough

MAKES 1 LB. DOUGH

- **8 oz. (1½ cups) plus 3 Tbs. unbleached all-purpose flour**
- **1 tsp. instant yeast (Red Star® Quick-Rise™, SAF® Perfect Rise, Fleischmann's® RapidRise™, or bread machine)**
- **1 very small potato, peeled, boiled, and sieved (to yield ¼ cup)**
- **2 large egg yolks**
- **2 tsp. pure vanilla extract**
- **¼ cup sour cream**
- **3 Tbs. granulated sugar**
- **½ tsp. table salt**
- **1½ oz. (3 Tbs.) cold unsalted butter**

Be sure to use a food processor that holds at least 7 cups.

1. In a large bowl, mix the 3 Tbs. flour with the yeast and then whisk in 3 Tbs. water. Cover and let the mixture sit until it has begun to puff, 10 to 15 minutes.

2. Fit a large-capacity food processor with the metal blade. Put the remaining flour in the bowl of the processor, and add the yeast mixture, potato, egg yolks, vanilla extract, and sour cream. Process the dough for about 1 minute. Remove it from the machine and knead it by hand on an unfloured countertop for 1 minute to redistribute the heat. The dough will be very stiff at this point. Continue this alternating kneading: Process for 30 seconds and then knead on the counter for about 30 seconds, until the dough is very smooth (this should take two to three rounds of processing).

3. Put the dough back in the food processor, and add the sugar and salt, kneading again in the processor and then on the counter until the sugar has dissolved (the dough will soften considerably and become very sticky; this is fine).

4. Return the dough to the processor, add the butter, and do another alternating kneading round until the butter is well incorporated and the dough is very soft and smooth, about 1 minute. The dough won't clean the bowl at this point. It's all right if it feels quite soft and warm after processing. Kneading the dough on the counter will help it to cool down and firm up.

5. Transfer the dough to a container at least four times its volume (no need to grease the container); seal well. (At this point, the dough can instead be rolled in flour and then sealed in a plastic bag and refrigerated for up to 4 days. If you do mix ahead and chill the dough, pull it out of the fridge 3 to 4 hours before baking.) Let the dough ferment at room temperature for about 3 hours or until it has expanded to three times its volume and an indent remains when you press it with a floured finger.

Much simpler to make than a true braided bread such as challah, chocolate-studded dough just gets twisted together so it bakes into a pretty pattern. Be careful to keep the cut side of the dough up as you work so the chocolate filling doesn't spill out.

chocolate truffle tart with
whipped vanilla mascapone
topping (recipe on p. 147)

pies & tarts

banana cream tarts with chocolate sauce

FOR THE CHOCOLATE CRUST

7⅞	oz. (1¾ cups)	unbleached all-purpose flour
1	oz. (⅓ cup)	unsweetened Dutch-processed cocoa powder
6	oz. (¾ cup)	cold unsalted butter, diced
1¾	oz. (6 Tbs.)	confectioners' sugar
1		large egg

FOR THE PASTRY CREAM

2	cups whole milk
6	large egg yolks
¾	cup granulated sugar
1¾	oz. (5 Tbs.) cornstarch
2	tsp. dark rum
1	vanilla bean, split and seeds scraped out
½	oz. (1 Tbs.) unsalted butter, softened

FOR THE CHOCOLATE SAUCE

½	lb. extra-bitter chocolate (67% to 72% cacao), preferably Valrhona®, coarsely chopped
¼	cup heavy cream
¼	cup whole milk
2	Tbs. light corn syrup
1	oz. (2 Tbs.) unsalted butter

This stunning tart is a riff on bananas Foster. Torched bananas and rum-spiked pastry cream are layered on a cocoa-fueled crust and drizzled with a warm chocolate sauce for a double dose of chocolate.

MAKE THE CHOCOLATE DOUGH

1. Sift the flour and cocoa powder into a medium bowl.

2. In a stand mixer fitted with a paddle attachment, cream the butter and sugar on medium speed until smooth, 3 to 4 minutes. Scrape the sides of the mixing bowl. Add the egg and beat well. In two batches, add the flour mixture and mix on medium-low speed until incorporated.

3. Scrape the dough onto plastic wrap, form into a flat square, and wrap well. Refrigerate the dough for at least 4 hours or overnight.

MAKE THE PASTRY CREAM

In a medium saucepan, heat the milk over medium-high heat until small bubbles form around the edges, about 3 minutes. Remove from the heat. In a medium bowl, whisk the egg yolks, sugar, cornstarch, rum, and vanilla seeds. Slowly whisk in the milk. Pour the mixture back into the pan and stir well. On medium heat, whisk until it boils and becomes thick and shiny, 3 to 4 minutes. Transfer to a stand mixer fitted with a paddle attachment. Add the butter and mix on medium speed until smooth, about 1 minute. Pass the cream through a fine-mesh sieve into a shallow bowl. Transfer to a disposable pastry bag. Squeeze it down to the tip and refrigerate until ready to use. (The pastry cream can be made up to 1 day ahead.)

MAKE THE CHOCOLATE SAUCE

Put the chocolate in a medium heatproof bowl. In a medium saucepan, heat the heavy cream, milk, corn syrup, and butter over medium heat. When steaming hot, pour the cream mixture over the chocolate and let sit for 5 minutes. Whisk until smooth. Set aside.

BAKE THE CRUSTS

1. Position a rack in the center of the oven, and heat the oven to 350°F.

2. Between two large sheets of parchment, roll the dough out into a ¼-inch-thick rectangle that's about 10x13½ inches. Slide it onto a rimmed baking sheet and freeze. Once the dough is firm, after about 30 minutes, trim to 9x12½ inches, then cut it into ten 2½x4½-inch rectangles. Arrange on a rimmed baking sheet and bake until set and dry, 10 to 15 minutes, rotating the pan after 5 minutes. Let cool completely on the baking sheet on a rack.

FOR THE WHIPPED CREAM

1 cup heavy cream

1 Tbs. confectioners' sugar

½ tsp. pure vanilla extract

FOR ASSEMBLY

4 to 6 large ripe bananas (7 to 8 oz. each)

10 tsp. turbinado sugar

Dutch-processed cocoa powder

Mint leaves (optional)

Rum-raisin ice cream, preferably Häagen-Dazs®

WHIP THE CREAM

In a stand mixer fitted with a whisk attachment, beat the cream on medium speed until it starts to thicken, about 2 minutes. Add the sugar and continue to beat until soft peaks form, about 1 minute. Add the vanilla and switch to a hand whisk, whipping until the cream forms stiff peaks.

ASSEMBLE THE TARTS

1. In a small saucepan, gently warm the chocolate sauce over low heat.

2. Cut a ½-inch hole at the tip of the bag of pastry cream. Pipe the cream in a zigzag pattern across each tart crust to cover completely.

3. Peel and cut the bananas into 2½-inch lengths, then slice them lengthwise ⅛ inch thick. Shingle the bananas across the pastry cream. Sprinkle each tart with 1 tsp. turbinado sugar. Pass the flame of a small kitchen torch over the bananas until the sugar bubbles and caramelizes. Let cool briefly.

4. Transfer the whipped cream to another pastry bag that's been fitted with a star tip, and pipe a string of ½-inch rosettes down one long side of each tart over the bananas. Dust with cocoa powder. Garnish with mint leaves (if using).

5. Serve the tarts with a scoop of ice cream on the side. Pour the warm chocolate sauce over the tart at the table.   —*Deborah Racicot*

PER SERVING: 750 CALORIES | 10G PROTEIN | 78G CARB | 45G TOTAL FAT | 27G SAT FAT | 8G MONO FAT | 1.5G POLY FAT | 260MG CHOL | 75MG SODIUM | 4G FIBER

bittersweet chocolate tart with salted caramelized pistachios

SERVES 12 TO 14

FOR THE TART SHELL

- **4** oz. (8 Tbs.) unsalted butter, melted
- **¼** cup granulated sugar
- **1** tsp. finely grated orange zest
- **¾** tsp. pure vanilla extract
- **⅛** tsp. table salt
- **4½** oz. (1 cup) unbleached all-purpose flour

FOR THE FILLING

- **1** cup half-and-half
- **2** Tbs. granulated sugar
- Pinch of table salt
- **7** oz. semisweet chocolate (up to 64% cacao), coarsely chopped
- **1** large egg, lightly beaten
- **1** recipe Salted Caramelized Pistachios (recipe on p. 144)
- Fleur de sel or other flaky sea salt

This buttery shortbread tart crust is filled with rich, dark chocolate and garnished with salty-sweet caramelized nuts and sea salt.

MAKE THE TART SHELL

1. In a medium bowl, combine the butter, sugar, orange zest, vanilla extract, and salt. Add the flour and mix just until well blended. If the dough seems too soft to work with, let it sit for a few minutes to firm up. Press the dough into a 9 ½-inch fluted tart pan with a removable bottom. Start with the sides, making them about ¼ inch thick, then press the remaining dough evenly over the bottom, pressing well into the corners. Let rest at room temperature for 30 minutes or chill until ready to bake (you can make the crust up to 3 days ahead).

2. Position a rack in the lower third of the oven, and heat the oven to 350°F. Put the pan on a cookie sheet and bake until the crust is a deep golden brown, 20 to 25 minutes, checking after about 15 minutes to see if the dough has puffed. Press the dough down with the back of a fork and prick a few times if necessary.

MAKE THE FILLING

1. In a small saucepan, bring the half-and-half, sugar, and salt to a simmer. Off the heat, add the chocolate and stir with a whisk until completely melted and smooth. Cover to keep warm.

2. Just before the crust is ready, whisk the egg thoroughly into the chocolate mixture. When the crust is done, lower the oven temperature to 300°F. Pour the filling into the hot crust. Return the tart (still on the baking sheet) to the oven and bake until the filling is set around the edges but still jiggles a little in the center when you nudge the pan, 10 to 15 minutes. Let cool on a rack.

3. Serve at room temperature or slightly cool. Garnish each slice with crushed Salted Caramelized Pistachios and a light sprinkling of fleur de sel. The tart is best on the day it's made but may be refrigerated for 2 to 3 days. Once the tart is completely chilled, cover it, but make sure no plastic wrap touches the surface by first putting the tart pan in a larger cake pan. Or cover the tart with an overturned plate.

—Alice Medrich

PER SERVING: 260 CALORIES | 4G PROTEIN | 31G CARB | 15G TOTAL FAT | 8G SAT FAT | 5G MONO FAT | 1G POLY FAT | 40MG CHOL | 95MG SODIUM | 2G FIBER

continued on p. 144

salted caramelized pistachios

MAKES 1 CUP

½ cup salted whole roasted shelled pistachios

½ cup granulated sugar

⅛ tsp. fine sea salt

You can make these up to a week in advance. Store in an airtight container while still warm to prevent the caramel from becoming sticky.

1. Line a baking sheet with foil.

2. Microwave the nuts on high for 1 minute so they will be warm when you add them to the caramel. Alternatively, heat them in a 200°F oven while you make the caramel.

3. Pour ¼ cup water into a heavy 3-quart saucepan. Pour the sugar and salt in the center of the pan and pat it down just until evenly moistened (there should be clear water all around the sugar). Cover the pan and cook over medium-high heat until the sugar dissolves, 2 to 4 minutes. Uncover and cook without stirring until the syrup begins to color slightly, about 1 minute. Reduce the heat to medium and continue to cook, swirling the pot gently if the syrup colors unevenly.

4. When the caramel is a pale to medium yellow, less than 1 minute more, add the warm nuts. With a heatproof silicone spatula, stir gently and slowly to coat the nuts with caramel. Continue to cook until a bead of caramel dribbled onto a white plate is reddish amber, about 1½ minutes more. Immediately scrape the mixture onto the baking sheet and spread it as thin as you can before it hardens. When the caramel is slightly cooled but still warm, slide the foil with the caramel nuts into a zip-top plastic bag and seal the bag. Let cool completely, then chop or crush.

chocolate silk pie

SERVES 8 TO 10

- 3 oz. unsweetened chocolate, finely chopped
- 8 oz. (1 cup) unsalted butter, slightly softened
- 1 cup superfine granulated sugar
- ½ tsp. pure vanilla extract
- ½ tsp. almond extract
- ⅛ tsp. table salt
- 3 large eggs
- 1 baked 9-inch pie crust (recipe on p. 157)
- 1 recipe Cacao-Nib Whipped Cream (recipe below)

  Semisweet or bittersweet chocolate shavings, for garnish

You can probably find this old-fashioned pie in your mother's recipe box, but with its intense filling, this version feels as sophisticated as any trendy ganache-based tart, especially when you use a good-quality chocolate. A touch of almond extract and a hint more salt than is traditional give the filling an extra flavor boost. The longer you beat the mixture after each egg is added, the fluffier the filling will be, so make it as dense and rich or as light and moussey as you like. The filling contains raw eggs, so if you're concerned, use pasteurized eggs or ¾ cup of egg substitute.

1. Melt the chocolate in a medium metal bowl set over a pan of simmering water (don't let the bowl touch the water); let cool slightly.

2. Put the butter and sugar in a mixing bowl and beat with an electric mixer until light and fluffy and the sugar doesn't feel grainy anymore, about 2 minutes. Slowly beat in the cooled melted chocolate, the vanilla and almond extracts, and the salt. Beat in the eggs one at a time, adding the next egg only once the mixture is smooth again.

3. Scrape the filling into the prepared pie crust and chill until firm, at least 2 hours or overnight.

4. To serve, dollop some Cacao-Nib Whipped Cream on each slice and sprinkle with some chocolate shavings. *—Martha Holmberg*

cacao-nib whipped cream

MAKES ABOUT 2 CUPS

- 1 cup heavy cream
- 2 Tbs. cacao nibs, roughly chopped if large
- 2 tsp. granulated sugar

1. Bring the cream and cacao nibs to a boil in a small saucepan. Remove from the heat, cover, and let steep for 20 minutes. Strain the cream, pressing on the nibs to extract any additional liquid, and chill until very cold, at least 4 hours in the refrigerator.

2. In a large bowl, whip the cream to soft peaks; sprinkle in the sugar and whip for another few seconds to blend. Use right away.

chocolate-raspberry tart with gingersnap crust

MAKES ONE 9½-INCH TART; SERVES 8 TO 10

Vegetable oil, for the pan

About 40 gingersnap wafers (to yield 1½ cups finely ground)

4   Tbs. melted unsalted butter

3½   cups fresh raspberries

8   oz. semisweet or bittersweet chocolate, finely chopped

1¼   cups heavy cream

Small pinch of salt

This tart can be made up to a day ahead. For the crust, you'll need nothing fancier than a bag of store-bought gingersnaps.

1. Position a rack in the center of the oven, and heat the oven to 325°F. Oil the sides and bottom of a 9½-inch fluted tart pan with a removable bottom. In a food processor, grind the gingersnaps until they're the texture of sand. Transfer to a bowl, add the melted butter, and work it in by squishing the mixture together with your hands. Press into the sides and bottom of the oiled tart pan. Set the pan on a baking sheet and refrigerate for 20 minutes to firm. Bake the tart crust on the baking sheet until fragrant, about 15 minutes, checking and rotating if needed to make the sure the crust doesn't get too dark. Set on a rack to cool.

2. Meanwhile, pass 1 cup of the berries through a food mill fitted with a fine disk or force them through a fine-mesh sieve, mashing with a wooden spoon, into a medium bowl. You'll have about ½ cup purée; set it aside and discard the contents of the strainer. Put the chopped chocolate in a medium bowl. Heat the cream in a small saucepan just until boiling. Pour the hot cream over the chopped chocolate; whisk to blend. Stir in the raspberry purée and the salt. Pour the mixture (called a ganache) into the cooled tart shell. Refrigerate until the ganache is fairly firm, about 1 hour. Arrange the remaining raspberries on top of the ganache; they should completely cover the surface. Chill until the ganache is completely firm, about 30 minutes, and serve.
—*Michelle Polzine*

PER SERVING: 350 CALORIES | 3G PROTEIN | 33G CARB | 25G TOTAL FAT | 14G SAT FAT | 7G MONO FAT | 2G POLY FAT | 55MG CHOL | 150MG SODIUM | 7G FIBER

chocolate truffle tart with whipped vanilla mascarpone topping

MAKES ONE 9½-INCH TART; SERVES 12 TO 16

FOR THE FILLING AND CRUST

- **12 oz. bittersweet chocolate, finely chopped**
- **1 cup whole milk**
- **2 oz. (¼ cup) unsalted butter, cut into 4 pieces**
- **1 tsp. pure vanilla extract**
- **¼ tsp. table salt**
- **1 Press-In Cookie Crust (recipe on p. 148), baked and cooled (graham cracker is delicious in this tart)**

FOR THE TOPPING

- **½ lb. mascarpone, at room temperature**
- **¾ cup heavy cream**
- **¼ cup granulated sugar**
- **½ tsp. pure vanilla extract**

The mascarpone, a thick and buttery triple-cream cow's milk cheese, in the topping is the perfect foil to the rich chocolate tart.

MAKE THE FILLING

1. Melt together the chocolate, milk, and butter in a medium bowl in a microwave or in a double boiler over medium heat. Add the vanilla extract and salt. Whisk the mixture until well blended and smooth. Set aside, whisking occasionally, until room temperature and slightly thickened, about 1 hour. (For faster cooling, refrigerate the filling until thickened to a pudding consistency, about 30 minutes, whisking and scraping the sides of the bowl with a rubber spatula every 5 minutes.)

2. With a rubber spatula, scrape the mixture into the crust and spread evenly, taking care not to disturb the edge of the crust. Let cool completely, cover, and refrigerate until the filling is set, about 4 hours and up to 8 hours before proceeding with the recipe.

MAKE THE TOPPING

1. In a medium bowl, combine the mascarpone, cream, sugar, and vanilla extract. Using an electric mixer, beat on low speed until almost smooth, 30 to 60 seconds. Increase the speed to medium high and beat until the mixture is thick and holds firm peaks, another 30 to 60 seconds. Don't overbeat.

2. With a rubber or metal spatula, spread the topping over the chocolate filling, leaving lots of swirls and peaks. Serve the tart right away or cover loosely and refrigerate, in the pan, for up to 4 hours.
—*Abigail Johnson Dodge*

continued on p. 148

press-in cookie crust

**MAKES 1 CRUST FOR ONE
9½-INCH TART**

- **1 cup finely ground cookies
(ground in a food proces-
sor); choose one from the
following: about 25 chocolate wafers, 8 whole graham
crackers, or 35 vanilla
wafers (preferably Nabisco
FAMOUS Chocolate Wafers,
Honey Maid® Grahams, and
Nilla® Vanilla Wafers)**
- **2 Tbs. granulated sugar**
- **1½ oz. (3 Tbs.) unsalted butter,
melted**

1. Position a rack in the center of the oven, and heat the oven to 350°F. Have ready an ungreased 9 ½-inch fluted tart pan with a removable bottom.

2. In a medium bowl, mix the cookie crumbs and sugar with a fork until well blended. Drizzle the melted butter over the crumbs, and mix with the fork or your fingers until the crumbs are evenly moistened. Put the crumbs in the tart pan and use your hands to spread the crumbs so that they coat the bottom of the pan and start to climb the sides. Use your fingers to pinch and press some of the crumbs around the inside edge of the pan to cover the sides evenly and create a wall about a scant ¼ inch thick. Redistribute the remaining crumbs evenly over the bottom of the pan, and press firmly to make a compact layer. (A metal measuring cup with straight sides and a flat base works well for this task.)

3. Bake the crust until it smells nutty and fragrant (crusts made with lighter-colored cookies will brown slightly), about 10 minutes. Set the baked crust on a rack and let cool. The crust can be made up to 1 day ahead and stored at room temperature, wrapped well in plastic.

chocolate caramel tart with macadamias and crème fraîche whipped cream

SERVES 12 TO 16

FOR THE CRUST

- **6** oz. (1⅓ cups) unbleached all-purpose flour; a little more for rolling
- **3** Tbs. granulated sugar
- **¼** tsp. kosher salt
- **4** oz. (8 Tbs.) cold unsalted butter, cut into small cubes
- **2** Tbs. heavy cream
- **1** large egg yolk

FOR THE FILLING

- **1¼** cups macadamia nuts
- **2** cups heavy cream
- **1½** oz. (3 Tbs.) unsalted butter, cut into chunks
- **1** cup plus 1½ Tbs. granulated sugar
- **¼** cup light corn syrup
- **½** vanilla bean, split and scraped
- **6** oz. bittersweet chocolate (70% cacao), chopped (about 1¼ cups)
- **½** cup whole milk
- **¼** cup crème fraîche

This dessert is a wonderful finish to a holiday meal. Be careful when cooking the caramel (turn off the heat and whisk in the milk carefully so it doesn't bubble over), and be sure it's set before you pour the chocolate on top.

MAKE THE CRUST

1. In a stand mixer fitted with a paddle attachment, combine the flour, sugar, salt, and butter, and mix on medium speed until the butter blends into the flour and the mixture resembles a coarse meal. Mix the cream and egg yolk together in a small bowl. With the mixer on low speed, gradually add the cream mixture and mix until just combined. Do not overwork the dough.

2. Transfer the dough to a work surface, and bring it together with your hands. Shape the dough into a 1-inch-thick disk. If the dough seems too soft to roll out, put it in the refrigerator for 5 to 10 minutes to firm it up a little. Set the dough on a lightly floured work surface, sprinkle a little flour over it, and roll it out into a ⅛-inch-thick circle 14 to 15 inches in diameter, reflouring the dough and work surface as necessary.

3. Starting at one side, roll and wrap the dough around the rolling pin to pick it up. Unroll the dough over an 11-inch fluted tart pan with a removable bottom and gently fit it loosely in the pan, lifting the edges and pressing the dough into the corners with your fingers. To remove the excess dough, roll the rolling pin lightly over the top of the tart pan, cutting a nice, clean edge. Cover loosely with plastic and chill for 1 hour.

MAKE THE TART

1. Position a rack in the center of the oven, and heat the oven to 375°F.

2. Prick the bottom of the crust with a fork, and line it with a piece of parchment paper or several opened-out basket-style coffee filters. Fill the lined tart shell with dried beans or pie weights and bake until set around the edges, about 15 minutes. Take the tart out of the oven, and carefully lift out the paper and pie weights (if using coffee filters, spoon out most of the weights first). Return the tart to the oven and bake until the crust is golden brown all over, another 10 to 15 minutes. Let cool completely on a rack.

3. While the crust is baking, spread the nuts on a baking sheet and toast (in the same oven) until they are golden brown and smell nutty, 10 to 12 minutes. Let them cool, and then chop coarsely.

4. In a small pot, bring ¾ cup of the cream and the butter to a simmer. Set aside.

continued on p. 151

5. Combine 1 cup of the sugar with the corn syrup, vanilla bean seeds and pod, and ¼ cup water in a 3- or 4-quart heavy-based pot. Boil over high heat, stirring frequently with a wooden spoon, until the mixture becomes caramel colored. Remove from the heat and immediately whisk in the hot cream mixture. (Do this slowly and carefully; you don't want the hot sugar to overflow or splatter.)

6. Pour the caramel into the baked tart shell, and pick out the vanilla bean halves with a fork or tongs. Sprinkle about two-thirds of the macadamia nuts on top of the caramel. Let cool completely in the refrigerator.

7. When the tart is cool, put the chocolate in a large bowl. In a small pot, bring ½ cup of the cream, the milk, and the remaining 1½ Tbs. sugar to a boil over medium-high heat. As soon as it boils, pour it over the chocolate. Let stand for 2 minutes, then stir very gently with a whisk until smooth and thoroughly combined. Let cool at room temperature for 5 minutes, and then pour the chocolate filling over the completely chilled tart, covering the nuts and caramel.

8. Chill in the refrigerator until completely set, at least 4 hours. Unmold the tart, using a long, thin metal spatula to release it from the pan bottom. Place it on a cutting board or a serving plate, depending on how you intend to serve it.

9. Just before serving, whip the remaining ¾ cup cream and the crème fraîche to soft peaks. Slice and plate the tart in the kitchen or at the table. Top each serving with a dollop of the whipped cream, and scatter the remaining macadamias over and around.   —*Suzanne Goin*

PER SERVING: 440 CALORIES | 4G PROTEIN | 36G CARB | 34G TOTAL FAT | 17G SAT FAT | 12G MONO FAT | 1G POLY FAT | 80MG CHOL | 40MG SODIUM | 2G FIBER

fried chocolate-hazelnut wontons with orange dipping sauce

SERVES 6

24	wonton wrappers, preferably square
1	13-oz. jar Nutella® (or other chocolate-hazelnut spread), chilled
¾	cup heavy cream
½	cup thawed orange juice concentrate
2	tsp. Grand Marnier
¼	tsp. pure vanilla extract
3	cups vegetable oil, for frying
	Confectioners' sugar, for serving

Look for wonton wrappers in the produce section of your supermarket. If not frying immediately, you can stuff the wontons and refrigerate them for up to 2 days. Just cover tightly with plastic wrap to prevent them from drying out. The sauce can also be made ahead and refrigerated for a day.

1. Set out a bowl of water and a pastry brush. If necessary, trim the wonton wrappers into squares. Lay the wrappers on a work surface, orienting them so they look diamond shaped instead of square. Working quickly, put 1 heaping tsp. of chilled Nutella in the lower half of each diamond. Brush the edges of one wonton with a little water and fold the top point of the diamond down to meet the bottom, forming a triangle. Gently press around the filling to force out any air and pinch the edges to seal. Repeat with the remaining wontons. Set the wontons on a baking sheet, cover, and keep chilled.

2. In a small bowl, combine the heavy cream with the orange juice concentrate, Grand Marnier, and vanilla extract. Refrigerate the sauce until ready to serve.

3. Heat the oil to 365°F in a heavy 3-quart saucepan over medium heat. Set a baking sheet lined with a thick layer of paper towels next to the pot. Slip 6 to 8 wontons into the oil and fry, turning occasionally, until golden brown, 2 to 3 minutes. Scoop them out with a slotted spoon and drain on the paper towels while you fry the rest.

4. Arrange 4 wontons on individual serving plates and sprinkle with confectioners' sugar. Serve with small individual dishes filled with the orange sauce for dipping. *—Gale Gand*

PER SERVING: 460 CALORIES | 6G PROTEIN | 53G CARB | 25G TOTAL FAT | 9G SAT FAT | 10G MONO FAT | 4G POLY FAT | 45MG CHOL | 210MG SODIUM | 3G FIBER

Use a second teaspoon to help drop a dollop of Nutella on the lower half of the wonton wrapper.

chocolate caramel-almond tart

SERVES 8

FOR THE CRUST

4½ oz. (1 cup) unbleached all-purpose flour; more for rolling the dough

3 Tbs. granulated sugar

Pinch of table salt

3 oz. (6 Tbs.) cold unsalted butter, cut into ½-inch pieces

FOR THE CARAMEL-ALMOND LAYER

¾ cup blanched whole almonds

½ cup heavy cream

1 recipe Basic Caramel (recipe on p. 155)

1 oz. (2 Tbs.) unsalted butter

1 tsp. pure vanilla extract

¼ tsp. table salt

Lightly sweetened whipped cream is the perfect counterpoint to chocolate and caramel.

MAKE THE CRUST

1. Put the flour, sugar, and salt in a food processor, and pulse a few times to combine. Add the butter pieces and pulse until the mixture is the texture of coarse meal with some pea-size butter pieces, five to seven 1-second pulses. Sprinkle 2 Tbs. ice-cold water over the flour mixture, and process until the dough just begins to come together in small, marble-size clumps. Don't overprocess; the dough should not form a ball.

2. Turn the dough out onto a work surface, and shape it into a thick 4-inch-diameter disk. Wrap the dough in plastic and chill until firm enough to roll, about 30 minutes.

3. On a lightly floured surface, roll the dough into an 11-inch circle, lifting and rotating it often, while lightly dusting the work surface and the dough with flour as necessary. Transfer the dough to a 9 ½-inch fluted tart pan with a removable bottom. Gently press the dough into the bottom and up the sides of the pan. Roll the pin over the top of the pan to trim the excess dough. Lightly prick the bottom of the dough with a fork at ½-inch intervals. Refrigerate for 20 minutes to firm it up.

4. Meanwhile, position a rack in the center of the oven, and heat the oven to 350°F.

5. Line the dough with aluminum foil and fill it with pie weights or dried beans. Put the tart pan on a baking sheet and bake for 20 minutes. Carefully lift the foil (and the weights) out of the tart pan, and bake the crust until golden brown along the top edge and in some spots on the bottom, 13 to 17 minutes. Transfer the tart pan to a wire rack and let cool completely. Raise the oven temperature to 375°F.

MAKE THE CARAMEL-ALMOND LAYER

1. Toast the almonds on a baking sheet in the oven until golden, 5 to 10 minutes. Let cool briefly and then chop coarsely.

2. Carefully add the heavy cream to the hot Basic Caramel. The mixture will bubble up furiously. Once the bubbling has subsided, add the butter and stir until completely melted. Whisk in the vanilla extract, salt, and almonds until the nuts are completely coated. Pour the hot caramel mixture into the cooled tart shell, using a heatproof spatula to scrape the pot clean and distribute the nuts evenly in the shell. Let cool for 30 minutes and then refrigerate until the caramel is completely chilled, about 1 hour.

continued on p. 154

FOR THE CHOCOLATE LAYER

- **2 oz. bittersweet chocolate, coarsely chopped**
- **⅓ cup heavy cream**
- **½ oz. (1 Tbs.) unsalted butter, cut into 3 pieces**
- **½ tsp. pure vanilla extract**

Lightly sweetened whipped cream or vanilla ice cream, for serving (optional)

MAKE THE CHOCOLATE LAYER

Put the chocolate and cream in a small saucepan over low heat and stir occasionally until the chocolate is melted, 3 to 5 minutes. Add the butter and stir until melted and the mixture is smooth. Stir in the vanilla extract. Pour over the caramel layer, and tilt the pan as needed to smooth the chocolate into an even layer that covers the caramel. Refrigerate until the chocolate is set, at least 1 hour and up to 1 day. Serve the tart with whipped cream or vanilla ice cream, if you like.

—*Tish Boyle*

PER SERVING: 470 CALORIES | 6G PROTEIN | 47G CARB | 30G TOTAL FAT | 15G SAT FAT | 11G MONO FAT | 2.5G POLY FAT | 65MG CHOL | 125MG SODIUM | 3G FIBER

basic caramel

MAKES ⅔ CUP

1   cup granulated sugar

¼   tsp. fresh lemon juice

1. Fill a cup measure halfway with water and put a pastry brush in it; this will be used for washing down the sides of the pan to prevent crystallization.

2. In a heavy-duty 2-quart saucepan, stir the sugar, lemon juice, and ¼ cup cold water. Brush down the sides of the pan with water to wash away any sugar crystals. Bring to a boil over medium-high heat and cook, occasionally brushing down the sides of the pan, until the mixture starts to color around the edges, 5 to 8 minutes. Gently swirl the pan once to even out the color and prevent the sugar from burning in isolated spots. Continue to cook until the sugar turns medium amber, about 30 seconds more. (Once the mixture begins to color, it will darken very quickly, so keep an eye on it.)

5 Tips for Perfect Caramel

One of two things can go wrong when making caramel: The caramel burns or sugar crystals form, so the caramel goes from liquid and smooth to crystallized and solid. Here are a few pointers for making a perfectly smooth caramel every time.

• **Watch bubbling caramel like a hawk.** Caramel cooks quickly and will turn from golden amber to a smoking mahogany in seconds. Burnt caramel has an unpleasantly bitter taste.

• **Use clean utensils.** Sugar crystals tend to form around impurities and foreign particles.

• **Acid helps**. Adding lemon juice to the sugar and water helps break down the sucrose molecules and prevents sugar crystals from forming.

• **Swirl, don't stir.** Stirring tends to splash syrup onto the sides of the pan, where sugar crystals can form. So once the sugar is completely dissolved in water, just gently swirl the pan to caramelize the sugar evenly.

• **A pastry brush is your friend.** Keep a pastry brush and some water next to the stove; you'll need it to wash off any crystals that might form on the sides of the pan.

chocolate-cherry cheesecake tart

SERVES 8 TO 10

- **6** oz. chocolate wafers, finely crushed (1⅓ cups)
- **⅓** cup plus 2 Tbs. granulated sugar
- **2½** oz. (5 Tbs.) unsalted butter, melted
- **1** cup pitted fresh or frozen sweet cherries, puréed
- **3** Tbs. cherry preserves
- **1** Tbs. kirsch
- **12** oz. cream cheese, softened
- **4** oz. sour cream (⅓ cup plus 1 Tbs.), at room temperature
- **1** Tbs. unbleached all-purpose flour
- **1** tsp. pure vanilla extract
- **½** tsp. kosher salt
- **2** large eggs, at room temperature

Black forest cake was the inspiration for this tart, which has a chocolate crust, a cherry-swirled topping, and a subtly tangy cream cheese filling.

1. Position a rack in the center of the oven, and heat the oven to 350°F.

2. In a small bowl, mix the crushed cookies with 2 Tbs. of the sugar. Add the melted butter and toss with your fingers until evenly moistened. Transfer the crumbs to a 9 ½-inch fluted tart pan with a removable bottom. With your fingers, gently pack the crumbs into the bottom and up the sides to form the crust. Bake on a rimmed baking sheet until set, 10 to 12 minutes. Set aside to cool. Reduce the oven temperature to 325°F.

3. Meanwhile, in a 1-quart saucepan over medium heat, bring the cherry purée to a simmer. Whisk in the cherry preserves and continue to simmer until the mixture thickens slightly, 3 to 5 minutes. Stir in the kirsch and continue to cook for 30 seconds more. Remove from the heat and let cool.

4. In a stand mixer fitted with a paddle attachment, beat the cream cheese and remaining ⅓ cup sugar on medium-low speed until the mixture is smooth and fluffy, about 3 minutes. Add the sour cream, flour, vanilla extract, and salt, and beat until well combined, about 1 minute more. Add the eggs one at a time, beating until just combined, about 15 seconds for each egg (do not overbeat).

5. Pour the batter into the crust and distribute evenly. Dot the batter with the cherry mixture and gently drag a butter knife through the filling to form decorative swirls.

6. Bake until the tart is just set but still slightly moist in the center, 18 to 24 minutes. Let cool on a wire rack. Refrigerate for at least 4 hours. Serve cold. The tart may be made up to 1 day ahead.
—Samantha Seneviratne

PER SERVING: 350 CALORIES | 5G PROTEIN | 31G CARB | 23G TOTAL FAT | 13G SAT FAT | 6G MONO FAT | 1.6G POLY FAT | 95MG CHOL | 310MG SODIUM | 1G FIBER

chocolate espresso pecan pie

SERVES 8 TO 10

FOR THE CRUST

6 oz. (1⅓ cups) unbleached all-purpose flour; more for rolling out the crust

1 tsp. granulated sugar

¼ tsp. plus ⅛ tsp. kosher salt

2 oz. (4 Tbs.) chilled unsalted butter, cut into ½-inch pieces

2 oz. (4 Tbs.) vegetable short-ening, chilled and cut into ½-inch pieces (put it in the freezer for 15 minutes before cutting)

FOR THE FILLING

3 oz. unsweetened chocolate, coarsely chopped

2 oz. (4 Tbs.) unsalted butter

4 large eggs

1 cup light corn syrup

1 cup granulated sugar

¼ tsp. kosher salt

2 Tbs. instant espresso pow-der (or instant coffee)

2 Tbs. coffee liqueur (Kahlúa or Caffé Lolita)

2 cups lightly toasted, coarsely chopped pecans

About ½ cup perfect pecan halves

This pie tastes best if cooled and then refrigerated for several hours or overnight. Serve it lightly chilled with a dollop of very lightly sweetened whipped cream.

MAKE THE CRUST

1. Pulse the flour, sugar, and salt in a food processor just to blend. Add the butter and shortening, and pulse several times until the mixture resembles coarse cornmeal, 8 to 10 pulses. Transfer the mixture to a medium bowl. Tossing and stirring quickly with a fork, gradually add enough cold water (2 to 4 Tbs.) that the dough just begins to come together. It should clump together easily if lightly squeezed but not feel wet or sticky. With your hands, gather the dough and form it into a ball. Flatten the ball into a disk and wrap it in plastic. Chill the dough for 2 hours or up to 2 days before rolling. The dough can also be frozen for up to 2 months; thaw it overnight in the refrigerator before using.

2. Remove the dough from the refrigerator and let it sit at room tem-perature until pliable, 10 to 15 minutes. On a lightly floured surface with a lightly floured rolling pin, roll the dough into a ⅛-inch-thick, 13-inch-diameter round. Be sure to pick up the dough several times and rotate it, reflouring the surface lightly to prevent sticking. A giant spatula or the bottom of a removable-bottom tart pan helps to move the dough around. (See the sidebar on p. 159 for tips on rolling out piecrust.) Transfer the dough to a 9-inch Pyrex pie pan, and trim the edges so there's a ½-inch overhang. Fold the overhang under-neath itself to create a raised edge and then decoratively crimp or flute the edge. (Save the scraps for patching the shell later, if neces-sary). Chill until the dough firms up, at least 45 minutes in the refrig-erator or 20 minutes in the freezer.

continued on p. 158

3. Position a rack in the center of the oven, and heat the oven to 350°F. Line the pie shell with parchment and fill with dried beans or pie weights. Bake until the edges of the crust are light golden brown, 25 to 30 minutes. Carefully remove the parchment and beans or weights. If necessary, gently repair any cracks with a smear of the excess dough. Transfer the shell to a rack to cool.

MAKE THE FILLING

1. Melt the chocolate and butter in a microwave or in a small metal bowl set in a skillet of barely simmering water, stirring with a rubber spatula until smooth.

2. In a medium mixing bowl, whisk the eggs, corn syrup, sugar, and salt. Dissolve the instant espresso in 1 Tbs. hot water and add to the egg mixture, along with the coffee liqueur and the melted chocolate and butter. Whisk to blend.

3. Evenly spread the toasted pecan pieces in the pie shell. To form a decorative border, arrange the pecan halves around the perimeter of the pie shell, on top of the pecan pieces, keeping the points of the pecans facing in and the backs just touching the crust. Carefully pour the filling over the pecans until the shell is three-quarters full. Pour the remaining filling into a liquid measuring cup or small pitcher. Transfer the pie to the oven and pour in the remaining filling. (The pecans will rise to the top as the pie bakes.)

4. Bake the pie until the filling puffs up, just starts to crack, and appears fairly set, 45 to 55 minutes. Transfer it to a rack and allow it to cool completely (at least 4 hours) before serving. *—Karen Barker*

PER SERVING: 650 CALORIES | 8G PROTEIN | 66G CARB | 42G TOTAL FAT | 12G SAT FAT | 18G MONO FAT | 8G POLY FAT | 110MG CHOL | 120MG SODIUM | 5G FIBER

How to Roll Out Perfect Piecrust

Piecrusts are one of the hardest things for a home cook to master. When it comes to rolling them out, experience counts for a lot, but good techniques are crucial, too. Here are some of our best pointers for rolling out lovely, even rounds of dough.

Start with dough at the right temperature

If it's too warm and soft, it'll stick like crazy to the rolling pin and the work surface, forcing you to add too much flour as you work it. Dough that's too cold and hard resists rolling and cracks if you try to force it. Press the dough lightly to check its rolling readiness—your fingertips should leave an imprint but shouldn't easily sink into the dough.

Roll around the clock

Start with the rolling pin in the center of your dough disk. Roll toward 12 o'clock, easing up on the pressure as you near the edge (this keeps the edge from getting too thin). Pick up the pin and return it to center. Roll toward 6 o'clock. Repeat this motion toward 3 o'clock and then 9 o'clock, always easing up the pressure near the edges and then picking up the pin rather than rolling it back to center. Continue to roll around the clock, aiming for different "times" (like 1, 7, 4, 10) on each round.

Turn the dough and check often for sticking. After each round of the clock, run a bench knife underneath the dough to make sure it's not sticking, and reflour the surface if necessary. When you do this, give the dough a quarter turn—most people inevitably use uneven pressure when rolling in one direction versus another, so the occasional turn helps average it out for a more even thickness. Continue to turn and roll until the dough is the right width and thickness.

Go easy on the flour

Even dough that's at the perfect temperature needs a little extra flour to keep it from sticking, but try not to use more than you really need—the more extra flour you work into the dough as you roll it, the drier and tougher the crust will be.

Try an alternative rolling surface

Beyond the usual lightly floured countertop, other options for rolling surfaces include a pastry cloth, a silicone rolling mat, and sheets of parchment, waxed paper, or plastic wrap. Choose whichever one you like best.

chocolate-glazed peanut butter tart

**MAKES ONE 9½-INCH TART;
SERVES 12**

FOR THE FILLING AND CRUST

- 1½ cups whole milk
- ¼ tsp. table salt
- 3 large egg yolks
- ⅓ cup firmly packed light brown sugar
- 4 tsp. unbleached all-purpose flour
- 4½ oz. (½ cup) creamy peanut butter (preferably natural, made with only peanuts and salt)
- ½ tsp. pure vanilla extract
- 1 **Press-In Cookie Crust (recipe on p. 148), baked and cooled (chocolate or graham cracker is delicious in this tart)**

FOR THE GLAZE

- 3 oz. bittersweet chocolate, finely chopped
- 2 oz. (¼ cup) unsalted butter, cut into 6 pieces
- 1 Tbs. light corn syrup

Cookie crumbs make a shortcut crust for this delicious tart.

MAKE THE FILLING

1. In a medium saucepan, bring the milk and salt to a simmer over medium heat, stirring occasionally. Meanwhile, in a small bowl, whisk the egg yolks, brown sugar, and flour until well blended. Slowly add the hot milk, whisking constantly. Pour the mixture back into the saucepan. Cook over medium heat, whisking constantly, until it thickens and comes to a full boil, about 3 minutes. Continue to cook, whisking constantly, for 1 minute. Remove the pan from the heat and add the peanut butter and vanilla extract; whisk until well blended.

2. Pour the hot peanut butter mixture into the crust, and spread evenly with a rubber or offset spatula. Gently press a piece of plastic wrap directly on the filling's surface to prevent a skin from forming. Refrigerate the tart until cold, about 2 hours, before proceeding with the recipe.

MAKE THE GLAZE

Melt the chocolate in a small bowl in a microwave or in a double boiler over medium heat. Add the butter and corn syrup, and whisk until the butter is melted and the mixture is smooth, about 1 minute. Carefully remove the plastic wrap from the top of the chilled filling. Drizzle the glaze over the filling and spread it evenly to cover the tart completely. Refrigerate the tart in the pan until the glaze sets, about 30 minutes or up to 12 hours. —*Abigail Johnson Dodge*

To remove a tart from the pan, set the pan on a wide can and let the outside ring fall away. If it's stubborn, grip the ring with your fingers to coax it off. Slide a long, thin metal spatula between the pan base and the crust and ease the tart onto a flat serving plate.

warm chocolate tarts

3 oz. (6 Tbs.) unsalted butter; more melted for the pans

Unbleached all-purpose flour, for the pans

13 oz. semisweet chocolate (to yield about 3 cups chopped)

Pinch of salt

9 egg yolks

½ cup granulated sugar

3 egg whites

1 recipe Espresso Crème Anglaise (recipe on p. 164) or Citrus-Peel Confit (recipe on p. 165), for serving (optional)

This intensely chocolate tart is cakey on the outside and gooey in the middle. Served in a pool of coffee-flavored crème anglaise and garnished with sweetened citrus zest and fresh raspberries, this dessert looks and tastes wonderful but is simple to make.

1. Brush each of twelve 4-inch tart pans or muffin pans with melted butter and coat with flour.

2. Using a chef's knife, chop the chocolate into small pieces on a cutting board. Cut up the butter and put it, together with the chocolate, in a clean, dry, microwave-safe bowl (a large porcelain soup or cereal bowl is just right). Add a pinch of salt to heighten the flavor of the dish. Microwave on high for 1 minute, stir, and repeat until the chocolate seems softened but still looks somewhat chunky, about 1 minute more. Remove from the microwave and stir to distribute the heat until the chocolate is completely smooth. If you don't have a microwave, you can melt the chocolate mixture over a hot water bath. Let the chocolate mixture cool to room temperature.

3. In a large bowl, put the egg yolks and all but 2 Tbs. of the sugar. Using an electric mixer with a whip attachment, beat on high speed until the mixture lightens in color and thickens in consistency, about 2 minutes. (If you prefer, you can whip the yolks and sugar by hand with a whisk.) Fold in the cooled chocolate mixture using a rubber spatula until the mixture is homogenous.

4. In a medium bowl, add the remaining 2 Tbs. of sugar to the egg whites and whip at high speed just until they form soft peaks, about 1½ minutes. Don't overbeat the eggs or they'll get dry and grainy.

5. Scoop one-third of the egg whites into the chocolate mixture and, using a rubber spatula or large whisk, fold the mixture together in a circular up-and-down motion until the egg whites are evenly incorporated. Add the remaining egg whites and lightly fold them in. Be sure to use good folding technique—if you stir or fold too roughly, you'll knock the air out of the mixture, decreasing the volume of the batter and leaving you with fewer tarts than you had planned.

6. Spoon the batter into the prepared tart or muffin pans so that the batter reaches about ½ inch from the top. Cover the tarts with plastic wrap and refrigerate until you're ready to bake them.

7. Position a rack in the center of the oven, and heat the oven to 475°F. If you've prepared the tarts ahead of time, take them directly from the refrigerator to a baking sheet and put them in the oven. Bake for 9 minutes if the batter has been chilled but only for 8 minutes if you're

continued on p. 164

baking them right away and the batter is room temperature. They won't look done when you pull them out—the tops may still have a spot or two of liquid batter and they'll jiggle like firm gelatin—but pull them out anyway. You want the outside of the tart to be like cake and the inside warm and runny. If you overbake them, the tart will be more cakey but still delicious. If you underbake them, the inside will be more saucy and won't be warm. Serve with the Espresso Crème Anglaise or Citrus-Peel Confit, if desired. —*Mary Beth Fama*

espresso crème anglaise

MAKES 2 CUPS

1 **pint (16 oz.) whole milk or heavy cream**

1 **Tbs. finely ground dark-roast coffee beans or 2 tsp. instant espresso powder**

5 **egg yolks**

½ **cup granulated sugar**

You can make this sauce up to a day ahead and keep it chilled in the refrigerator. Depending on how rich you want the sauce to be, you can make it with either milk or heavy cream. Finely ground coffee beans speckle the sauce and give it a subtle coffee flavor. Since the chocolate supplies enough of a jolt, use decaffeinated dark-roast coffee beans.

1. Put the milk or cream in a heavy, medium saucepan and slowly heat it until it just comes to a boil, stirring occasionally. Remove the milk from the heat and stir in the ground coffee.

2. In a medium bowl, combine the egg yolks with the sugar and whisk, either by hand or in an electric mixer, until they lighten in color, about 1 minute.

3. With the mixer on low speed, pour half of the hot milk into the egg yolks and stir until incorporated. Transfer all the egg-yolk mixture into the saucepan and stir thoroughly.

4. Return the pan to the stove and slowly heat the sauce over low heat, taking care to scrape the bottom of the pan as you stir (a wooden spatula with a flat edge works great for this). Heat the sauce for several minutes until it reaches the nappe stage—that is, until it coats the back of the wooden spatula and when you draw your finger through the sauce, the mark doesn't fill in. This should happen just before the sauce reaches the boiling point. Don't let the sauce boil or the eggs will coagulate and you'll have lumps in the sauce.

5. Transfer the sauce to an ice bath to cool. You may want to strain it through a fine-mesh sieve to ensure a smooth consistency, but if you've taken care not to overcook the sauce, this shouldn't be necessary.

citrus-peel confit

MAKES ½ CUP

- **1 orange**
- **1 lemon**
- **½ cup granulated sugar**
- **1 Tbs. light corn syrup**

These sweet, tender strips of lemon and orange zest confit (pro-nounced kohn-fee) provide a sparkle of color and flavor that con-trasts with the intense chocolate of the tart.

1. Slice off the peel from the orange and the lemon, taking care to cut away as much of the bitter, white inner rind, or pith, as possible. To do this easily, first cut off the stem and navel ends, cut the fruit in half between the two ends, then cut each half into two semicircles. Prop each quarter of fruit on a cutting board, skin side down. Hold your knife parallel to the cutting board and slice away the pulp and the pith. You'll have four neat rectangular strips of zest, which you can then julienne into matchstick-size pieces.

2. Put the sliced zest in a small saucepan of cold water, bring it to a boil, and drain. Repeat twice to thoroughly remove all bitterness.

3. In another small saucepan, combine the sugar, corn syrup, and ¼ cup water, and heat until the sugar dissolves, stirring occasionally. Add the blanched zest, and simmer them in the syrup until they're very tender (but not broken down) and the syrup is still runny, about 15 minutes. Let the zests cool, then store them with the syrup in a glass jar. They'll keep for many months in the refrigerator.

dark-chocolate mousse
with caramelized allspice
oranges (recipe on p. 173)

puddings, mousses & more

bittersweet chocolate pots de crème

SERVES 2

½ cup half-and-half

¼ cup whole milk

2 large egg yolks

½ cup bittersweet chocolate chips

2 Tbs. granulated sugar

Pinch of kosher salt

This quick version of a classic French pudding comes together on the stovetop in minutes and then chills during dinner.

1. Heat the half-and-half and milk in a small saucepan over medium heat until scalding hot. Meanwhile, whisk the egg yolks in a small bowl. Slowly whisk the hot milk mixture into the eggs.

2. Return the milk mixture to the pan, reduce the heat to low, and whisk until it thickens, about 1 minute. Remove from the heat and add the chocolate chips, sugar, and salt; whisk until melted. Strain through a medium-mesh sieve into a medium bowl.

3. Divide the mixture among two 6-oz. ramekins or serving glasses. Refrigerate until set, at least 1 hour. —*Allison Fishman*

PER SERVING: 430 CALORIES | 9G PROTEIN | 43G CARB | 25G TOTAL FAT | 155G SAT FAT | 9G MONO FAT | 1G POLY FAT | 235MG CHOL | 105MG SODIUM | 5G FIBER

chocolate steamed pudding

**MAKES 2 PUDDINGS;
EACH SERVES 12**

FOR THE FUDGE SWIRL

¼ cup granulated sugar

½ cup light corn syrup

¾ cup Dutch-processed cocoa

2½ tsp. instant coffee

8 oz. bittersweet chocolate, chopped

3 Tbs. Cognac or brandy

FOR THE PUDDING

8 oz. (16 Tbs.) unsalted butter, softened; more melted butter for the molds

½ cup Dutch-processed cocoa; more for dusting

½ cup buttermilk

2 tsp. instant espresso powder

6 oz. bittersweet chocolate, chopped

½ cup sour cream

¾ cup lightly packed light brown sugar

6 oz. almond paste

8 eggs, separated

2 cups pitted prunes, chopped

10 oz. (2 ¼ cups) unbleached all-purpose flour, sifted

2½ tsp. baking soda dissolved in 2 Tbs. boiling water

¼ cup granulated sugar

Crème fraîche, for garnish

Steaming lends a creamy texture and brings out the chocolate's deep richness. Pudding molds with latched tops are best, but if you don't have them, use molds with aluminum foil crimped tightly over the top.

PREPARE THE FUDGE SWIRL

In a large saucepan over medium-high heat, combine the sugar, corn syrup, ½ cup plus 1 Tbs. water, the cocoa, and coffee; bring to a boil. Cook for 1 to 2 minutes, stirring constantly to prevent burning on the bottom. Remove the pan from the heat, and whisk in the chocolate until melted and smooth. Stir in the brandy and set aside to cool. Refrigerate the swirl if you won't be using it that day.

MAKE THE PUDDING

1. Choose two pots large enough to hold the pudding molds. Set a trivet at the bottom of each. Fill the pots with water and bring to a boil. (If you can only steam one pudding at a time, refrigerate the other until needed.)

2. Brush two 8-cup molds with melted butter and let them set for a minute in the freezer; dust with cocoa. In a small saucepan over medium-high heat, whisk ½ cup water, the cocoa, and the buttermilk. Bring to a boil, whisking constantly until the cocoa is dissolved. Remove the pan from the heat; whisk in the espresso powder and chocolate, mixing until melted. Add the sour cream; set aside to cool.

3. With an electric mixer, beat the butter on low speed. As it starts to soften, increase the speed to medium and beat until smooth, 1 to 2 minutes. Beat in the brown sugar, almond paste, egg yolks, prunes, the chocolate mixture, half the flour, the baking soda mixture, and finish with the remaining flour. Set aside.

4. With an electric mixer on low speed, beat the egg whites until frothy. Increase the speed to medium and beat until soft peaks form. Increase the speed to high and gradually beat in the sugar until stiff, glossy peaks form. Quickly fold half the egg whites into the chocolate mixture, and then gently but thoroughly add the other half. Drizzle the fudge swirl onto the mixture, folding only once or twice to marble the batter, leaving large streaks of fudge.

5. Pour half the batter into each mold; it should come to 1½ inches below the rim. Latch the molds securely and set them into the hot water on top of the trivets. The water should reach halfway up the sides of the mold. Cover the pots and steam the puddings over medium heat until they're firm to the touch, about 90 minutes. After 30 minutes, check the water level; add more water if it's below halfway down the mold. Let the puddings cool in their molds on a rack for 20 minutes before inverting and unmolding them. Slice the pudding and serve warm or at room temperature with a dollop of crème fraîche. —*Nancy Silverton*

PER SERVING: 680 CALORIES | 12G PROTEIN | 85G CARB | 39G TOTAL FAT | 20G SAT FAT | 14G MONO FAT | 2G POLY FAT | 190MG CHOL | 350MG SODIUM | 8G FIBER

bourbon-chocolate mousse

MAKES 3 CUPS; SERVES 4

½   **cup heavy cream**

3   **Tbs. confectioners' sugar**

2   **Tbs. bourbon**

1   **tsp. pure vanilla extract**

4   **oz. bittersweet chocolate, finely chopped (¾ cup)**

4   **large egg whites, preferably at room temperature**

    Pinch of table salt

    Whipped cream or crème fraîche, for garnish (optional)

    Fresh berries, for garnish (optional)

The egg whites in this recipe are not cooked, but don't use pasteurized egg whites because they tend to separate after they're folded into the ganache. If you like, top the mousse with a dollop of whipped cream or crème fraîche and sprinkle with cocoa powder. Garnish with fresh raspberries or strawberries.

1. Put 4 small (at least ¾ cup) individual serving bowls in the refrigerator to chill.

2. Bring the heavy cream and sugar to a boil in a small saucepan and remove the pan from the heat (don't just turn off the burner). Stir in the bourbon and vanilla extract. Add the chocolate and let it sit for 5 minutes without stirring. Whisk the chocolate and cream until smooth and then transfer the ganache to a large bowl. Don't refrigerate.

3. In a medium bowl, beat the egg whites and salt with a hand mixer on high speed just until they form stiff peaks when you lift the beaters.

4. With a rubber spatula, fold about one-quarter of the beaten whites into the ganache to lighten it. Then gently fold in the remaining whites, taking care not to deflate them. Divide the mousse among the chilled bowls and refrigerate for at least 30 minutes but preferably 1 hour and up to 24 hours. —*Allison Ehri Kreitler*

PER SERVING: 300 CALORIES | 6G PROTEIN | 21G CARB | 23G TOTAL FAT | 13G SAT FAT | 3G MONO FAT | 0G POLY FAT | 40MG CHOL | 140MG SODIUM | 2G FIBER

> **Egg whites can go from perfectly stiff to lumpy in a matter of seconds, so as you get close, stop the mixer frequently to check on them. They're ready when the peaks stand up straight but still have visible air bubbles.**

white-chocolate bread pudding with white-chocolate sauce

SERVES 8

- 1 roll, 10 inches long and 2½ inches in diameter or the equivalent amount of bread
- 2 cups heavy cream
- ½ cup whole milk
- ¼ cup granulated sugar
- 9 oz. white chocolate, chopped
- 1 egg
- 4 egg yolks
- Semisweet chocolate, for garnish (optional)

Long French rolls are crisp on the outside, light and airy within. They're great for this recipe because they soak up custard more readily than heavier breads. Use whatever is available to you that's good but light— perhaps an Italian or Viennese bread. Serve the pudding warm or make it a day ahead and cut it into squares or triangles.

1. Heat the oven to 250°F. Cut the roll into eight slices, place it on the middle rack of the oven, and leave until dry, about 20 minutes.

2. In a saucepan, heat 1½ cups of the cream, the milk, and the sugar over low heat, stirring until the sugar is dissolved. Add 5 oz. of the white chocolate, stir until melted, and remove from the heat. In a large bowl, whisk the egg and yolks together. Whisk the chocolate mixture into the eggs a little at a time.

3. Tear the bread into 1-inch pieces, add to the chocolate custard, and stir to mix. Leave to soak, stirring occasionally, until all the custard has been absorbed by the bread, 1 to 2 hours. Put the mixture into an 8-inch-square, 2-inch-deep baking dish. Put the dish in a slightly larger pan and add hot water to come halfway up the sides of the baking dish. Bake the pudding in the water bath at 350°F until the custard is set and the top is golden brown, 45 to 50 minutes.

4. Serve warm or cold. If you chill it, loosen the sides with a metal spatula and invert the pudding onto a serving plate.

5. For the sauce, heat the remaining cream in a small saucepan. Add the remaining 4 oz. white chocolate and melt. Pour over the pudding. If you like, grate some semisweet chocolate and sprinkle on top of the pudding. *—Ti Martin*

chocolate-banana bread pudding

MAKES ONE 9X13-INCH BREAD PUDDING; SERVES 12

7	large egg yolks
3	large eggs
1	cup granulated sugar
1	tsp. table salt
6	cups half-and-half
2	cups chopped bittersweet or semisweet chocolate
1	Tbs. pure vanilla extract
10	cups 1-inch cubes of day-old croissant
3	ripe bananas, thinly sliced

A bread pudding can sound like a humble dessert, but when you make it with generous amounts of bittersweet choco-late, ripe bananas, and buttery croissants, "delectable" is probably a better descriptor.

1. In a large heatproof bowl, whisk the yolks and eggs. Slowly whisk in the sugar and salt until thoroughly combined. Pour the half-and-half into a medium saucepan. Heat over medium-high heat until steaming but not bubbling. Add the chocolate to the half-and-half and whisk until the chocolate is completely melted. Slowly whisk the half-and-half mixture into the egg mixture until thoroughly combined. Strain the mixture through a fine-mesh sieve into a large Pyrex measuring cup or heatproof bowl. Add the vanilla extract.

2. Put the bread cubes in a 9x13-inch baking dish and pour the custard on top. Make sure the bread is as submerged in the custard as possible and let cool at room temperature for about 1 hour. Cover with plastic wrap and refrigerate for at least 5 hours and up to 24 hours.

3. Position a rack in the center of the oven, and heat the oven to 325°F. Transfer the bread mixture to a large mixing bowl and gently fold in the bananas. Return the mixture to the baking dish.

4. Cover the pudding loosely with foil and bake for 70 minutes. Remove the foil and continue to bake until no liquid custard is visible when you poke a small hole in the center with a paring knife, 20 to 40 minutes more.

5. Let the pudding cool on a rack. Serve warm, at room temperature, or chilled. —*Joanne Chang*

dark-chocolate mousse with caramelized allspice oranges

SERVES 8

FOR THE ORANGES

- 5 navel oranges
- ¾ cup granulated sugar
- 1½ tsp. ground allspice
- Pinch of salt
- ¼ tsp. freshly ground black pepper

FOR THE MOUSSE

- 8 oz. high-quality bittersweet chocolate, melted and cooled
- 1½ cups heavy cream, whipped to soft but firm peaks
- ½ tsp. ground cinnamon

- Pistachios, chocolate shavings, or whipped cream, for garnish (if desired)

The mousse needs to chill before serving, so have it ready before you cook the oranges.

CARAMELIZE THE ORANGES

1. Remove the zest from one of the oranges, cut it into thin strips, and set aside. Remove the peel and pith from all the oranges. Working over a bowl to catch the juice, cut the oranges into sections. After all the sections are removed, squeeze the membranes to extract their juice. Discard the membranes; reserve the juice and sections separately.

2. In a large saucepan, melt the sugar over medium heat. Cook, stirring and shaking the pan often, until the sugar turns a dark amber color. Carefully pour the reserved orange juice into the pan. Continue stirring as the mixture bubbles until the sugar dissolves completely. Add the orange sections, allspice, salt, pepper, and zest. Bring to a simmer and cook for 2 minutes. Remove from the heat.

MAKE THE MOUSSE

Whisk ¾ cup warm water into the cooled, melted chocolate. Allow to cool completely. Fold the whipped cream and cinnamon into the chocolate until thoroughly combined. Fold carefully and don't overmix or the cream may go flat. Chill for at least 15 minutes.

ASSEMBLE AND SERVE

Put the warm oranges and their syrup in dessert bowls or goblets. Top with a scoop of chocolate mousse. Garnish with pistachios, chocolate shavings, or whipped cream, if desired. *—Andrew MacLauchlan*

PER SERVING: 400 CALORIES | 4G PROTEIN | 44G CARB | 28G TOTAL FAT | 17G SAT FAT | 9G MONO FAT | 1G POLY FAT | 60MG CHOL | 55MG SODIUM | 2G FIBER

chocolate terrine with whipped cream and almond brittle

SERVES 12

- 8 oz. good-quality semi-sweet chocolate, coarsely chopped
- 6 oz. (12 Tbs.) unsalted butter, cut into 12 pieces; more for the pan
- ¾ cup granulated sugar
- ½ cup brewed coffee (fresh or leftover)
- 4 large eggs, beaten
- 1 cup heavy cream
- 1 recipe Almond Brittle (recipe on the facing page)

The crunchy almond brittle exaggerates the silky feel of the terrine. Coffee adds depth of flavor.

1. Position a rack in the lower middle of the oven, and heat the oven to 350°F. Grease an 8x5-inch loaf pan and line it with heavy-duty foil, making sure not to puncture it.

2. Fill a medium saucepan halfway with water and bring the water to a simmer. Put the chocolate and butter in a stainless-steel bowl large enough to fit over the pan without dipping into the water. Set the bowl over the simmering water, stirring the chocolate and butter with a whisk until melted and blended. Add the sugar and coffee, slowly stirring to dissolve the sugar. Continue cooking until the mixture is hot to the touch and the sugar is dissolved. Remove the bowl from the heat and whisk in the beaten eggs. Pour the chocolate mixture into the lined loaf pan.

3. Set a large baking dish on the oven rack. Set the loaf pan in the center of the baking dish and surround it with 1 inch of very hot water. Bake until the chocolate has begun to lose its shine, doesn't shimmy when jostled, and just begins to puff slightly around the edges, 40 to 50 minutes. Remove the terrine from the oven and set it on a wire rack to cool to room temperature. Cover with plastic wrap and chill in the refrigerator for at least 4 hours or overnight.

4. Lift the terrine out of the loaf pan, using the foil as a sling. Turn it over onto a platter or cutting board and peel off the foil. Using a knife that has been dipped in hot water and wiped dry, cut the terrine into ½-inch-thick slices. (For even slices, trim off the ends of the loaf first.)

5. In a chilled medium stainless-steel bowl, beat the heavy cream with a whisk or an electric mixer at medium-high speed until it holds soft peaks when the beaters are lifted. Serve each slice of the terrine with a dollop of the whipped cream and a tablespoon-size sprinkling of the chopped almond brittle. —*Gale Gand*

PER SERVING: 280 CALORIES | 6G PROTEIN | 39G CARB | 12G TOTAL FAT | 7G SAT FAT | 3.5G MONO FAT | 0.5G POLY FAT | 35MG CHOL | 130MG SODIUM | 2G FIBER

almond brittle

MAKES ABOUT 1¼ LB.

Vegetable oil, for the baking sheet

2½ cups granulated sugar

2 Tbs. unsalted butter

5 oz. (1 cup) whole almonds, toasted, cooled, and coarsely chopped

Grease a rimmed baking sheet with oil or cover with a nonstick liner (not parchment). Put the sugar in a medium saucepan without catching any crystals on the walls of the pan. Add ¾ cup water, pouring it around the walls to rinse down any sugar that might be there. Let the mixture sit for 1 minute (don't stir) so that the water infiltrates the sugar. Over high heat, boil the mixture without stirring until it turns very light amber, about 10 minutes. (Test the color of the caramel by dripping a bit onto a white plate.) Remove from the heat and stir in the butter with a wooden spoon just until melted and evenly blended. Stir in the nuts, then immediately pour the mixture across the prepared baking sheet. Let cool. Break the brittle into manageable pieces and then chop half of it for the terrine (save the rest for snacking). The brittle can be stored in an airtight container for up to 1 week.

white-chocolate mousse parfaits

**MAKES 8 SMALL PARFAITS;
3 CUPS MOUSSE**

- **4** **oz. good-quality white chocolate, chopped**
- **1½** **cups heavy cream**
- **¼** **tsp. pure vanilla extract**
- **Pinch of salt**
- **1** **ripe mango, cut into small chunks**
- **20** **gingersnaps or chocolate wafers, crushed**

Don't like mango and gingersnaps? Try these other combinations: fresh raspberries or quartered strawberries with crushed chocolate cookies, reconstituted dried apricots with gingersnaps, or blueberries with vanilla wafers.

1. Melt the white chocolate in a small heatproof bowl over simmering water or in a microwave. Stir until smooth. Set the chocolate aside and proceed with the rest of the recipe immediately; the chocolate needs to be very warm for this speedy recipe to succeed.

2. Pour the cream into a medium bowl and add the vanilla extract and salt. Beat with an electric mixer on medium-high speed until the cream forms firm but not stiff peaks, 2 to 3 minutes. (Don't go too far or the cream will curdle when the chocolate is beaten in.) Scrape the very warm white chocolate into the cream. Continue beating on medium-high speed until well blended and firm, about 30 seconds. The mousse should form a dollop when dropped from a spoon.

3. To serve, spoon the mousse into tall glasses, alternating with layers of the mango chunks and crushed cookies. —*Abigail Johnson Dodge*

PER SERVING: 280 CALORIES | 6G PROTEIN | 39G CARB | 12G TOTAL FAT | 7G SAT FAT | 3.5G MONO FAT | 0.5G POLY FAT | 35MG CHOL | 130MG SODIUM | 2G FIBER

Be careful when you melt the white chocolate—it burns easily, so use very low heat.

devil's food cake verrine

SERVES 12

FOR THE CAKE

4	oz. (½ cup) unsalted butter; more for the pan
3½	oz. (1 cup) unbleached cake flour
1	cup plus 2 Tbs. granulated sugar
2	oz. (⅔ cup) Dutch-processed cocoa powder
1	tsp. baking soda
½	tsp. baking powder
½	tsp. table salt
½	cup hot freshly brewed coffee
½	cup buttermilk
1	large egg
1	large egg yolk

FOR THE MOUSSE

3	oz. bittersweet chocolate, coarsely chopped
3	oz. milk chocolate, coarsely chopped
2	large eggs, separated
½	Tbs. Lyle's Golden Syrup, honey, or light corn syrup
¾	cup heavy cream

Make Ahead

- The cake can be made 1 day ahead.
- The mousse can be made up to 4 hours ahead.
- The streusel can be made 1 day ahead.

This decadent parfait-like treat of cake, mousse, and chocolate sauce is topped with an unexpected crunchy, salty cocoa nib streusel.

MAKE THE CAKE

1. Position a rack in the center of the oven, and heat the oven to 325°F. Butter an 8-inch square cake pan, line the bottom with parchment, and butter the parchment.

2. Sift the cake flour, sugar, cocoa powder, baking soda, baking powder, and salt onto a piece of parchment. In a small saucepan, combine the butter and the coffee over medium heat to melt the butter. Transfer to a medium bowl. Whisk in the buttermilk, egg, and yolk and then the flour mixture until incorporated.

3. Pour the batter into the prepared cake pan, and bake until a toothpick inserted in the center comes out clean, about 50 minutes. Let cool on a rack for 15 minutes. Invert onto the rack, remove the parchment, and let cool completely.

MAKE THE MOUSSE

1. Melt the bittersweet and milk chocolates in a medium heatproof bowl over a pan of barely simmering water. Set aside.

2. In another medium bowl, whisk the egg yolks and the syrup over the water bath just until warm. Remove from the heat and whisk briefly to cool.

continued on p. 178

FOR THE STREUSEL

- **6 oz. (¾ cup) unsalted butter, softened**
- **½ cup granulated sugar**
- **1 tsp. pure vanilla extract**
- **5 oz. (1 cup plus 2 Tbs. unbleached all-purpose flour**
- **2½ oz. (¾ cup) Dutch-processed cocoa powder**
- **1½ oz. cocoa nibs (about ⅓ cup)**
- **¾ tsp. fine sea salt**

FOR THE SAUCE

- **8 oz. bittersweet chocolate, finely chopped**
- **⅔ cup heavy cream**
- **2 Tbs. Lyle's Golden Syrup or light corn syrup**
- **Pinch of kosher salt**
- **2 Tbs. Nocino or dark rum**

3. Using an electric hand mixer on medium speed, whip the egg whites in a medium bowl until stiff peaks form, 1 to 2 minutes.

4. With the mixer on medium-high speed, whip the cream in another medium bowl until soft peaks form.

5. Whisk the yolk mixture into the melted chocolate. Whisk in a spoonful of the whipped cream. With a rubber spatula, fold in the remaining whipped cream and then the egg whites. Refrigerate.

MAKE THE STREUSEL

1. In a stand mixer fitted with a paddle attachment, beat the butter and sugar on medium-high speed until light and fluffy, 3 to 4 minutes. Reduce the speed to low and add the vanilla extract.

2. In a medium bowl, stir the flour and cocoa powder. With the mixer running on low speed, add the flour mixture in three increments, including the cocoa nibs and salt with the final addition. Mix until the dough comes together. (The dough can be refrigerated for 1 week or frozen for up to 2 months.)

3. Line a rimmed baking sheet with parchment, and press the dough into the pan in a ¼-inch-thick layer. Bake at 325°F for 8 minutes, and then rake with a fork to break into medium clumps. Bake for 7 minutes more, and rake again to create small pieces. The streusel will look sandy and will crisp as it cools.

MAKE THE SAUCE

Put the chocolate in a medium bowl. Put the cream, syrup, salt, and ¼ cup water in a small saucepan and bring to a boil over medium-high heat. Remove from the heat, pour over the chocolate, and stir to melt.

ASSEMBLE AND SERVE

Divide the warm chocolate sauce among twelve 8-oz. glasses. Cut the cake into 1-inch cubes and put 4 cubes in each glass. Drizzle ½ tsp. of the Nocino on the cake cubes. Scoop a spoonful or a quenelle (see the sidebar on the facing page) of mousse into each glass. Sprinkle about 2 Tbs. of streusel on top of the mousse, and serve.

—Elizabeth Falkner

PER SERVING: 280 CALORIES | 6G PROTEIN | 39G CARB | 12G TOTAL FAT | 7G SAT FAT | 3.5G MONO FAT | 0.5G POLY FAT | 35MG CHOL | 130MG SODIUM | 2G FIBER

how to make quenelles

Traditionally, the word "quenelle" refers to a small, oval-shaped dumpling of poached fish or meat, but today, chefs form everything from ice cream to mashed potatoes into the distinctive dumpling shape. Quenelles made of chocolate mousse add an extra touch of elegance to this dessert. To create a quenelle, you'll need two spoons of the same size. The size of the spoon will determine the size of your quenelle.

With a spoon in each hand, scoop a generous amount of mousse into one spoon. Gently press the bowl of the second spoon against the mousse, scooping the contents from the first spoon into the second.

Transfer the mousse back to the first spoon in the same manner. This begins to create a smooth, rounded surface where the mousse is molded to the spoon.

Keep scooping back and forth until you have a nice, smooth oval shape.

gianduia mousse

FOR THE MOUSSE

- 6 oz. bittersweet or semi-sweet chocolate, finely chopped
- 1½ cups heavy cream
- ⅔ cup Hazelnut Butter, at room temperature (recipe on the facing page)
- 2 tsp. pure vanilla extract

FOR THE GARNISH

- ½ cup heavy cream
- ½ tsp. pure vanilla extract
- 2 Tbs. finely ground toasted hazelnuts (follow the instructions for toasting in the Hazelnut Butter recipe)

The hazelnut butter in this quick-to-make, creamy mousse adds a bit of texture that's a real palate pleaser. Try the mousse as a pie filling in your favorite graham cracker crust or tart crust; serve well chilled. This mousse is best when served within 6 hours of the time it's made.

MAKE THE MOUSSE

1. In a 2-quart metal bowl set over a saucepan of simmering water, melt the chocolate, stirring with a rubber spatula until the chocolate is completely smooth. In a separate small saucepan, heat ½ cup of the cream over medium heat to just below the boiling point. Remove the bowl of chocolate from the pan of water and wipe the bottom and sides dry. Pour the hot cream into the melted chocolate, and stir together with the spatula until well blended. Add the Hazelnut Butter and stir until well combined. Stir in the vanilla extract.

2. In a chilled mixing bowl, using chilled beaters, beat the remaining 1 cup of cream until it holds soft peaks. With a rubber spatula, fold the whipped cream into the chocolate mixture in four batches, blending thoroughly after each addition. Pour the mousse into a 1½-quart soufflé dish or serving bowl, or into individual serving bowls or glasses. Cover with plastic wrap and refrigerate until set, at least 2 hours.

MAKE THE GARNISH

In a chilled mixing bowl with chilled beaters, beat the cream until frothy. Add the vanilla extract and continue beating until the cream holds soft peaks. Pipe or spoon the whipped cream on top of the mousse. Sprinkle the chopped hazelnuts over the whipped cream and serve. *—Carol Bloom*

PER SERVING: 280 CALORIES | 6G PROTEIN | 39G CARB | 12G TOTAL FAT | 7G SAT FAT | 3.5G MONO FAT | 0.5G POLY FAT | 35MG CHOL | 130MG SODIUM | 2G FIBER

hazelnut butter

8 oz. (1⅔ cups) hazelnuts

¼ cup vegetable oil, such as canola or sunflower

Pinch of table salt

1. Position a rack in the center of the oven, and heat the oven to 350°F. Spread the hazelnuts in a single layer on a baking sheet, and toast in the oven until the skins are mostly split and the nuts are light golden brown and quite fragrant, 15 to 18 minutes. Don't overcook the nuts or they'll become bitter.

2. Put the warm hazelnuts in a clean dishtowel. Fold the towel around the hazelnuts and let them steam for at least 5 minutes. Then rub the nuts in the towel to remove most of the skins (try to get at least 50% of the skins off). Let the hazelnuts sit for another 10 to 15 minutes to cool completely. Toasted, peeled hazelnuts can be cooled and frozen in a sealed plastic container for up to 3 months.

3. Put the nuts in a food processor; add the oil and salt, and pulse a few times. Then process, checking the consistency every few seconds, until the texture resembles that of natural, unhomogenized peanut butter or wet sand, 1 to 2 minutes.

Make Ahead

This butter can be refrigerated in a sealed container for up to 3 months or frozen for up to 6 months. If frozen, thaw it slowly in the refrigerator overnight. Always bring the hazelnut butter to room temperature before use.

individual orange and chocolate bread puddings

SERVES 4

- 2 Tbs. unsalted butter, softened; more for the ramekins
- 8 slices good-quality American-style white bread (about 8 oz.)
- ⅓ cup orange marmalade
- 3 oz. (½ cup) chopped semisweet chocolate (or ½ cup semisweet chocolate chips)
- 2 large eggs
- 1 cup whole milk
- ½ cup heavy cream
- ⅓ cup granulated sugar
- ½ tsp. pure vanilla extract

You can assemble the bread puddings and keep them in the refrigerator up to a day ahead. Remove them from the refrigerator 30 minutes before baking, let them come up to room temperature, and bake them when ready to serve.

1. Position a rack in the center of the oven, and heat the oven to 375°F. Lightly butter four 1¼-cup ramekins. Remove the crusts from the bread and spread one side with the butter and marmalade. Cut the bread into quarters and arrange four quarters in the base of each ramekin, overlapping to fit. Sprinkle with half of the chocolate and repeat with the remaining bread and chocolate to make two layers.

2. Whisk the eggs, milk, cream, sugar, and vanilla extract in a medium bowl or large glass measuring cup. Pour the egg mixture over the bread. Set the ramekins on a baking sheet and bake until puffed and golden brown, 20 to 25 minutes. Let cool for 5 minutes before serving.
—Eva Katz

PER SERVING: 280 CALORIES | 6G PROTEIN | 39G CARB | 12G TOTAL FAT | 7G SAT FAT | 3.5G MONO FAT | 0.5G POLY FAT | 35MG CHOL | 130MG SODIUM | 2G FIBER

milk chocolate pudding

SERVES 6

1½ oz. (½ cup) Dutch-processed cocoa powder

¼ cup granulated sugar

¼ tsp. table salt

½ cup heavy cream

3 Tbs. cornstarch

2 cups whole milk

7 oz. milk chocolate, finely chopped, preferably Lindt (about 1¾ cups)

1 tsp. pure vanilla extract

Most puddings contain eggs for added creaminess, but here, creamy milk chocolate makes eggs unnecessary. This pudding is delicious served warm, but you can also chill it if you like.

1. In a medium bowl, whisk together the cocoa powder, sugar, and salt. In a small bowl, whisk the cream and cornstarch until smooth.

2. Bring the milk to a boil in a heavy-duty 3-quart saucepan over medium heat. Whisk ¾ cup of the hot milk into the cream mixture. Add to the dry ingredients and whisk until fully incorporated. Add the cocoa mixture to the remaining milk. Cook, whisking constantly, until the mixture thickens and bubbles, about 1 minute. Remove from the heat and add the chocolate and vanilla extract. Let stand for 1 minute. Whisk until smooth.

3. Divide the mixture among six 6-oz. ramekins or small serving dishes and serve. Or if you prefer chilled pudding, put plastic wrap directly on the surfaces of the puddings and refrigerate for at least 30 minutes and no longer than 2 hours. *—Nicole Rees*

PER SERVING: 280 CALORIES | 6G PROTEIN | 39G CARB | 12G TOTAL FAT | 7G SAT FAT | 3.5G MONO FAT | 0.5G POLY FAT | 35MG CHOL | 130MG SODIUM | 2G FIBER

no-cook chocolate pudding

MAKES 3 CUPS; SERVES 6

1¾ cups heavy cream

2 Tbs. unsweetened cocoa powder, preferably Dutch processed

8 oz. bittersweet chocolate, finely chopped (1½ cups)

2 oz. (¼ cup) unsalted butter, cut into 4 pieces

2 Tbs. granulated sugar

1 tsp. pure vanilla extract

Pinch of table salt

Sweetened whipped cream and chocolate shavings, for garnish (optional)

Microwave the cream in an 8-cup Pyrex measuring cup and then use that vessel as your mixing bowl—the pour spout is extremely useful.

Have ready six 4- to 6-oz. ramekins or teacups. Heat the heavy cream in a small saucepan or microwave until just boiling. Remove from the heat and whisk in the cocoa powder until smooth. Add the chocolate, butter, sugar, vanilla extract, and salt, and whisk until the chocolate and butter are melted and the mixture is smooth. Pour the mixture into the ramekins or cups. Depending on the size of your ramekins, they'll be filled about two-thirds to three-quarters of the way. Cover with plastic (not touching the surface of the puddings) and refrigerate until chilled and thickened, at least 6 hours or up to 3 days. Serve with a dollop of sweetened whipped cream and a few chocolate shavings, if you like. *—Abigail Johnson Dodge*

PER SERVING: 520 CALORIES | 5G PROTEIN | 26G CARB | 50G TOTAL FAT | 29G SAT FAT | 10G MONO FAT | 2G POLY FAT | 115MG CHOL | 75MG SODIUM | 3G FIBER

quick chocolate bread pudding

SERVES 4

- 1 cup whole milk
- 6 Tbs. firmly packed light brown sugar
- 2 large eggs
- ½ tsp. pure vanilla extract
- ⅛ tsp. table salt
- 1 oz. (2 Tbs.) unsalted butter
- 5 oz. crusty sourdough bread, cut into ¾-inch cubes (4 cups)
- 4 oz. semisweet or bittersweet chocolate, broken into small pieces or chopped

Although sourdough bread is particularly good in this recipe, you can use any leftover crusty bread you have on hand. Whipped cream or your favorite flavor of ice cream is a perfect accompaniment.

1. Position an oven rack about 6 inches from the broiler, and heat the broiler on high.

2. In a large bowl, whisk the milk, brown sugar, eggs, vanilla extract, and salt.

3. Melt 1 Tbs. of the butter in a 9- to 10-inch cast-iron skillet over medium heat. Add the bread and cook, tossing often, until toasted and golden brown in spots, about 5 minutes. Add the bread to the milk mixture, toss to coat, and let soak for at least 5 minutes.

4. Wipe the skillet clean and return to medium heat. Melt the remaining 1 Tbs. butter in the skillet until just browned and fragrant, about 2 minutes. Spread the bread mixture evenly in the skillet. Nestle the chocolate pieces into the bread. Cook until the pudding is browned around the edges and just set in the center, 4 to 5 minutes.

5. Transfer the skillet to the oven and broil until golden brown on top and completely set, 1 to 2 minutes more. (Watch closely to ensure that any chocolate pieces poking out of the pudding don't burn.) Scoop the bread pudding into bowls and serve warm or at room temperature. —*Liz Pearson*

PER SERVING: 440 CALORIES | 11G PROTEIN | 61G CARB | 19G TOTAL FAT | 11G SAT FAT | 6G MONO FAT | 1G POLY FAT | 125MG CHOL | 370MG SODIUM | 3G FIBER

real chocolate mousse

SERVES 4

6   oz. semisweet or bitter-
    sweet chocolate, preferably
    60% to 62% cacao, chopped

2   Tbs. unsalted butter, cut
    into 8 pieces

3   large egg whites

    Pinch of table salt

3   Tbs. granulated sugar

¾   cup cold heavy cream

    Chocolate shavings, for
    garnish (optional)

Rich, indulgent, light as air. Chocolate mousse is all of those things. And given how easy it is to make, it's a dessert that should have prime real estate in your recipe box. With this basic recipe, the right tools, and a little know-how, you'll soon be on your way to sweet success.

Although the risk of salmonella infection from consuming raw egg whites is low, use pasteurized egg whites if you want to be completely safe.

1. Put the chopped chocolate in a medium heatproof bowl and set the bowl in a skillet of barely simmering water. Stir the chocolate with a heatproof spatula just until it is melted. Remove the bowl from the skillet, add the butter to the chocolate, and stir until the butter is completely melted and the mixture is smooth.

2. In a medium bowl with an electric hand mixer on medium-high speed (or with a balloon whisk), whip the egg whites and salt until they barely hold soft peaks. While whipping, gradually sprinkle in the sugar—go slowly, as adding it too fast may cause the whites to fall. Continue whipping until the whites just start to hold stiff peaks. Don't overbeat or the dissolved sugar may weep out of the whites.

3. Wipe the beaters (or whisk) clean and then whip the cream in a large bowl until it's fairly thick and holds a soft peak when the beaters are lifted.

tips for success

Making this classic French dessert is easy; follow these tips to ensure success.

Knowing when to stop beating your egg whites is key. Soft peaks barely hold their shape; the peaks flop over when the beaters are lifted. Stiff peaks (like those above) stand up when the beaters are lifted.

For an airy mousse, use a light touch and a large rubber spatula to fold the egg whites and whipped cream into the chocolate.

4. With a large spatula, gently fold about one-third of the egg whites into the chocolate until the mixture is no longer streaky. Fold in the remaining whites. Scrape the chocolate mixture into the whipped cream. Add a flavoring, if using (see the sidebar below). Fold gently until the mixture is uniform in color and texture.

5. Divide among 4 dessert dishes and serve immediately, or refriger-ate for at least 30 minutes for a slightly firmer texture. Garnish with chocolate shavings, if using. *—Dabney Gough*

PER SERVING: 470 CALORIES | 6G PROTEIN | 39G CARB | 33G TOTAL FAT | 20G SAT FAT | 10G MONO FAT | 1G POLY FAT | 75MG CHOL | 135MG SODIUM | 3G FIBER

Flavor Twists

Check out these flavor twists for something a little different:

- **Hazelnut:** 3 Tbs. Frangelico

- **Bourbon:** 1 Tbs. bourbon

- **Coconut:** ½ cup toasted sweetened coconut (serve immediately to retain texture)

black forest trifle

SERVES 16

Layer the flavors of black forest cake for this showstopping, make-ahead dessert.

FOR THE CAKE

3   oz. (6 Tbs.) unsalted butter, softened at room temperature; more for the pan

2   oz. semisweet chocolate, chopped

1   oz. unsweetened chocolate, chopped

5   oz. (1 cup plus 2 Tbs.) unbleached all-purpose flour

½   oz. (2 Tbs.) unsweetened Dutch-processed cocoa powder

½   tsp. baking powder

½   tsp. baking soda

¼   tsp. table salt

1   cup granulated sugar

2   large eggs

1   tsp. pure vanilla extract

½   cup sour cream

⅓   cup strong brewed coffee

FOR THE CHERRIES AND KIRSCH SYRUP

One   15- or 16-oz. can pitted sweet cherries in heavy or extra-heavy syrup

¼   cup kirsch (cherry brandy)

Granulated sugar

FOR THE WHIPPED CREAM

3   cups cold heavy cream

½   cup granulated sugar

1   Tbs. kirsch

FOR ASSEMBLING THE TRIFLE

1   cup semisweet chocolate shavings (from a 3- to 4-oz. block of chocolate)

MAKE THE CAKE

1. Position a rack in the middle of the oven, and heat the oven to 350°F. Butter the bottom and sides of a 9x2-inch round cake pan. Line the bottom of the pan with parchment and butter the parchment.

2. Fill a medium skillet with about ½ inch water and heat until just below a simmer. Put both the semisweet and unsweetened chocolate in a medium heatproof bowl and put the bowl in the barely simmering water. Stir until the chocolate is melted and smooth. Remove from the water bath and let cool slightly.

3. Sift together the flour, cocoa powder, baking powder, baking soda, and salt. In an electric mixer (use the paddle attachment), beat the butter and sugar on medium speed until light and fluffy, 2 to 4 minutes. Mix in the slightly cooled melted chocolate on low speed just until incorporated. Increase the speed to medium and add the eggs one at a time, beating well after each addition. Scrape the bowl, add the vanilla extract, and beat on medium speed for 1 minute. On low speed, mix in the sour cream just until it's incorporated. Add the flour mixture (in three additions), alternating with the coffee (in two additions); scrape the bowl as needed. The batter will be very thick, like chocolate mousse or frosting.

4. Scrape the cake batter into the prepared pan and smooth the top. Bake until the top feels firm and a toothpick inserted in the center comes out clean, about 35 minutes. The cake may sink a bit in the center, but that's fine. Let the cake cool for 20 minutes in the baking pan on a wire rack. Using a small, sharp knife, loosen the sides of the cake from the pan, invert the cake onto the rack, and discard the paper liner. Let cool completely.

PREPARE THE CHERRIES AND KIRSCH SYRUP

Drain the cherries in a colander set over a large bowl (to catch the syrup) for 30 minutes. Reserve ½ cup of the syrup. Transfer the cherries to a small bowl, drizzle with 1 Tbs. of the kirsch, and set aside. Taste the syrup; it should be slightly tart and not too sweet. If necessary, stir in 1 to 2 tsp. sugar. Put the syrup in a small saucepan and simmer over medium heat until reduced by about half, about 3 minutes. Remove the pan from the heat and stir in the remaining 3 Tbs. kirsch. Set aside to cool.

MAKE THE WHIPPED CREAM

Just before serving, put the cream, sugar, and kirsch in the large bowl of an electric mixer and whip on high speed until it holds firm peaks.

ASSEMBLE THE TRIFLE

Pick out the 10 best-looking cherries and blot them dry with paper towels. With a long, serrated knife, cut the cooled cake vertically into ½-inch-thick slices. Line the bottom of a 2½- to 3-quart glass bowl or trifle bowl with about a third of the cake slices to create an even layer. Don't worry if the pieces break, as long as they fill in the spaces. Brush this layer of cake lightly with some of the kirsch syrup, top with a third of the whipped cream, and randomly nestle half of the remaining cherries into the cream. Sprinkle with a third of the chocolate shavings. Repeat with two more layers. On the top layer of cream, arrange the best-looking cherries in a ring near the rim of the bowl and scatter the rest of the chocolate shavings inside the cherry ring. Refrigerate for at least 30 minutes and up to 6 hours. Serve chilled.
—*Elinor Klivans*

PER SERVING: 400 CALORIES | 4G PROTEIN | 40G CARB | 26G TOTAL FAT | 16G SAT FAT | 6G MONO FAT | 4G POLY FAT | 105MG CHOL | 120MG SODIUM | 2G FIBER

Look for cherries labeled "in heavy syrup" or "in extra-heavy syrup." Some canned cherries come in fruit juice concentrate, which doesn't have quite the same flavor or texture and will give you a different result.

chocolate ice cream sandwiches
(recipe on p. 200)

ice creams
& frozen treats

bittersweet chocolate-bourbon pops

MAKES 8 POPS

½ cup granulated sugar

3½ oz. bittersweet chocolate (70% to 72% cacao), chopped

2 Tbs. Dutch-processed cocoa powder

⅛ tsp. table salt

2 Tbs. good-quality bourbon (like Knob Creek®)

Dark chocolate and bourbon make for a truly decadent treat. Since the bourbon doesn't get cooked, it's worth splurging on the high-end stuff.

1. Put the sugar, chocolate, cocoa powder, salt, and 2 cups water in a large saucepan. Bring to a boil over medium heat, whisking constantly. Transfer to a 4-cup glass measure (or any container with a spout for easy pouring). Let cool at room temperature for 30 minutes.

2. Stir in the bourbon and divide the mixture among eight 3-oz. pop molds or wax-lined paper cups. Freeze until just set, about 3 hours. Insert craft sticks and freeze until completely set, about 4 hours more. When ready to serve, unmold or peel off the paper cups. The pops can be frozen for up to 3 days. —*Genevieve Ko*

PER SERVING: 120 CALORIES | 1G PROTEIN | 19G CARB | 6G TOTAL FAT | 2.5G SAT FAT | 0G MONO FAT | 0G POLY FAT | 0MG CHOL | 35MG SODIUM | 1G FIBER

Tips for Success

• Almost any mold—from classic cylinders to whimsical rockets—will work. Or keep it simple and use small wax-lined paper cups, which peel off easily.

• To ensure that the pops freeze firmly, make certain your freezer is set to 0°F.

• You can pile the ice pops on a platter and pass it, or serve them individually in glasses (which do a good job of catching drips).

frozen hot chocolate

SERVES 4

- **1 cup whole milk**
- **½ cup heavy cream**
- **½ cup natural unsweetened cocoa powder**
- **½ cup firmly packed light brown sugar**
- **¾ tsp. pure vanilla extract**
- **Pinch of kosher salt**
- **2 cups ice cubes**
- **3 Tbs. bittersweet or semi-sweet chocolate shavings (made with a vegetable peeler)**

This delicious cross between a milk shake and a slushie makes for a surprisingly refreshing (and easy) summertime dessert. You can add about ¼ cup of chocolate or coffee liqueur for a boozy kick, if you like.

Blend the milk, cream, cocoa powder, brown sugar, vanilla extract, and salt in a blender until well combined and the sugar is dissolved. Add the ice and blend just until slushy. Transfer to glasses, top with the chocolate shavings, and serve immediately with spoons.

—Lori Longbotham

PER SERVING: 310 CALORIES | 5G PROTEIN | 43G CARB |
17G TOTAL FAT | 10G SAT FAT | 4G MONO FAT | 0.5G POLY FAT |
45MG CHOL | 85MG SODIUM | 4G FIBER

triple chocolate ice cream pie

SERVES 12

- **5 Tbs. unsalted butter, melted; more for the pan**
- **6 oz. (about 30) chocolate wafer cookies**
- **2 pints chocolate ice cream, slightly softened**
- **1 recipe Quick Hot Fudge Sauce (recipe on the facing page), at room temperature**
- **1 pint coffee ice cream, slightly softened**
- **1 pint vanilla ice cream, slightly softened**

This pie features a chocolate crust, chocolate ice cream, and chocolate sauce, with a few scoops of coffee and vanilla added for contrast.

1. Position a rack in the center of the oven, and heat the oven to 350°F. Butter a 9-inch Pyrex or metal pie plate.

2. Put the cookies in a zip-top bag and crush them with a rolling pin (or process in a food processor) until you have fine crumbs. Measure 1½ cups of crumbs (crush more cookies, if necessary) and put them in a medium bowl. Add the melted butter and stir until the crumbs are evenly moistened. Transfer to the pie plate and, using your fingers, press the mixture evenly into the bottom and sides (but not on the rim). Bake for 10 minutes. Let cool completely on a wire rack.

3. Scoop 1 pint of the chocolate ice cream into the cooled crust and spread it evenly with a rubber spatula. Place in the freezer to firm up for about 30 minutes. Remove the pie from the freezer and, working quickly, drizzle ½ cup of the room-temperature fudge sauce over the ice cream. Using a small ice cream scoop (1½ inches diameter), scoop round balls of the chocolate, coffee, and vanilla ice creams and arrange them over the fudge sauce layer (you may not need all of the ice cream). Drizzle with about ¼ cup of the remaining fudge sauce, using a squirt bottle if you have one. Freeze until the ice cream is firm, about 2 hours. If not serving right away, loosely cover the pie with waxed paper and then wrap with aluminum foil. Freeze for up to 2 weeks.

4. To serve, let the pie soften in the refrigerator for 15 to 30 minutes (premium ice cream brands need more time to soften). Meanwhile, gently reheat the remaining fudge sauce in a small saucepan over medium-low heat. Pry the pie out of the pan with a thin metal spatula. (If the pie doesn't pop out, set the pan in a shallow amount of hot water for 1 to 2 minutes to help the crust release.) Set the pie on a board, cut into wedges, and serve drizzled with more hot fudge sauce, if you like. —*Lori Longbotham*

PER SERVING: 495 CALORIES | 7G PROTEIN | 48G CARB | 34G TOTAL FAT | 20G SAT FAT | 6G MONO FAT | 1G POLY FAT | 90MG CHOL | 190MG SODIUM | 3G FIBER

quick hot fudge sauce

MAKES 1½ CUPS

- 1 cup heavy cream
- 2 Tbs. light corn syrup
  Pinch of table salt
- 8 oz. bittersweet chocolate, finely chopped (to yield about 1⅓ cups)

This sauce will keep for at least 2 weeks in the refrigerator and for several months in the freezer.

Bring the cream, corn syrup, and salt just to a boil in a heavy medium saucepan over medium-high heat, whisking until combined. Remove the pan from the heat, add the chocolate, and whisk until smooth. Let cool to a bit warmer than room temperature before using in the ice cream pie. The sauce thickens as it cools; you want it warm enough to drizzle but not so warm that it melts the ice cream.

luscious milk chocolate ice cream

MAKES ABOUT 1 QUART

1½ cups whole milk

1½ cups heavy cream

1 Tbs. natural cocoa powder

⅓ cup granulated sugar

7 oz. good-quality milk chocolate, finely chopped

8 large egg yolks

This is an ice cream for those who love to luxuriate in the creaminess of milk chocolate, which is enhanced by the cream in the custard base. Tuck in a butter cookie next to your scoop.

1. In a medium heavy-based saucepan, combine the milk and cream. Sift the cocoa powder over the mixture and whisk thoroughly to combine. Sprinkle about half the sugar into the saucepan and slowly bring the mixture to a simmer; don't let it boil.

2. Put the chopped chocolate in a medium bowl and fill a large bowl with ice water.

3. While you're waiting for the milk mixture to simmer, whisk the egg yolks with the remaining sugar in a medium bowl. Whisk vigorously until the yolks thicken and become a paler shade of yellow, 3 to 4 minutes.

4. To combine the egg and milk mixtures, slowly pour half the simmering milk into the yolks while whisking constantly to temper it. Whisk that mixture back into the milk in the saucepan. Reduce the heat to low, and stir constantly with a wooden spoon or rubber spatula in a figure-eight motion until the custard is thick enough to coat the back of a spoon (about 170°F), 10 to 15 minutes.

5. Pour the cooked custard over the chocolate. Whisk until all the chocolate is melted. Set the custard bowl over the bowl of ice water; stir until the custard is completely cool. Pour through a fine-mesh sieve if there are any lumps and then refrigerate for several hours or overnight.

6. Pour the custard into an ice cream machine with at least a 1-quart capacity and freeze following the manufacturer's directions.
—*Steven Durfee*

chocolate-cinnamon sherbet

SERVES 6

- ½ **cup plus 2 Tbs. unsweetened Dutch-processed cocoa powder**
- 1 **cup granulated sugar**
- 1 **tsp. ground cinnamon**
- **Pinch of freshly ground black pepper**
- **Pinch of freshly grated nutmeg**
- 1 **12-oz. can evaporated skim milk**
- 1 **Tbs. pure vanilla extract**

Although it's extremely low in fat, this sherbet has a deep, chocolate taste. If you're used to making ice cream, be patient; low-fat sherbets take longer to freeze than richer frozen desserts. An ice cream maker is handy but not essential.

In a small saucepan, mix the cocoa powder, sugar, cinnamon, pepper, and nutmeg. Whisk in 1 cup water and bring to a boil, continuing to whisk to break up lumps and prevent burning. Turn down the heat and simmer for 2 to 3 minutes, until the sugar is completely dissolved, leaving the whisk in the pan to prevent a boil-over. Off the heat, add the evaporated skim milk and vanilla extract and let the mixture cool.

TO MAKE THE SHERBET IN AN ICE CREAM MAKER
When the mixture is room temperature, put it in an ice cream maker and follow the manufacturer's directions. The sherbet may take as long as 40 minutes to freeze to "soft-serve" texture or a little softer. Transfer to a container with a cover and freeze longer for a firmer texture.

TO MAKE THE SHERBET IN A LARGE DISH
If you don't have an ice cream maker, the sherbet can be frozen in a large, nonreactive baking container, like a glass lasagne dish. The texture of the sherbet done in this manner is a little icier, closer to a granita. Pour the room-temperature mixture into the dish and put it in the freezer. When it starts to chill, stir at least once an hour until it has the texture of very soft ice cream. The length of time it takes depends on how cold your freezer is.

Serve in small chilled bowls or martini glasses. —*Amy Cotler*

PER SERVING: 190 CALORIES | 5G PROTEIN | 44G CARB | 1G TOTAL FAT | 0.5G SAT FAT | 1G MONO FAT | 1G POLY FAT | 75MG CHOL | 200MG SODIUM | 1G FIBER

chocolate-raspberry cookies and cream

**MAKES 2½ CUPS CREAM
AND ¾ CUP SAUCE; SERVES 6**

- 3 cups frozen raspberries (about 12 oz.), thawed
- 5 Tbs. granulated sugar; more if needed

  Lemon juice

  Kosher salt
- ⅔ cup heavy cream
- ⅓ cup crème fraîche
- 21 Nabisco FAMOUS Chocolate Wafer cookies
- 6 sprigs mint, for garnish

This is delicious with both crème fraîche and heavy cream, but you can use all cream if that's easier.

1. Put 1 cup of the raspberries in a small bowl, sprinkle with 2 Tbs. of the sugar, mash with a fork, and let sit for a few minutes.

2. Meanwhile, put the remaining 2 cups of berries and 2 Tbs. of the sugar in a food processor (or blender) and process until the berries form a purée. Strain through a fine-mesh strainer into a small bowl, pressing with a rubber spatula to get the seeds out. Squeeze in a few drops of lemon juice and a tiny pinch of salt. Taste and add more sugar or lemon if needed. The sauce should be thin enough to drizzle. If it seems too thick, add a few drops of water. Cover and refrigerate.

3. In a medium bowl, combine the cream, crème fraîche, and the remaining 1 Tbs. sugar, and whip with a hand mixer until the mixture forms firm, thick peaks. Stir the mashed berries and sugar and lightly fold into the cream mixture with a rubber spatula, leaving streaks.

4. Reserving six cookies for decoration, crunch up the rest into uneven pieces—don't make them too small. Fold the cookies into the cream. Cover with plastic wrap, pressing the wrap onto the surface of the cream, and chill until the cookie pieces are thoroughly softened, at least 2 hours and preferably overnight.

5. To serve, use an ice cream scoop or large spoon to scoop out a mound of cookies and cream into a small bowl or onto a plate. Drizzle a ribbon of raspberry sauce around the plate, tuck a cookie into the cream, and decorate with a mint sprig. *—Martha Holmberg*

PER SERVING: 310 CALORIES | 3G PROTEIN | 36G CARB | 18G TOTAL FAT | 10G SAT FAT | 5G MONO FAT | 1G POLY FAT | 50MG CHOL | 200MG SODIUM | 4G FIBER

chocolate ice cream sandwiches

**MAKES 12 ICE CREAM
SANDWICHES, EACH
2¾ INCHES SQUARE**

A sophisticated twist on this childhood favorite combines a tender chocolate cookie, store-bought ice cream, and crunchy garnishes.

FOR THE SOFT CHOCOLATE COOKIE

- 3 oz. (6 Tbs.) **unsalted butter, softened at room temperature; more for the pan**
- 5⅔ oz. (1¼ cups) **unbleached all-purpose flour**
- 1½ oz. (½ cup) **unsweetened, natural cocoa powder**
- ½ tsp. **baking soda**
- ¼ tsp. **table salt**
- ¾ cup **granulated sugar**
- 1½ tsp. **pure vanilla extract**
- ⅔ cup **cold milk**
- **Vegetable oil or cooking spray, for the parchment**

FOR ASSEMBLY

- 1 quart or 2 pints **ice cream (see the sidebar on p. 202 for ideas)**
- 1½ cups **press-on garnish (optional; see the sidebar on p. 202 for ideas)**

MAKE THE COOKIE

1. Position a rack in the center of the oven, and heat the oven to 350°F. Lightly grease the bottom of an 18x13-inch rimmed baking sheet. Line the pan with parchment to cover the bottom and the edges of the pan's longer sides.

2. Combine the flour, cocoa powder, baking soda, and salt in a medium bowl; whisk to blend. In a large bowl, beat the butter and sugar with a hand-held electric mixer on medium high until well blended and lightened in color, about 3 minutes. Beat in the vanilla extract. Add about one-third of the flour mixture and beat on medium low until just blended. Pour in half the milk and beat until just blended. Add another third of the flour and blend. Pour in the remaining milk and blend, then beat in the remaining flour.

3. Distribute the dough evenly over the prepared pan in small dollops. Using one hand to anchor the parchment, spread the dough with a spoon or spatula. Drag a rectangular offset spatula over the dough to smooth it into an even layer, rotating the pan as you work. Brush or spray a sheet of parchment the same size as the pan with oil, and lay it, oiled side down, on the dough. Roll a straight rolling pin or a straight-sided wine bottle over the paper (or swipe it with a dough scraper) to level the batter. Carefully peel away the parchment. Bake until a pick inserted in the center comes out clean, 10 to 12 minutes. Set the pan on a wire rack and let cool to room temperature.

ASSEMBLE THE LAYERS

1. Lay two long pieces of plastic wrap in a cross shape on a baking sheet. Slide a knife along the inside edge of the pan containing the cookie to loosen it. Invert the cookie onto a large cutting board. Peel off the parchment. Using a ruler as a guide, cut the cookie crosswise into two equal pieces. Place one layer, top side down, in the middle of the plastic wrap (a wide, sturdy spatula will help the transfer).

2. Remove the ice cream from the freezer and take off the lid. It's important to work quickly from this point on. (If the ice cream gets too soft, pop it onto a plate and back into the freezer to harden up.) Using scissors or a sharp knife, cut the container lengthwise in two places and tear away the container. Set the ice cream on its side. Cut the ice cream into even slices, ½ to ¾ inch thick, and arrange them on top of the cookie layer in the pan, pairing the smallest piece next to the largest.

3. Using a rubber spatula, gently yet firmly smear the ice cream to spread it evenly. (It helps to put a piece of plastic wrap on the ice cream and smear with your hands; remove the plastic before proceeding.)

4. Position the remaining cookie layer, top side up, over the ice cream. Press gently to spread the ice cream to the edges. Put a clean piece of plastic on top and wrap the long ends of the bottom sheet of plastic up and over the layers and ice cream. Put the baking sheet in the freezer and chill until the sandwich is hard, about 4 hours and up to 2 days.

CUT AND GARNISH THE SANDWICHES

1. Take the baking sheet out of the freezer. Lift the package from the pan, transfer it to a cutting board, and line the pan with a fresh piece of plastic. Peel the top layer of plastic off the sandwich (you can leave on the bottom layer).

2. Working quickly, use a ruler and a long, sharp chef's knife to score the cookie, dividing it into 12 pieces: three across the short side and four across the long side. Cut the sandwiches, wiping the blade clean as needed. (If your kitchen is very warm, put the pieces back into the freezer to firm, or work with one strip at a time, keeping the rest in the freezer.)

3. Garnish the sandwiches, if you like. Fill a small, shallow bowl with your chosen garnish (see the ideas in the sidebar on p. 202) and set it next to your work surface. Press some of the garnish onto some or all of the sides of the sandwich. Set the sandwiches back on the baking sheet and return to the freezer immediately. (If your kitchen is warm, keep the sandwiches in the freezer and garnish one at a time.) Once the sandwiches are hard, wrap them individually in plastic and store in the freezer. They'll keep for up to 2 weeks. *—Abigail Johnson Dodge*

PER SERVING: 290 CALORIES | 4G PROTEIN | 37G CARB | 15G TOTAL FAT | 9G SAT FAT | 4G MONO FAT | 1G POLY FAT | 65MG CHOL | 180MG SODIUM | 2G FIBER

continued on p. 202

Ice Cream Sandwich Variations

Garnishes
Try one of these garnishes on your ice cream sandwiches. Be sure they're finely chopped and uniform in size.

- finely crushed hard peppermint candies

- finely chopped or grated bittersweet or semisweet chocolate

- minced crystallized ginger

- finely chopped and toasted pecans

- toasted sweetened coconut flakes

- crushed amaretti cookies

- crushed toffee chips

Cookie Variations
- **Chocolate-Mint:** Add ½ tsp. peppermint extract when you add the vanilla.

- **Chocolate-Orange:** Add ½ tsp. natural orange flavor or orange extract when you add the vanilla.

- **Chocolate-Espresso:** Mix in 1 level Tbs. instant coffee granules when you add the vanilla.

- **Chocolate-Ginger:** Add ½ tsp. ground ginger to the dry ingredients.

Mix and Match
You can design your own sandwich combinations by choosing the ice cream, adding flavor to the chocolate cookie, and picking your favorite garnish. The flavoring possibilities are endless, but here are some to get you started.

- chocolate-mint cookie with vanilla ice cream and crushed peppermints

- chocolate-orange cookie with raspberry sorbet

- chocolate-ginger cookie with vanilla ice cream and minced crystallized ginger

- chocolate-espresso cookie with coffee or mocha swirl ice cream and chopped pecans

chocolate ice cream with cinnamon, dulce de leche & toasted pecans

MAKES ABOUT 1 QUART

½ cup granulated sugar

2½ tsp. cornstarch

Pinch of table salt

1¾ cups whole milk

7 oz. Mexican chocolate, coarsely chopped (such as Ibarra® brand)

¼ cup Dulce de Leche (recipe below)

3 large egg yolks

½ cup chilled evaporated milk

¾ cup chilled whipping or heavy cream

½ cup coarsely chopped pecans

This chocolate ice cream has a distinctive, almost roasty flavor. You can substitute semisweet chocolate for the Mexican chocolate, increasing the sugar to ¾ cup and adding a scant ½ tsp. ground cinnamon (preferably Ceylon) along with the chocolate. Some specialty shops or Hispanic markets carry dulce de leche in jars, but it's easy to make your own.

1. In a medium saucepan, combine the sugar, cornstarch, and salt. Gradually stir in the milk over medium heat and add the chocolate, whisking often until the chocolate has melted and the milk is hot and just about to simmer, about 5 minutes. Add the Dulce de Leche and whisk until it melts, 1 to 2 minutes. Remove the pan from the heat.

2. In a large bowl, beat the egg yolks until blended, about 30 seconds. Whisk about ½ cup of the hot milk-chocolate mixture into the yolks and then beat in another ½ cup. Slowly whisk in the remaining hot liquid, then pour the mixture back into the pan. Heat the mixture over medium to medium-high heat, stirring constantly, until it reaches 180°F and just begins to thicken. Remove from the heat and whisk in the evaporated milk and cream, whisking until the mixture begins to cool. Strain to remove any cooked pieces of egg, and refrigerate until it's colder than about 60°F, at least 2 hours or as long as 24 hours, stirring occasionally.

3. Add the pecans and freeze the mixture in an ice cream machine (following the manufacturer's instructions) until the ice cream is very thick and cold. Transfer to a resealable plastic or stainless-steel container and freeze until it's firm enough to scoop, at least 3 hours.
—*James Peyton*

PER SERVING: 350 CALORIES | 6G PROTEIN | 44G CARB | 18G TOTAL FAT | 10G SAT FAT | 5G MONO FAT | 1G POLY FAT | 125MG CHOL | 105MG SODIUM | 1G FIBER

dulce de leche

1 14- or 14½-oz. can sweetened condensed milk

¼ tsp. pure vanilla extract

This recipe makes more caramel than you'll need for the ice cream recipe, but that's a good thing. It keeps in the refrigerator for at least a week, at the ready for nibbling or drizzling on grilled fresh pineapple.

In a small saucepan, combine the sweetened condensed milk with the vanilla extract. Simmer very gently, stirring frequently, until very thick and golden brown (it may get lumpy but will eventually smooth out), about 20 minutes.

coffee ice cream with sour cream ganache, toffee chips & toasted almonds

SERVES 4 TO 6

- **6** oz. semisweet chocolate, chopped (or use chocolate chips)
- **⅓** cup sour cream, at cool room temperature
- **¼** tsp. pure vanilla extract
- **1** quart coffee ice cream, slightly softened
- **¼** cup toffee chips
- **3** Tbs. sliced almonds, toasted

Here's a dessert that's perfect for impromptu entertaining because you can toss it together using ingredients from the pantry. The sour cream in the chocolate sauce gives it a nice tang, keeping the sweetness of this dish in check.

Melt the chocolate in the top of a double boiler over barely simmering water, stirring frequently, until completely melted. (Or put the chocolate in a Pyrex bowl and heat in the microwave, uncovered, until melted and hot, about 1 minute on high.) Stir in the sour cream and vanilla extract. Continuing to stir, drizzle 3 to 4 Tbs. water into the sauce until it reaches a smooth, pourable consistency. Ladle the warm sauce on top of individual scoops of coffee ice cream and scatter with the toffee chips and almond slices. —*Lauren Groveman*

PER SERVING: 400 CALORIES | 6G PROTEIN | 45G CARB | 25G TOTAL FAT | 14G SAT FAT | 6G MONO FAT | 3G POLY FAT | 50MG CHOL | 120MG SODIUM | 4G FIBER

> If you can't find toffee chips at the store, make your own by putting a toffee candy bar, such as a Heath® bar, into a heavy zip-top bag and crushing with a rolling pin.

double chocolate malted milk shake

SERVES 1 OR 2

- ⅓ to ½ cup very cold whole milk; more as needed

- 3 scoops chocolate ice cream (about 2 oz. each), slightly softened; more as needed

- 1 Tbs. chocolate syrup, such as Hershey's Special Dark

- 1 Tbs. plain malted milk powder; more to taste

If you have extra ice cream in your freezer, make malteds! For the thickest shakes, use a dense, premium brand of ice cream, like Ben & Jerry's®. And if you'd rather have just a chocolate milk shake, skip the malt powder at the end.

Pour the milk into the mixing cup of a milk shake mixer or hand blender or into the jar of a regular blender. Add the ice cream and chocolate syrup. Blend on high speed until smooth. The blending time depends on the machine and the temperature of the ingredients. If necessary, add more milk or ice cream to adjust to your preferred consistency. When the shake is just about smooth, briefly blend in the malted milk powder. Serve immediately in a chilled glass. —*Jennifer Armentrout*

PER SERVING: 280 CALORIES | 6G PROTEIN | 39G CARB | 12G TOTAL FAT | 7G SAT FAT | 3.5G MONO FAT | 0.5G POLY FAT | 35MG CHOL | 130MG SODIUM | 2G FIBER

More about Malted Milk Powder

For the uninitiated, a malted (or malt) is a milk shake flavored with malted milk powder—a blend of dried milk, wheat flour, and barley malt (and sometimes sugar and other flavors depending on the brand). Barley malt, which is best known as a baking and beer-brewing ingredient, is made from barley that's been germinated and roasted, causing a number of chemical and physical changes that create a distinctive sweet, "malty" flavor.

To turn a milk shake into a malted, simply add malted milk powder once the shake is nearly blended. Not only does malted milk lend its unique flavor to the shake, but it also enriches and amplifies the shake's base flavor.

frozen mocha

MAKES 3 CUPS

½ cup Dutch-processed cocoa

¾ cup granulated sugar

4 tsp. instant espresso powder

2 cups plus 2 Tbs. whole milk

Dutch-processed cocoa gives this dessert its rich chocolate flavor.

1. Fill a measuring cup with ½ cup water. In a medium saucepan, combine the cocoa, sugar, espresso powder, and just enough of the water to make a smooth paste. Add the rest of the water. Bring to a simmer over medium heat, whisking constantly to prevent scorching. Continue to whisk and simmer for 1 minute. Remove the pan from the heat and stir in 2 cups of the milk. Pour into a shallow cake pan or ice-cube trays and freeze until hard.

2. Break up the frozen mixture with a fork and put it in a food processor. Add the remaining 2 Tbs. milk. Process until no lumps remain and the mixture is thick, slushy, and lightens in color. Immediately pour into goblets and serve. Or, refreeze the slush overnight to harden and serve it in scoops. *—Alice Medrich*

PER SERVING: 340 CALORIES | 9G PROTEIN | 67G CARB | 8G TOTAL FAT | 5G SAT FAT | 2G MONO FAT | 0G POLY FAT | 25MG CHOL | 90MG SODIUM | 4G FIBER

Tips for Cooking with Cocoa

• **Substituting cocoa for chocolate.** Cocoa can often be substituted for baking chocolate. Use 3 level Tbs. cocoa and 1 Tbs. butter for each ounce of unsweetened baking chocolate.

• **Measure cocoa like flour.** Spoon the unsifted cocoa into a measuring cup and level it off without compacting it. Sift it after measuring to remove any lumps. If the recipe calls for measuring sifted cocoa, sift the cocoa over the measuring cup and then level it off without compacting it.

• **Getting the lumps out.** When dissolving cocoa in liquid, stir just enough of the liquid into the cocoa to make a stiff paste. Stir and mash the paste until it's smooth and then stir in the rest of the liquid gradually. If you'll be adding sugar to the cocoa, do it before the liquid goes in.

hot fudge sauce
(recipe on p. 227)

fudge, truffles & more

creamy chocolate fudge

**MAKES TWENTY-FIVE
1½-INCH PIECES**

3 **Tbs. cold unsalted butter;
more at room temperature
for buttering the thermometer and pan**

3¾ **cups granulated sugar**

1½ **cups heavy cream**

4 **oz. unsweetened chocolate,
coarsely chopped**

3 **Tbs. light corn syrup**

1 **tsp. table salt**

*The fudge will keep for 7 to 10 days stored in an airtight container at
room temperature.*

1. Lightly butter the face of a candy thermometer and set aside.

2. Put the sugar, cream, chocolate, corn syrup, and salt in a large
(4-quart) heavy-duty saucepan, and stir with a spoon or heatproof
spatula until the ingredients are moistened and combined. Stirring
gently and constantly, bring the mixture to a boil over medium heat,
7 to 12 minutes. Cover the saucepan and let the steam clean the sides
of the pan for 2 minutes.

3. Clip the candy thermometer to the pot, being careful not to let the
tip of the thermometer touch the bottom of the pot or you might get
a false reading. Let the mixture boil without stirring until it reaches
236°F to 238°F, 2 to 5 minutes. Take the pan off the heat and add the
butter, but do not stir it into the mixture. Set the pan on a rack in a cool
part of the kitchen. Don't disturb the pan in any way until the mixture
has cooled to 110°F, 1 to 1½ hours.

4. Meanwhile, line the bottom and sides of an 8x8-inch baking pan
with foil, leaving a 2-inch overhang on two opposite sides of the pan.
Butter the foil. Set the pan aside.

5. Remove the thermometer from the fudge mixture. Using a hand
mixer, beat the mixture on high speed until it is a few shades lighter
in color and thickens enough that the beaters form trails that briefly
expose the bottom of the pan as they pass through, 10 to 20 minutes. Pour the thickened fudge into the prepared pan, using a rubber
spatula to help nudge it out of the pot. You can scrape the bottom of
the pot but not the sides; any crystals that stick to the pot stay in the
pot. Smooth the top of the fudge with the spatula. Set the pan on a
rack and let the fudge cool completely, about 2 hours. The fudge will
be slightly soft the day it's made but will firm up overnight.

6. Turn the fudge out onto a clean cutting board and peel off the foil.
Turn the slab of fudge right side up and cut it into 25 equal pieces.
—Bonnie Gorder-Hinchey

PER SERVING: 190 CALORIES | 1G PROTEIN | 30G CARB | 9G TOTAL FAT | 6G SAT FAT |
2.5G MONO FAT | 0G POLY FAT | 25MG CHOL | 100MG SODIUM | 1G FIBER

secrets to smooth fudge

Making melt-in-your-mouth chocolate fudge is simple: You boil sugar, heavy cream, and chocolate, let the mixture cool, and then beat it to the right consistency. As the mixture boils, the sugar crystals dissolve, and the sugar concentration gradually increases. Then, once beating starts, the sugar begins to recrystallize. If the crystals stay small, the result is a smooth fudge. But if larger crystals form, the fudge will be grainy. Because large crystals can form at any time during fudge making, you need to be vigilant. Here's what to do every step of the way for perfect results.

USE CORN SYRUP AND BUTTER
Both interfere with sugar crystallization, so adding them to the fudge prevents the crystals from growing too large. Butter should be added only after the boiling is done. If added before boiling, it coats the crystals and keeps them from dissolving, resulting in grainy fudge.

CLEAN THE PAN SIDES It's important to keep the boiling mixture from coming in contact with sugar crystals on the sides of the pan; otherwise, the sugar will start to recrystallize too soon, causing large crystals to form. To prevent this, cover the pot with a lid for 2 minutes after it starts boiling—the steam will wash the crystals down the sides.

BRING IT TO THE RIGHT TEMPERA-TURE Boiling the mixture to 236°F to 238°F (known as the soft-ball stage) results in the correct concentration of sugar, so the fudge sets up to the proper firmness after beating. Fudge boiled below this temperature is too soft to hold its shape, and fudge boiled above this point becomes too firm.

DON'T STIR THE FUDGE Shaking or stirring the fudge mixture while it's boiling or cooling causes premature crystal growth. If the crystals form too early, they continue to grow and become too large.

LET IT COOL Start beating the fudge only when it has cooled down to 110°F. It will be glossy and dark brown. If it's hotter, the crystals will form too fast and the fudge will be grainy. If the fudge is too cool, it will set up and be difficult to beat.

KNOW WHEN TO STOP BEAT-ING Beat the fudge vigorously to form many small crystals and create a smooth texture; stop beating when it turns a lighter brown and becomes more opaque and when the ripples made by the beaters hold their shape long enough to briefly expose the bottom of the pan.

toffee-chocolate candy

MAKES ABOUT THIRTY-FIVE 2-INCH PIECES

- **6 oz. semisweet chocolate, chopped**
- **6 oz. bittersweet chocolate, chopped**
- **½ lb. (1 cup) unsalted butter**
- **1 cup granulated sugar**
- **1 tsp. light corn syrup**
- **½ tsp. kosher salt**
- **1 tsp. pure vanilla extract**
- **½ cup finely chopped toasted pecans**

Variations on this addictive candy show up in older American cook-books. This version has been adapted a bit by the addition of vanilla, bittersweet chocolate, and toasted pecans. You could use all semi-sweet chocolate, or even milk chocolate, if you like. Put some of this candy in a festive holiday tin for gift giving.

1. Combine the two chocolates and set aside.

2. Set a small bowl of water and a pastry brush next to the stove.

3. In a heavy-based saucepan fitted with a candy thermometer, cook the butter, sugar, ¼ cup water, corn syrup, and salt over medium heat. Stir frequently with a wooden spoon until the butter melts and the sugar dissolves, then stir gently and only occasionally as the mixture approaches 300°F and begins to darken. Brush the sides of the pan down with a little water once in a while to keep the sugar from crystal-lizing. When the mixture reaches 300°F (this will take 18 to 20 min-utes), remove the pan from the heat, carefully add the vanilla extract, and stir it in. With a heatproof rubber spatula, scrape the mixture into a metal 9x11-inch baking pan set on a cooling rack. Tilt the pan until the toffee covers the bottom of the pan evenly. Let cool for 2 minutes.

4. Sprinkle the toffee with the chopped chocolate, and cover the pan with another baking pan (to keep things warm and help the chocolate melt) for a few minutes. Smooth the melted chocolate with a spatula (use a narrow offset spatula if you have one) and sprinkle on the pecans. Let cool completely (3 to 4 hours) and then break or chop into pieces; use a metal spatula or a blunt knife to pry the toffee out of the pan. To help the chocolate set faster on a warm day, refrigerate the candy. *—Susie Middleton*

chocolate bark with ginger and pistachios

SERVES 4

6 oz. bittersweet dark chocolate (70% to 72% cacao),
  chopped (1 cup)

2 oz. white chocolate, chopped
  (⅓ cup) (optional)

3 Tbs. chopped salted
  pistachios

3 Tbs. chopped dried apricots

2 Tbs. chopped crystallized
  ginger

This is a quick and sweet end to dinner, perfect with a cup of coffee or tea.

1. In a small bowl, melt the dark chocolate in a microwave on high, 1 to 2 minutes. Stir until smooth.

2. Line a baking sheet with a silicone baking mat or waxed paper. Spread the melted dark chocolate into an approximately 8x5-inch rectangle.

3. If using the white chocolate, melt it in the same manner as the dark chocolate and drizzle it in a zigzag pattern across the dark chocolate.

4. Sprinkle with the chopped pistachios, apricots, and ginger, and press gently to set them into the chocolate. Chill in the refrigerator for 10 minutes. Break into pieces and serve. Store any leftovers in the refrigerator. —*Bruce Weinstein* and *Mark Scarbrough*

PER SERVING: 380 CALORIES | 6G PROTEIN | 45G CARB | 19G TOTAL FAT | 11G SAT FAT | 7G MONO FAT | 1G POLY FAT | 0MG CHOL | 80MG SODIUM | 6G FIBER

bourbon balls

MAKES 3½ TO 4 DOZEN

- **1 cup heavy cream**
- **¼ cup bourbon**
- **½ tsp. pure vanilla extract**
- **12 oz. bittersweet chocolate, chopped (about 2½ cups)**
- **8 oz. pecans, toasted and cooled (about 2 cups)**
- **8 oz. plain homemade or store-bought pound cake (thawed if frozen), cut into cubes (about 2½ cups)**
- **⅔ cup cocoa powder, preferably Dutch processed**
- **⅓ cup confectioners' sugar**

For some of us, it wouldn't be Christmas without these rich, potent treats. Make them with chocolate or vanilla cake scraps from a leftover cake layer or use a store-bought pound cake.

1. In a small saucepan, bring the cream just to a boil over medium-high heat. Remove from the heat and stir in the bourbon and vanilla extract. Sprinkle the chocolate evenly over the cream and let sit without stirring for 5 minutes.

2. Meanwhile, pulse the pecans in a food processor until coarsely chopped. Add the pound cake and pulse until the nuts and cake are finely chopped.

3. Stir the chocolate and cream until smooth. Pour the chocolate over the pecan and pound cake mixture in the food processor and pulse until combined. Transfer to a medium bowl and refrigerate, stirring occasionally, until firm enough to scoop, about 1 hour.

4. Sift the cocoa powder and confectioners' sugar together into a medium bowl. Line a rimmed baking sheet with waxed paper or parchment. Scoop out a heaping tablespoon of the bourbon-chocolate mixture and roll it in your hands to form a ball. Transfer the bourbon ball to the cocoa-sugar mixture, roll it around to coat, and transfer to the baking sheet. Repeat with the remaining bourbon-chocolate mixture. Sift some of the remaining cocoa-sugar mixture over the bourbon balls just to dust them. Refrigerate the bourbon balls until firm, about 2 hours. For a nice presentation, you can put them in mini muffin cups. —*Allison Ehri Kreitler*

PER SERVING: 110 CALORIES | 2G PROTEIN | 9G CARB | 8G TOTAL FAT | 3G SAT FAT | 3.5G MONO FAT | 1G POLY FAT | 10MG CHOL | 30MG SODIUM | 2G FIBER

chocolate brigadeiros

MAKES ABOUT 3 DOZEN

- **1 14-oz. can sweetened condensed milk**
- **2 Tbs. unsalted butter**
- **2 Tbs. heavy cream**
- **1 tsp. light corn syrup**
- **1½ oz. semisweet or bittersweet chocolate (preferably 60% to 62% cacao), chopped**
- **1 tsp. Dutch-processed cocoa powder**
- **1 cup chocolate sprinkles (preferably Guittard®)**

Learning when to stop cooking the batter is the trickiest part of making brigadeiros. If the batter is undercooked, your brigadeiros will be too soft; if the batter is overcooked, they will be hard and chewy. The batter is done when it slides to one side of the pan in a blob and leaves a thick residue on the bottom.

Like many Brazilian sweets, brigadeiros are named after a famous personality. Brigadier Eduardo Gomes was a well-known Brazilian Air Force commander who loved chocolate. Legend has it that chocolate brigadeiros were created for and named after him.

1. Put the condensed milk, butter, cream, and corn syrup in a 3-quart heavy-duty saucepan and bring to a boil over medium heat, whisking constantly. Add the chocolate and cocoa powder and continue to whisk, making sure there are no pockets of cocoa powder. As soon as the mixture comes back to a boil, turn the heat to medium low and cook, whisking constantly, until the mixture thickens and pulls together into a dense, fudgy batter, about 8 minutes. When the mixture is ready, the whisk will leave trails in the batter, allowing you to briefly see the pan bottom, and when you tilt the pan, the mixture should slide to the side in a blob, leaving a thick residue on the bottom of the pan.

2. Slide the mixture into a medium bowl. (Don't scrape the pan—you don't want to use any of the batter stuck to the bottom.) Let the mixture cool to room temperature and then refrigerate, uncovered, until very firm, 3 to 4 hours.

3. Put the sprinkles in a bowl. Using a teaspoon or a melon baller, scoop the mixture by the teaspoonful, and with your hands, roll each into a ball about 1 inch in diameter. Drop each ball into the sprinkles as you finish rolling it. When you have 4 to 6 brigadeiros, toss them in the sprinkles to coat. You may need to exert a little pressure to ensure that the sprinkles stick. *—Leticia Moreinos*

PER PIECE: 50 CALORIES | 1G PROTEIN | 8G CARB | 2.5G TOTAL FAT | 1.5G SAT FAT | 0.5G MONO FAT | 0G POLY FAT | 5MG CHOL | 15MG SODIUM | 0G FIBER

chocolate-dipped strawberries

MAKES ABOUT 1 DOZEN

- **3** oz. bittersweet chocolate, chopped into almond-size pieces
- **2** tsp. neutral vegetable oil, such as grapeseed or canola
- **1** pint medium-size ripe fresh strawberries (preferably with stems), rinsed and dried

The secrets to perfection: Use the best strawberries and chocolate you can, and be sure your strawberries are bone-dry before you dip them into the melted chocolate or the chocolate will seize into a mass.

1. Melt the chocolate with the oil in a small, deep, heatproof bowl set in a skillet holding about 1 inch of barely simmering water, whisking occasionally until smooth. Remove the bowl from the heat.

2. Line a small, rimmed baking sheet with waxed paper. Tilt the bowl to pool the chocolate on one side. Dip each strawberry into the chocolate to cover about two-thirds of the berry, or until the chocolate reaches the strawberry's shoulders. Turn the berry to coat it evenly, lift it out of the chocolate, and gently shake off any excess. Carefully lay it on the waxed paper. If the dipping chocolate begins to cool and thicken, return the bowl to the water bath to heat it briefly.

3. Let the berries stand at room temperature for 15 minutes and then refrigerate until the chocolate is set, 20 to 30 minutes. Carefully remove the berries from the waxed paper. Serve immediately or refrigerate for up to 8 hours before serving. —*Lori Longbotham*

PER 2 STRAWBERRIES: 105 CALORIES | 1G PROTEIN | 12G CARB | 6G TOTAL FAT | 3G SAT FAT | 2G MONO FAT | 1G POLY FAT | 0MG CHOL | 14MG SODIUM | 3G FIBER

pecan-nougat chocolates

MAKES ABOUT 3 DOZEN CANDIES

Unsalted butter, for the pans

¾ cup granulated sugar

¾ cup toasted pecans

1   lb. good-quality dark chocolate

These candies are quite easy to make, but the taste—crunchy, caramelized pecans and dark chocolate—is pure elegance.

1. Lightly grease two baking sheets or line them with kitchen parchment. In a heavy saucepan, melt the sugar until it turns a golden caramel color. Remove from the heat and quickly stir in the toasted pecans. Spread the mixture as thin as possible on one of the prepared baking sheets. Allow the nougat to harden completely.

2. Meanwhile, chop ¾ lb. of the chocolate, leaving the rest in a large chunk. Put the chopped chocolate in a bowl set over hot but not simmering water. The bowl should not touch the water. Put a chocolate thermometer in the chocolate, and heat the chocolate, stirring constantly, until the temperature reaches 120°F. When the chocolate is completely melted, remove it from the heat and let it cool slightly. Add the remaining chunk of chocolate and continue stirring until the temperature drops below 91°F. Remove any unmelted chocolate. (If the chocolate melts completely before the temperature reaches 91°F, continue stirring until it reaches the proper temperature.) While working with the chocolate, you want to keep it between 84°F and 91°F—placing the bowl on a heating pad set at the lowest temperature is a good way to do this. As you work, stir the chocolate occasionally, and if it cools too much, simply increase the temperature by adjusting the heat setting.

3. Crush the hardened nougat into small pieces with a rolling pin. You should have about 1½ cups of nougat pieces. In a food processor or blender, pulverize ¼ cup of the nougat pieces to a fine powder. Fold the remaining nougat pieces into the tempered chocolate. Using a teaspoon, drop small circles of the chocolate-nougat mixture onto the other prepared baking sheet. Sprinkle the top of each candy with some of the powdered nougat. Allow to harden. —*Mark Gray*

PER SERVING: 90 CALORIES | 1G PROTEIN | 12G CARB | 5G TOTAL FAT | 3G SAT FAT | 2G MONO FAT | 0G POLY FAT | 0MG CHOL | 0MG SODIUM | 1G FIBER

chocolate mint truffles

MAKES 16 TRUFFLES

½ **cup heavy cream**

4 **4-inch-long sprigs of fresh peppermint or chocolate mint**

½ **lb. good-quality semisweet chocolate, chopped**

Cocoa, for rolling

Peppermint, with its head-clearing aroma and expansive, menthol-cool flavor, is the perfect match for rich, dark chocolate. When infusing mint in a liquid, as you do here, there's no need to strip the leaves from the stem. Just use whole sprigs.

1. Bring the cream to a boil in a small saucepan. Add the mint. Turn the heat off and let it steep for 15 minutes. Strain the cream and return it to the saucepan.

2. Place the chocolate in the bowl of a food processor. Bring the mint-flavored cream to a boil again. Pour it over the chocolate and process until smooth. Transfer the mixture to a small mixing bowl and chill until solid.

3. Scoop out tablespoon-size dollops of the chocolate and place them on a plate. Chill for 10 minutes. Dip your hands in ice water and dry them. Roll the chocolate into uniform balls and toss them in a bowl of the cocoa. Chill and dry your hands again if the chocolate begins to melt. Shake off any excess cocoa and store the truffles in the refrigerator. *—Jerry Traunfeld*

chocolate-nut bark

MAKES ABOUT 1¾ LB. CANDY

1 lb. good-quality chocolate

¾ lb. toasted nuts, such as
   hazelnuts or almonds

*Toasting brings out the flavor
in nuts, but let them cool completely before you add them to
the chocolate or you'll destroy
the temper.*

1. Line a baking sheet with
kitchen parchment.

2. Meanwhile, chop ¾ lb. of the
chocolate, leaving the rest in a
large chunk. Put the chopped chocolate in a bowl set over hot but not
simmering water. The bowl should not touch the water. Put a chocolate thermometer in the chocolate, and heat the chocolate, stirring
constantly, until the temperature reaches 120°F. When the chocolate
is completely melted, remove it from the heat and let it cool slightly.
Add the remaining chunk of chocolate and continue stirring until the
temperature drops below 91°F. Remove any unmelted chocolate.
(If the chocolate melts completely before the temperature reaches
91°F, continue stirring until it reaches the proper temperature.) While
working with the chocolate, you want to keep it between 84°F and
91°F—placing the bowl on a heating pad set at the lowest temperature
is a good way to do this. As you work, stir the chocolate occasionally,
and if it cools too much, simply increase the temperature by adjusting
the heat setting.

3. Fold the nuts into the tempered chocolate, and spread the mixture
in an even layer about ¼ inch thick on the prepared pan. Let set
completely. Cut into squares with a sharp knife or break into bite-
size pieces. *—Mark Gray*

PER SERVING: 160 CALORIES | 3G PROTEIN | 10G CARB | 14G TOTAL FAT | 3G SAT FAT |
10G MONO FAT | 1G POLY FAT | 0MG CHOL | 0MG SODIUM | 2G FIBER

macadamia trios

MAKES ABOUT 40 CANDIES

1½   lb. good-quality chocolate

120   (about 12 oz.) whole roasted macadamia nuts

Walnut halves or peanuts and raisins can be used instead of macadamias.

1. Line two baking sheets with kitchen parchment.

2. Chop 1¼ lb. of the chocolate, leaving the rest in a large chunk. Put the chopped chocolate in a bowl set over hot but not simmering water. The bowl should not touch the water. Put a chocolate thermometer in the chocolate, and heat the chocolate, stirring constantly, until the temperature reaches 120°F. When the chocolate is completely melted, remove it from the heat and let it cool slightly. Add the remaining chunk of chocolate and continue stirring until the temperature drops below 91°F. Remove any unmelted chocolate. (If the chocolate melts completely before the temperature reaches 91°F, continue stirring until it reaches the proper temperature.) While working with the chocolate, you want to keep it between 84°F and 91°F—placing the bowl on a heating pad set at the lowest temperature is a good way to do this. As you work, stir the chocolate occasionally, and if it cools too much, simply increase the temperature by adjusting the heat setting.

3. Fill a small plastic bag with about 8 oz. of the chocolate, and cut a small hole in one corner of the bag. Squeeze out 40 teaspoon-size drops of chocolate onto one of the baking sheets. Arrange three nuts in a triangle on top of each chocolate drop and allow to set.

4. Drop the nut trios, one at a time, into the tempered chocolate. With a dry fork, gently submerge the nuts until completely coated. Lift out of the chocolate, tapping gently on the edge of the bowl to shake off any excess chocolate. Set on a parchment lined baking sheet to dry.
—Mark Gray

PER SERVING: 140 CALORIES | 1G PROTEIN | 12G CARB | 11G TOTAL FAT | 4G SAT FAT | 7G MONO FAT | 0G POLY FAT | 0MG CHOL | 0MG SODIUM | 2G FIBER

Temperature Ranges for Tempered Chocolate

The temperature ranges here indicate the point at which the tempering is complete. To maintain the proper temperature, keep the chocolate set over a bowl of warm water. If the temperature falls below the indicated range, the chocolate will be too thick to form a smooth coating; if it rises above the proper temperature, the chocolate will have to be retempered.

- Semisweet and bittersweet chocolate: 86°F to 91°F

- Milk chocolate: 84°F to 86°F

- White chocolate: 84°F to 86°F

old-fashioned fudge with crunchy cacao nibs

MAKES 5 DOZEN 1-INCH SQUARES

- 2 Tbs. unsalted butter; more for the pans
- 2 cups granulated sugar
- ¾ cup whole milk
- Pinch of table salt
- 1 Tbs. light corn syrup
- 4 oz. unsweetened chocolate, coarsely chopped
- 1 tsp. pure vanilla extract
- ⅓ cup cacao nibs

Old-fashioned fudge isn't difficult to make, but it may give your forearms a workout during the beating stage. A successful batch of fudge is all about controlling the crystals that form at different stages; all it takes is one misstep to find yourself with a pan full of grainy candy. Follow the steps carefully and you'll be in the clear. Adding the cacao nibs gives this classic candy a crunchy new twist.

1. Line an 8x8-inch pan with foil, folding the excess over the sides to form handles. Grease the foil and set the pan aside.

2. Butter the inside of a heavy 2-quart saucepan. Put the sugar, milk, salt, corn syrup, and chocolate in the saucepan and place over medium heat, stirring until the sugar dissolves and the mixture boils. Clip on a candy thermometer and cook until the mixture reaches 234°F (soft-ball stage).

3. Immediately remove the pan from heat. Add the butter and, without stirring or swirling, cool the mixture until the thermometer reads 110°F (you may either allow this to happen naturally or plunge the base of the saucepan into an ice bath). Add the vanilla extract and beat vigorously with a wooden spoon until the fudge becomes quite stiff and loses its gloss (this may take up to 5 minutes). Quickly add the nibs and turn the fudge into the prepared pan, being careful not to scrape the insides of the saucepan too much, so you don't incorporate dried-out bits of fudge. Smooth the fudge so that the top is relatively even, and allow to set before cutting. *—Fine Cooking editors*

truffles

1 recipe Basic Ganache (recipe on p. 79)

2 Tbs. unsalted butter, softened

1 cup cocoa powder (preferably Dutch processed); more as needed

8 oz. semisweet chocolate, chopped (about 1½ cups)

When coating the truffles, it's important to work quickly and in batches so the coating doesn't harden before you roll them in the cocoa powder. Any leftover cocoa powder can be sifted and saved. Using Dutch-processed cocoa powder to coat the truffles is preferable because it's brighter in color and less acidic than natural cocoa powder. But if you can find only natural cocoa, you can use it instead.

1. Make the ganache and add the butter to the warm ganache still in the food processor. Process until smooth, about 10 seconds. Transfer to a medium bowl, cover tightly with plastic wrap, and refrigerate until firm, at least 2 hours or overnight.

2. Put the cocoa powder in a large bowl. Using two teaspoons, drop rounded, heaping teaspoonfuls of truffle mixture onto a large, parchment-lined baking sheet.

Flavor Variations

Once you learn how to make truffles, the flavor possibilities are endless.

Liqueur filling

Add 3 Tbs. of a flavored liqueur of your choice to the ganache before refrigerating. Try Frangelico, Baileys®, Godiva®, Kahlúa, and amaretto.

Nut coating

After coating the truffles with melted chocolate, coat them with 1 cup (6 oz.) of your choice of finely chopped toasted nuts instead of cocoa powder. Try almonds, hazelnuts, walnuts, pecans, peanuts, and pistachios. Note that when you use nuts instead of cocoa for the coating, you will still need cocoa to shape the truffles.

Mexican chocolate

Add 2 Tbs. Kahlúa liqueur, 2 tsp. instant espresso, and ½ tsp. ground cinnamon to the ganache. Coat the truffles with 1 cup (6 oz.) ground toasted almonds.

Toffee and fleur de sel

Add ½ cup ground toffee bits (you can use Heath Bars and grind them coarsely in a food processor) and ¼ tsp. fleur de sel to the ganache. Use 1¼ cups finely ground toffee bits mixed with 1 tsp. fleur de sel for the coating. (You'll need a total of six 1.4-oz. Heath Bars.)

PB&J

Add ⅔ cup strawberry jam to the ganache and process until smooth. Coat the truffles with 2 cups (10 oz.) ground salted peanuts. (This makes about 54 truffles because of the added jam.)

Mint

Add ½ tsp. pure peppermint extract to the ganache.

3. When all of the truffles are scooped, dip them in the cocoa and use your palms to roll the truffles into smooth 1-inch balls (don't worry about making them perfect; slightly irregular truffles have an appealing homemade appearance). Transfer the truffles to the refrigerator.

4. Melt the chocolate in a medium heatproof bowl set in a small skillet of barely simmering water, stirring occasionally until smooth.

5. Transfer the bowl to a work surface. Working in batches, use your fingers or a couple of forks to coat the truffles with the melted chocolate, coat them again with cocoa powder or nuts, and return them to the baking sheet. If using your hands, you'll have to stop and wash off the chocolate in between batches.

6. Let the truffles sit at room temperature for at least 15 minutes before serving. If not serving right away, store them in an airtight container in the refrigerator, where they will keep for up to 5 days. Bring them to room temperature before serving. —*Greg Case*

PER TRUFFLE: 90 CALORIES | 1G PROTEIN | 9G CARB | 7G TOTAL FAT | 4G SAT FAT | 2G MONO FAT | 0.2G POLY FAT | 10MG CHOL | 4MG SODIUM | 1G FIBER

chocolate-raspberry truffles

**MAKES ABOUT SIXTY
1-INCH TRUFFLES**

- **1** cup fresh raspberries
- **1** lb. semisweet or bittersweet chocolate, finely chopped
- **1½** cups heavy cream

  Small pinch of salt
- **1** cup unsweetened Dutch-processed cocoa

Use the best-quality chocolate you can find. When warmed, the chocolate mixture doubles as a killer sauce for ice cream.

1. Pass the berries through a food mill fitted with a fine disk or force them through a fine-mesh sieve, mashing with a wooden spoon, into a medium bowl. You'll have about ½ cup purée; set it aside and discard the contents of the strainer.

2. Put the chopped chocolate in a medium bowl. In a small saucepan, heat the cream just until boiling. Pour the hot cream over the chopped chocolate; whisk to blend. Stir in the raspberry purée and the salt. Refrigerate the mixture until completely chilled, about 1 hour.

3. Pour the cocoa powder onto a plate. Using a melon baller or a spoon, scoop the chocolate and shape it into 1-inch balls. If the truffles are very soft, put them on a baking sheet and refrigerate briefly to firm. Roll the shaped truffles in the cocoa, coating them thoroughly. If sealed and refrigerated, they'll keep for about 1 week.
—Michelle Polzine

PER TRUFFLE: 60 CALORIES | 1G PROTEIN | 6G CARB | 4.5G TOTAL FAT | 3G SAT FAT | 1G MONO FAT | 0.5G POLY FAT | 10MG CHOL | 5MG SODIUM | 2G FIBER

A food mill makes quick work of raspberry purée, mashing and straining in one sweep.

fast and easy nibby fudge

MAKES 5 DOZEN 1-INCH SQUARES

- 2 oz. (¼ cup) unsalted butter; more for the pan
- ⅔ cup evaporated milk
- 1 7-oz. jar marshmallow creme
- 1½ cups granulated sugar
- ¼ tsp. table salt
- 12 oz. semisweet chocolate, finely chopped
- 1 tsp. pure vanilla extract
- ⅓ cup cacao nibs, divided

Cacao nibs are roasted and lightly crushed cacao beans—in other words, pure chocolate! Their bittersweet, toasty flavor and irresistible crunch are wonderful contrasts to this super-creamy fudge. You won't need a thermometer to make this fudge because marshmallow creme ensures a smooth texture.

1. Line an 8x8-inch pan with foil, folding the excess over the sides to form handles. Grease the foil and set the pan aside.

2. Put the evaporated milk, marshmallow creme, butter, sugar, and salt in a large, heavy-bottomed saucepan. Bring to a boil over medium heat, stirring constantly with a heatproof spatula. Scrape the bottom and sides of the pan often, as this mixture is apt to burn.

3. Once the mixture comes to a boil, cook for 5 minutes, stirring constantly; it will caramelize a bit, which is fine. Remove from the heat, add the chocolate and vanilla extract, and stir until the chocolate is melted and the mixture is smooth. Add half of the nibs, stir to combine, and pour into the prepared pan. Top with the remaining nibs and allow to set.

4. Once the fudge is firm, lift it out of the pan using the foil handles and cut it into small squares with a long, sharp knife on a cutting board.
—*Martha Holmberg*

bittersweet chocolate bark with marcona almonds

MAKES ABOUT 2 LB.

- **1** cup plus 2 Tbs. granulated sugar
- **9** oz. Marcona almonds, coarsely chopped and sifted
- **1** lb. bittersweet chocolate, coarsely chopped

If you can't find Spanish Marcona almonds, which are generally sold salted, use toasted blanched almonds and add a good pinch of salt to the brittle.

MAKE THE ALMOND BRITTLE

1. Line a heavy-duty rimmed baking sheet with foil. Put the sugar in a 2-quart heavy-duty saucepan. Add ¼ cup water and swirl (don't stir) to moisten. Cover and boil over high heat until starting to turn golden around the edges, about 4 minutes. Remove the lid and cook, swirling occasionally, until the caramel is deep amber, 3 to 4 minutes more. Stir in half of the almonds. Pour the mixture onto the foil-covered baking sheet, and spread to ⅛ inch thick. Let cool completely at room temperature.

2. Peel the brittle off the foil, chop coarsely, and sift through a medium-fine–mesh sieve to remove the extra-small pieces and the brittle dust, which will make the chocolate bark too sweet. At this point, you can proceed with making the bark, or store the brittle in an airtight container in the freezer for up to a week.

MAKE THE CHOCOLATE BARK

1. Line two 8x8-inch pans with foil. In a 12-inch skillet, bring 1 inch of water to a boil over high heat. Reduce the heat to maintain a bare simmer. Put the chocolate in a dry stainless-steel bowl that fits in the skillet and put the bowl in the simmering water bath. Stir until most of the chocolate is melted, about 5 minutes. Remove the bowl from the water—be careful not to get any water in the chocolate—and stir until smooth. Stir in the remaining almonds and the almond brittle.

2. Divide the chocolate mixture between the prepared pans, making sure that none of the brittle is exposed. (The brittle will sweat and soften if not coated in chocolate.) Shake the pan a little to level the chocolate. Refrigerate until firm, about 30 minutes. Turn out the bark and remove the foil. Cut into small, rustic pieces and refrigerate for up to 1 week before serving. —*Tasha DeSerio*

PER SERVING: 240 CALORIES | 5G PROTEIN | 27G CARB | 14G TOTAL FAT | 5G SAT FAT | 7G MONO FAT | 1.5G POLY FAT | 0MG CHOL | 65MG SODIUM | 4G FIBER

hot fudge sauce

MAKES ABOUT 2 CUPS

- **1** **recipe Basic Ganache (recipe on p. 79)**
- **2** **Tbs. light corn syrup**
- **2** **tsp. pure vanilla extract**
- **1** **Tbs. unsalted butter, softened**

This gooey, stick-to-your spoon hot fudge sauce will please both kids and grown-ups. It's delicious served over vanilla or coffee ice cream.

Make the ganache and add the corn syrup, vanilla extract, and butter to the warm ganache still in the food processor. Process until smooth, about 10 seconds. Serve immediately over ice cream, or transfer to a container, cool, cover, and refrigerate for up to 1 week. To reheat, pour into a small saucepan and warm over medium-low heat.

—*Greg Case* and *Keri Fisher*

PER 1 TBS: 80 CALORIES | 1G PROTEIN | 8G CARB | 6G TOTAL FAT | 4G SAT FAT | 2G MONO FAT | 0.2G POLY FAT | 10MG CHOL | 5MG SODIUM | 1G FIBER

METRIC EQUIVALENTS

LIQUID/DRY MEASURES	
U.S.	**METRIC**
¼ teaspoon	1.25 milliliters
½ teaspoon	2.5 milliliters
1 teaspoon	5 milliliters
1 tablespoon (3 teaspoons)	15 milliliters
1 fluid ounce (2 tablespoons)	30 milliliters
¼ cup	60 milliliters
⅓ cup	80 milliliters
½ cup	120 milliliters
1 cup	240 milliliters
1 pint (2 cups)	480 milliliters
1 quart (4 cups; 32 ounces)	960 milliliters
1 gallon (4 quarts)	3.84 liters
1 ounce (by weight)	28 grams
1 pound	454 grams
2.2 pounds	1 kilogram

OVEN TEMPERATURES		
°F	**GAS MARK**	**°C**
250	½	120
275	1	140
300	2	150
325	3	165
350	4	180
375	5	190
400	6	200
425	7	220
450	8	230
475	9	240
500	10	260
550	Broil	290

CONTRIBUTORS

Bruce Aidells is a chef, cookbook author, and meat and grilling expert. His Live Well network television show is called Good Cookin' with Bruce Aidells, and he has written 10 cookbooks.

Jennifer Armentrout is the editor-in-chief at *Fine Cooking*.

Karen Barker is a pastry chef and cookbook author. She co-owns Magnolia Grill in Durham, North Carolina. She won the James Beard Outstanding Pastry Chef Award in 2003.

Carol Bloom has been teaching the pastry arts for more than 25 years and has written many books and numerous articles about baking.

Tish Boyle is the editor of *Dessert Professional* magazine. She studied at La Varenne in Paris and has been a pastry chef, caterer, food stylist, recipe developer, and cookbook author.

Greg Case was a pastry chef at Dean & DeLuca in New York City and Hammersley's Bistro in Boston before setting out on his own. He owns the G. Case Baking Company in Somerville, Massachusetts.

Joanne Chang is the pastry chef and owner of Flour Bakery + Café, which has two locations in Boston.

Andy Corson is an avid baker and former owner of American Artisan Food & Bakery in Newtown, Connecticut.

Amy Cotler is a longtime culinary professional and farm-to-table advocate, who speaks, teaches, writes, and consults about the pleasures of local farm-fresh food.

David Crofton and his wife, **Dawn Casale**, are bakers and business partners at One Girl Cookies in Brooklyn, New York.

Regan Daley is a food writer from Toronto, Canada. Her cookbook, *In the Sweet Kitchen*, won several awards, including the IACP's Award for Best Baking and Dessert Book and Best Overall Book.

Tasha DeSerio is a cooking teacher, food writer, and caterer in Berkeley, California. Her latest book, *Salad for Dinner*, was published in 2012.

Paula Disbrowe was the chef at Hart & Hind Fitness Ranch in Rio Frio, Texas, from January 2002 to December 2005. Prior to that she spent ten years in Manhattan working as a food and travel writer. Her work has appeared in the *New York Times, T Living, Food & Wine, Spa, Health, Cooking Light*, and *Saveur*, among others.

Abigail Johnson Dodge, a former pastry chef, is a widely published food writer, cooking instructor, and *Fine Cooking* contributor editor. She has also written numerous cookbooks, including *Mini Treats & Hand-Held Sweets.*

Steven Durfee has been a pastry instructor at CIA Greystone since 2000. Previously, he was executive pastry chef at the French Laundry in Yountville, California, during which time he won the 1998 James Beard Award for Pastry Chef of the Year.

Elizabeth Falkner is chef/partner of Citizen Cake and Ice Cream Parlor and Orson, both in San Francisco. She also was a competitor on Top Chef Masters, Iron Chef America, and Food Network's Challenge. In addition, she's been a judge on some of those same shows.

Keri Fisher is a food writer and cookbook author who cut her teeth at restaurants in Florida and Boston.

Allison Fishman is a cooking teacher, healthy living and home cooking consultant, and food writer for numerous publications.

Gale Gand is a pastry chef, restaurateur, and cookbook author. She was recognized in 2001 as Outstanding Pastry Chef by The James Beard Foundation and Pastry Chef of the Year in 2001 by *Bon Appetit* magazine.

Maggie Glezer is an American Institute of Baking-certified baker. Her first book, *Artisan Baking Across America*, won a James Beard Foundation award. Maggie also teaches and writes about bread baking for numerous publications.

Suzanne Goin is chef-owner of Lucques in West Hollywood, California. She has received five concurrent nominations for Outstanding Chef of the Year by the James Beard Foundation from 2008-2011, and her cookbook, *Sunday Suppers at Lucques,* received the James Beard Foundation award for Best Cookbook from a Professional Viewpoint in 2006.

Bonnie Gorder-Hinchey, a food scientist and cooking teacher, has more than 25 years of experience developing recipes and food products for Nestlé and General Mills.

Dabney Gough is a Honolulu-based food writer, cookbook author, and recipe developer. Her latest cookbook is *Sweet Cream and Sugar Cones.*

Mark Gray is the former chocolatier at The Greenbrier and owner of Cacao Handmade Chocolates in Charleston, South Carolina.

Lauren Groveman is a cooking and baking teacher and host of the public television series "Home Cooking with Lauren Groveman."

David Guas is a pastry chef, restaurant consultant, and cooking teacher. David is the chef-owner of Bayou Bakery in Arlington, Virginia, as well as the author of *DamGoodSweet*.

Karen Hatfield has worked in the pastry kitchens at Café Boulud, Jean-Georges, and Gramercy Tavern in New York City. She and her husband are co-owners of Hatfield's restaurant in Los Angeles.

Patricia Ann Heyman is the author of *American Regional Cooking: A Culinary Journey* and *International Cooking: A Culinary Journey.*

Heather Ho was an executive pastry chef at Windows on the World restaurant in New York City.

Martha Holmberg is a cookbook author and food writer based in Portland, Oregon. Her latest book is *Crepes.*

Eva Katz has worked as a chef, caterer, teacher, recipe developer and tester, food stylist, and food writer. She is a member of the Program Advisory Committee at the Cambridge School of Culinary Arts in Massachusetts.

Jeanne Kelley, the author of the award-winning cookbook *Blue Eggs and Yellow Tomatoes*, is a food stylist and recipe developer.

Elinor Klivans has written numerous cookbooks, including *Fast Breads: 50 Recipes for Easy, Delicious Breads*. Klivans also writes for the *Washington Post, Real Food, Fresh,* and *Cooking Pleasures.*

Genevieve Ko is a cookbook author and the senior food editor at *Good Housekeeping*. She was previously an editor at *Gourmet* and *Martha Stewart Living* and co-authored *The Sweet Spot* with renowned pastry chef Pichet Ong.

Allison Ehri Kreitler is a *Fine Cooking* contributing editor. She has also worked as a freelance food stylist, recipe tester and developer, and writer for several national food magazines and the Food Network.

Beth Kujawski is a baker from Crown Point, Indiana.

Lori Longbotham is a chef and food writer who has written 10 cookbooks; her most recent is *Luscious Coconut Desserts.*

Emily Luchetti is the executive pastry chef at Farallon and Water Bar in San Francisco.

Andrew MacLauchlan is the author of three cookbooks: *The Making of a Pastry Chef, Tropical Desserts,* and *New Classic Desserts.*

Ti Martin is co-owner of Commander's Palace in New Orleans. In 2011, New Orleans *City Business* magazine named her Woman of the Year.

Alice Medrich is a three-time Cookbook of the Year Award winner and teacher. Her book, *Pure Dessert,* was named one of the top cookbooks of 2007.

Susie Middleton is *Fine Cooking*'s editor at large, a food writer, recipe developer, and cookbook author. Her latest book is *The Fresh and Green Table.* She lives and grows her own vegetables on Martha's Vineyard, Massachusetts.

Leticia Moreinos is a cooking teacher, food writer, and cookbook author. Her first cookbook, *The Brazilian Kitchen,* was published in 2010.

David Norman is a former *Fine Cooking* contributor.

Nancy Oakes is chef and co-owner of Boulevard and Prospect restaurants in San Francisco. She is the author of *Boulevard: The Cookbook.*

David Page and **Barbara Shinn** are co-owners of Shinn Estate Vineyards in Mattituck, New York. They also are chefs, cookbook authors, and IACP award winners for their cookbook, *Recipes from Home.*

Greg Patent studies and writes about food and cooking. The author of seven cookbooks, Greg won a James Beard Award for Baking in America. He hosts The Food Guys on Montana public radio and blogs at thebakingwizard.com.

Liz Pearson worked as the kitchen director for *Saveur* magazine before moving back to her native Texas, where she's a freelance writer and recipe developer.

James Peyton has studied Mexican cuisine for more than 30 years and has written many books on the subject. He also runs the web site LoMexicano.com, which features recipes, cooking information, and Mexican cooking ingredients.

Michelle Polzine is a pastry chef at Range Restaurant in San Francisco. She was named 2010's Best Pastry Chef by San Francisco Weekly.

Deborah Racicot is the pastry chef at Gotham Bar & Grill in New York City. In 2008, she was named one of *Pastry Art & Design*'s Top Ten Pastry Chefs in America.

Rebecca Rather is a baker and owner of the Rather Sweet Bakery café in Fredericksburg, Texas. She is the author of *The Pastry Queen.*

Nicole Rees, author of *Baking Unplugged*, is a food scientist and professional baker. She is the research and development manager for a baking ingredient company in Wilsonville, Oregon.

Tony Rosenfeld, a *Fine Cooking* contributing editor, is the author of two cookbooks. He's also the co-owner of b.good, a Boston-based healthy fast food chain, and the creator of cookangel.com, a culinary troubleshooting website.

Katherine Eastman Seeley runs a catering company, Sweet & Savory, and also is a recipe developer and tester.

Samantha Seneviratne, *Fine Cooking*'s former associate food editor is a graduate of the Fresh Culinary Institute and an avid baker.

Nancy Silverton is chef-owner of Pizzeria Mozza and Osteria Mozza, the latter of which was nominated as Best New Restaurant by the James Beard Foundation for 2007. She is also the author of 7 cookbooks.

Kathleen Stewart is a master baker and the owner of Downtown Bakery and Creamery in Healdsburg, California. Kathleen's recipes have been featured in *Fine Cooking, Gourmet Magazine,* 101cookbooks.com, and seriouseats.com.

Jerry Traunfeld, formerly the executive chef of The Herbfarm in Seattle, recently opened Poppy on Seattle's Capitol Hill. Jerry was named one of the "chefs who made a difference" in *Bon Appetit*'s 2003 Decade of Dining issue.

Carole Walter is a master baker, cooking instructor, and author of many cookbooks, including *Great Coffee Cakes,* which is based on years of studying with pastry chefs in France, Austria, Italy, Denmark, and the United States as well as two decades of teaching baking classes.

Kathleen Weber is a bread baker and owns Della Fattoria bakery in Northern California.

Bruce Weinstein, a one-time advertising creative director and a Johnson & Wales graduate, and **Mark Scarbrough**, a former professor of American literature, write and develop recipes. They have co-authored more than 15 cookbooks.

INDEX

Numbers in **bold** indicate pages with photographs

If you like this book, you'll love *Fine Cooking*.

Read *Fine Cooking* Magazine:

Get six idea-filled issues including FREE iPad digital access. Every issue is packed with triple-tested recipes, expert advice, step-by-step techniques – everything for people who love to cook!

Subscribe today at:
FineCooking.com/4Sub

Discover our *Fine Cooking* Online Store:

It's your destination for premium resources from America's best cookbook writers, chefs, and bakers: cookbooks, DVDs, videos, special interest publications, and more.

Visit today at:
FineCooking.com/4More

Get our FREE *Fine Cooking* eNewsletter:

Our *Make It Tonight* weekday email supplies you with no-fail recipes for quick, wholesome meals; our weekly eNewsletter inspires with seasonal recipes, holiday menus, and more.

Sign up, it's free:
FineCooking.com/4Newsletter

Become a CooksClub member

Join to enjoy unlimited online access to member-only content and exclusive benefits, including: recipes, menus, techniques, and videos; our Test Kitchen Hotline; digital issues; monthly giveaways, contests, and special offers.

Discover more information online:
FineCooking.com/4Join